4/50
- CHRISTIANITY

I0665412

SON OF MAN

GREAT WRITING ABOUT JESUS CHRIST

SON OF MAN

GREAT WRITING ABOUT JESUS CHRIST

EDITED BY CLINT WILLIS

Thunder's Mouth Press
New York

Son of Man: Great Writing about Jesus Christ

Compilation copyright © 2002 by Clint Willis
Introductions copyright © 2002 by Clint Willis

Adrenaline ® and the Adrenaline® logo are trademarks of
Avalon Publishing Group Incorporated, New York, NY.

An Adrenaline Book®

Published by
Thunder's Mouth Press
An Imprint of Avalon Publishing Group Incorporated
161 William Street, 16th floor
New York, NY 10038

A Balliett & Fitzgerald book

Book design: Sue Canavan

frontispiece photo: Carmelite Friar Carving Statue of Christ
© Philip Gould/Corbis

All rights reserved. No part of this book may be reproduced in any form without prior written permission from the publishers and the copyright owner,
except by reviewers who wish to quote brief passages.

Library of Congress Cataloging-in-Publication Data is available.

ISBN: 1-56025-383-5

Printed in the United States of America
Distributed by Publishers Group West

For Hampton Davis

The Belief in Christianity that now prevails is the Unbelief of men. They will have Christ for a Lord and not for a Brother. Christ preaches the greatness of man, but we hear only the greatness of Christ.

—RALPH WALDO EMERSON

My views of the Christian religion are the result of a life of inquiry and reflection, and very different from that anti-Christian system imputed to me by those who know nothing of my opinions. To the corruptions of Christianity I am, indeed, opposed; but not to the genuine precepts of Jesus himself. I am a Christian, in the only sense in which he wanted anyone to be: sincerely attached to his doctrines, in preference to all others; ascribing to himself every *human* excellence; and believing he never claimed any other.

—THOMAS JEFFERSON

contents

p h o t o g r a p h s

introduction

W hen I was twenty-seven years old, an older man—a Jewish writer named Harold—diagnosed me: "You have a Jesus complex," he said. Harold meant that I thought I was Jesus, and he was partly right.

I had come to Jesus as a small child in need of a story. Early on, I stole the story or versions of it for myself. I took on the notion that I could be perfect—without sin—and that my sinless state would fix the broken world. I made suffering one of my jobs, in part because Jesus endowed suffering with glamour. He had power; he was like a younger, better-looking God. And he loved me; this I knew from nursery rhymes and Sunday School pictures.

My trying-on of Jesus' story began early, and it was intense from the start. When I was four or five years old my family lived in a pink shot-gun house on Joseph Street in New Orleans. One night I dreamed that my family took part in a contest at the enormous Presbyterian Church on Saint Charles Avenue—the church where I attended Sunday School and listened to Bible stories every week. The contest went like this: The mothers in the congregation carried their children onto a stage in front of the church, where each mother tried to prove that she loved her child more than the other mothers loved their children. My mother lost, and as a consequence I was seized and handed into the crowd of churchgoers to be crucified. Someone hoisted me up and onto a cross while my family and a boy from day camp milled around at my feet.

I woke up and wandered out to the living room. My father was reading on the couch. He'd spent four years standing watches on ships during World War II, and never relearned how to sleep through the night. I wasn't visibly upset, so he took me back to bed. But finding my father on that couch is one of the moments by which I remember my childhood—what it felt like to be so nearly empty of knowledge, raw to the experience of coming out of sleep to come upon my unknowable father; no other sights or voices to distract me from the mystery and quiet of extreme youth and innocence. Looking back, I wonder: Is that what Jesus felt like when he woke from his long and painful and confusing dream to come upon his mysterious and powerful father in Heaven? Did the light look different to Jesus? Was his father more mysterious than mine? Even now, I don't think so.

So I already was using the story of Jesus to create an emotional life for myself—a life that was painful but also dramatic and entertaining and beautiful. My crucifixion dream is an early example, and one of the most striking; but my inner life continued to unfold in the shadow of Jesus and his story—and in my almost unconscious wish and belief that he could and would look after me.

My best friend in middle school was a Catholic boy named Hampton. I often slept at his house on Saturday nights, and in the morning we went with his family (eventually there were eight children) to Mass at a cathedral. One Saturday night when we were supposed to be asleep we stayed up late giggling in his room until the talk got onto religion. Hampton was horrified to learn that I'd never been baptized: If I suddenly died, I'd be stuck in Limbo with the unbaptized babies who die before they can be christened. At the time—I was ten or eleven years old—I thought babies were incredibly boring. I believe I pictured them in Limbo hanging upside down like bananas, like the embryo at the end of the film version of *2001: A Space Odyssey*.

The next day I told my parents I wanted to be baptized. We'd moved away from New Orleans, three hours west, and hadn't joined a new church yet, so my mother offered to take me church hunting. Every Sunday we tried a different one: Catholic, Presbyterian, Episcopalian and finally Baptist. I was tempted by the Catholics—one dark cathedral reminded me of ghost stories—but the Baptists snagged me. The preacher had the same first name as my father and my older brother (Perry) and he wore a white suit and shouted at the congregation a little like Jimmy Swaggart (whom no one had heard of yet). The Baptists also sang more than the Catholics.

At some point—the chronology is fuzzy—I stood up at the end of one of Perry's sermons, in response to his call for souls ready to be saved. I approached the altar, thereby demonstrating my intention to accept the Lord Jesus Christ into my heart and to be washed in the blood of the lamb. Later that week my mother drove me to the church, where I met alone with the preacher. I sat next to him in his office and listened to him while he paged through a paperback copy of the New Testament, reading aloud and highlighting in yellow certain crucial passages having to do with the promise of eternal life. He baptized me on Easter Sunday in a giant fishtank above the altar: The congregation watched as I waded into the tank from stage right and leaned back on the arm of the preacher, who wore wading boots under his robe; he held my forehead and pinched my nostrils as he lowered my body until I was entirely submerged. It was the highlight of my career as a Baptist, which petered out after a year or two.

I have told that story to entertain people; it's easy to laugh at Bible-thumping suburban Baptist ministers. But it wasn't funny to me then; in my experience it was rare for an important grown-up to pay that kind of attention to a child and it mattered to me. Beyond that, it was high stakes: salvation and life after death. And for a brief time I was a leading character in some kind of drama.

My friend Hampton went on to become a priest. When he was at seminary, in New Orleans, I visited him. We got drunk and climbed up a terrifying ladder in an attic at the seminary—fifty feet straight up, and then an awkward maneuver to clamber onto the roof. We stood there across from the spire of the cathedral, staring drunkenly out at rooftops and up at stars and me worrying about how I'd get back onto that top rung and down the ladder. I was also worried about Hampton—that he was running away from some things—but it seemed a fine and dangerous thing to become a priest, like being Irish. I wished I had the kind of courage I imagined it required; I envied the drama and decisiveness of that choice. I worried, too, that his commitment would get him closer to Jesus than I could get without making some equally daunting and costly commitment of my own.

I've since come to believe that commitment isn't a matter of cost. Jesus is a friend of mine. I've known him all my life in just the ways we know anyone: pictures and stories; hearsay and guesses; maybe an occasional moment of clarity and surrender. Clearly, I'm not alone in all of this. It's nine-thirty in the morning, and I've come across Jesus in four or five strikingly different contexts since four o'clock yesterday afternoon, when I opened my office mailbox; there I found a magazine that features a review of two new books about what scholars call the historical Jesus. I went home and stayed up late with my family to watch the second half of *Ben-Hur*, a film drenched in Christian ideology. This morning I came across a local alternative paper with a cover story on Jesus and Buddha; the paper was stacked on a chair outside of a yoga studio. A few minutes ago my eyes fell upon a Rolodex opened to a business card that features a picture of Jesus wearing his crown of thorns. The *New York Times* this morning offers a story about terrorists opening fire in a Christian church in Pakistan.

It is everywhere apparent that the story of Jesus, as told in the four gospels of the New Testament, holds staggering power for many of us—and not only for believers. The novelist Reynolds Price has translated the Gospel of Mark, and he has this to say about that document:

> Mark commands a degree of attention in the reader—an attention which soon becomes a conviction that what he or she is reading or hearing is in fact a possible tale, a possible figure made by humans against the background sight of

the Earth and the distant sky, pregnant with meaning for every soul.

What meaning? There is of course the idea that anyone can live forever—whether literally or in some metaphorical sense. Some Christian ideology suggests that life everlasting is Jesus' gift to all of us; our job is just to believe that he suffered so that we sinners could live for eternity. This meaning doesn't convince everyone. There's something difficult about the notion that another man should do all the work; that our role in our own salvation should be at least partly a passive one.

It's also possible to derive from Jesus' story the notion that we can save ourselves and in doing so perhaps redeem the world; that we can be heroes, strong and fearless; loving and worthy of love. The story also provides examples of the clarity, compassion and courage such a task might require. Among other things, the story of Jesus suggests how we might try to face, accept and love in all their mystery the stories we discover and invent and inhabit—stories that contain our lives and our deaths; stories no less dramatic or meaningful than the ones we inherit or imagine about Jesus.

How does loving a story help us? It helps us—Jesus knew this—to love each other. I love Jesus for his story—if only because I know it and because it's a good one, in many ways deeply convincing to me. I'll go even further to say that we can't love each other without loving each other's stories. I love my mother for telling me stories about her long-dead grandmother—and I love my mother (as well as the great-grandmother I never met) for inhabiting those stories. This is true even if the stories as I carry them are very different (as I think they must be) from the ones the girl and the old woman lived together long ago.

This mother of mine is a church-going sings-in-the-choir Christian; she's married to my father, a so-called atheist who believes in ghosts. My wife is a Jew by birth and upbringing; her version of religion has something to do with that, I think, and something to do with yoga. We celebrate Christmas and Passover with our children in mixed companies of Jews and Christians; we often say a Buddhist prayer before supper, and some mornings I meditate in my basement before a statue of the Buddha. None of this rattles the notion I carry from my earliest childhood that Jesus loves me and that I love him back; I love his story and I love him for living it.

—CLINT WILLIS

The Conversion of the Jews
by Philip Roth

Phillip Roth's (born 1933) early stories about the American Jewish experience upset some orthodox members of the Jewish community. In this story from Roth's first collection of fiction, a young Jewish boy considers the possibility of the virgin birth.

Y ou're a real one for opening your mouth in the first place," Itzie said. "What do you open your mouth all the time for?"

"I didn't bring it up, Itz, I didn't," Ozzie said.

"What do you care about Jesus Christ for anyway?"

"I didn't bring up Jesus Christ. He did. I didn't even know what he was talking about. Jesus is historical, he kept saying. Jesus is historical." Ozzie mimicked the monumental voice of Rabbi Binder.

"Jesus was a person that lived like you and me," Ozzie continued. "That's what Binder said—"

"Yeah? . . . So what! What do I give two cents whether he lived or not. And what do you gotta open your mouth!" Itzie Lieberman favored closed-mouthedness, especially when it came to Ozzie Freedman's questions. Mrs. Freedman had to see Rabbi Binder twice before about Ozzie's questions and this Wednesday at four-thirty would be the third time. Itzie preferred to keep *his* mother in the kitchen; he settled for behind-the-back subtleties such as gestures, faces, snarls and other less delicate barnyard noises.

"He was a real person, Jesus, but he wasn't like God, and we don't believe he is God." Slowly, Ozzie was explaining Rabbi Binder's position to Itzie, who had been absent from Hebrew School the previous afternoon.

"The Catholics," Itzie said helpfully, "they believe in Jesus Christ, that he's God." Itzie Lieberman used "the Catholics" in its broadest sense—to include the Protestants.

Ozzie received Itzie's remark with a tiny head bob, as though it were a footnote, and went on. "His mother was Mary, and his father probably was Joseph," Ozzie said. "But the New Testament says his real father was God."

"His *real* father?"

"Yeah," Ozzie said, "that's the big thing, his father's supposed to be God."

"Bull."

"That's what Rabbi Binder says, that it's impossible—"

"Sure it's impossible. That stuff's all bull. To have a baby you gotta get laid," Itzie theologized. "Mary hadda get laid."

"That's what Binder says: 'The only way a woman can have a baby is to have intercourse with a man.' "

"He said *that*, Ozz?" For a moment it appeared that Itzie had put the theological question aside. "He said that, intercourse?" A little curled smile shaped itself in the lower half of Itzie's face like a pink mustache. "What you guys do, Ozz, you laugh or something?"

"I raised my hand."

"Yeah? Whatja say?"

"That's when I asked the question."

Itzie's face lit up. "Whatja ask about—intercourse?"

"No, I asked the question about God, how if He could create the heaven and earth in six days, and make all the animals and the fish and the light in six days—the light especially, that's what always gets me, that He could make the light. Making fish and animals, that's pretty good—"

"That's damn good." Itzie's appreciation was honest but unimaginative: it was as though God had just pitched a one-hitter.

"But making light . . . I mean when you think about it, it's really something," Ozzie said. "Anyway, I asked Binder if He could make all that in six days, and He could *pick* the six days he wanted right out of nowhere, why couldn't He let a woman have a baby without having intercourse."

"You said intercourse, Ozz, to Binder?"

"Yeah."

"Right in class?"

"Yeah."

Itzie smacked the side of his head.

"I mean, no kidding around," Ozzie said, "that'd really be nothing. After all that other stuff, that'd practically be nothing."

Itzie considered a moment. "What'd Binder say?"

"He started all over again explaining how Jesus was historical and how he lived like you and me but he wasn't God. So I said I under*stood* that. What I wanted to know was different."

What Ozzie wanted to know was always different. The first time he had wanted to know how Rabbi Binder could call the Jews "The Chosen People" if the Declaration of Independence claimed all men to be created equal. Rabbi Binder tried to distinguish for him between political equality and spiritual legitimacy, but what Ozzie wanted to know, he insisted vehemently, was different. That was the first time his mother had to come.

Then there was the plane crash. Fifty-eight people had been killed in a plane crash at La Guardia. In studying a casualty list in the newspaper his mother had discovered among the list of those dead eight Jewish names (his grandmother had nine but she counted Miller as a Jewish name); because of the eight she said the plane crash was "a tragedy." During free-discussion time on Wednesday Ozzie had brought to Rabbi Binder's attention this matter of "some of his relations" always picking out the Jewish names. Rabbi Binder had begun to explain cultural unity and some other things when Ozzie stood up at his seat and said that what he wanted to know was different. Rabbi Binder insisted that he sit down and it was then that Ozzie shouted that he wished all fifty-eight were Jews. That was the second time his mother came.

"And he kept explaining about Jesus being historical, and so I kept asking him. No kidding, Itz, he was trying to make me look stupid."

"So what he finally do?"

"Finally he starts screaming that I was deliberately simple-minded and a wise guy, and that my mother had to come, and this was the last time. And that I'd never get bar-mitzvahed if he could help it. Then, Itz, then he starts talking in that voice like a statue, real slow and deep, and he says that I better think over what I said about the Lord. He told me to go to his office and think it over." Ozzie leaned his body towards Itzie. "Itz, I thought it over for a solid hour, and now I'm convinced God could do it."

Ozzie had planned to confess his latest transgression to his mother as soon as she came home from work. But it was a Friday night in November and already dark, and when Mrs. Freedman came through the door she tossed off her coat, kissed Ozzie quickly on the face, and went to the kitchen table to light the three yellow candles, two for the Sabbath and one for Ozzie's father.

When his mother lit the candles she would move her two arms slowly towards her, dragging them through the air, as though persuading people whose minds were half made up. And her eyes would get glassy with tears. Even when his father was alive Ozzie remembered that her eyes had gotten glassy, so it didn't have anything to do with his dying. It had something to do with lighting the candles.

As she touched the flaming match to the unlit wick of a Sabbath candle, the phone rang, and Ozzie, standing only a foot from it, plucked it off the receiver and held it muffled to his chest. When his mother lit candles Ozzie felt there should be no noise; even breathing, if you could manage it, should be softened. Ozzie pressed the phone to his breast and watched his mother dragging whatever she was dragging, and he felt his own eyes get glassy. His mother was a round, tired, gray-haired penguin of a woman whose gray skin had begun to feel the tug of gravity and the weight of her own history. Even when she was dressed up she didn't look like a chosen person. But when she lit candles she looked like something better; like a woman who knew momentarily that God could do anything.

After a few mysterious minutes she was finished. Ozzie hung up the phone and walked to the kitchen table where she was beginning to lay the two places for the four-course Sabbath meal. He told her that she would have to see Rabbi Binder next Wednesday at four-thirty, and then he told her why. For the first time in their life together she hit Ozzie across the face with her hand.

All through the chopped liver and chicken soup part of the dinner Ozzie cried; he didn't have any appetite for the rest.

On Wednesday, in the largest of the three basement classrooms of the synagogue, Rabbi Marvin Binder, a tall, handsome, broad-shouldered man of thirty with thick strong-fibered black hair, removed his watch from his pocket and saw that it was four o'clock. At the rear of the room Yakov Blotnik, the seventy-one-year-old custodian, slowly polished the large window, mumbling to himself, unaware that it was four o'clock or six o'clock, Monday or Wednesday. To most of the students Yakov Blotnik's mumbling, along with his brown curly beard, scythe nose, and two heel-trailing black cats, made of him an object of wonder, a foreigner, a relic, towards whom they were alternately fearful and disrespectful. To Ozzie the mumbling had always seemed a monotonous, curious prayer; what made it curious was that old Blotnik had been mumbling so steadily for so many years, Ozzie suspected he had memorized the prayers and forgotten all about God.

"It is now free-discussion time," Rabbi Binder said. "Feel free to talk about any Jewish matter at all—religion, family, politics, sports—"

There was silence. It was a gusty, clouded November afternoon and it did not seem as though there ever was or could be a thing called baseball. So nobody this week said a word about that hero from the past, Hank Greenberg—which limited free discussion considerably.

And the soul-battering Ozzie Freedman had just received from Rabbi Binder had imposed its limitation. When it was Ozzie's turn to read aloud from the Hebrew book the rabbi had asked him petulantly why he didn't read more rapidly. He was showing no progress. Ozzie said he could read faster but that if he did he was sure not to understand what he was reading. Nevertheless, at the rabbi's repeated suggestion Ozzie tried, and showed a great talent, but in the midst of a long passage he stopped short and said he didn't understand a word he was reading, and started in again at a drag-footed pace. Then came the soul-battering.

Consequently when free-discussion time rolled around none of the students felt too free. The rabbi's invitation was answered only by the mumbling of feeble old Blotnik.

"Isn't there anything at all you would like to discuss?" Rabbi Binder asked again, looking at his watch. "No questions or comments?"

There was a small grumble from the third row. The rabbi requested that Ozzie rise and give the rest of the class the advantage of his thought.

Ozzie rose. "I forget it now," he said, and sat down in his place.

Rabbi Binder advanced a seat towards Ozzie and poised himself on the edge of the desk. It was Itzie's desk and the rabbi's frame only a dagger's-length away from his face snapped him to sitting attention.

"Stand up again, Oscar," Rabbi Binder said calmly, "and try to assemble your thoughts."

Ozzie stood up. All his classmates turned in their seats and watched as he gave an unconvincing scratch to his forehead.

"I can't assemble any," he announced, and plunked himself down.

"Stand up!" Rabbi Binder advanced from Itzie's desk to the one directly in front of Ozzie; when the rabbinical back was turned Itzie gave it five-fingers off the tip of his nose, causing a small titter in the room. Rabbi Binder was too absorbed in squelching Ozzie's nonsense once and for all to bother with titters. "Stand up, Oscar. What's your question about?"

Ozzie pulled a word out of the air. It was the handiest word. "Religion."

"Oh, now you remember?"

"Yes."

"What is it?"

Trapped, Ozzie blurted the first thing that came to him. "Why can't He make anything He wants to make!"

As Rabbi Binder prepared an answer, a final answer, Itzie, ten feet behind him, raised one finger on his left hand, gestured it meaningfully towards the rabbi's back, and brought the house down.

Binder twisted quickly to see what had happened and in the midst of the commotion Ozzie shouted into the rabbi's back what he couldn't have shouted to his face. It was a loud, toneless sound that had the timbre of something stored inside for about six days.

"You don't know! You don't know anything about God!"

The rabbi spun back towards Ozzie. "What?"

"You don't know—you don't—"

"Apologize, Oscar, apologize!" It was a threat.

"You don't—"

Rabbi Binder's hand flicked out at Ozzie's cheek. Perhaps it had only been meant to clamp the boy's mouth shut, but Ozzie ducked and the palm caught him squarely on the nose.

The blood came in a short, red spurt on to Ozzie's shirt front.

The next moment was all confusion. Ozzie screamed, "You bastard, you bastard!" and broke for the classroom door. Rabbi Binder lurched a step backwards, as though his own blood had started flowing violently in the opposite direction, then gave a clumsy lurch forward and bolted out the door after Ozzie. The class followed after the rabbi's huge blue-suited back, and before old Blotnik could turn from his window, the room was empty and everyone was headed full speed up the three flights leading to the roof.

If one should compare the light of day to the life of man: sunrise to birth; sunset—the dropping down over the edge—to death; then as Ozzie Freedman wiggled through the trapdoor of the synagogue roof, his feet kicking backwards bronco-style at Rabbi Binder's outstretched arms—at that moment the day was fifty years old. As a rule, fifty or fifty-five reflects accurately the age of late afternoons in November, for it is in that month, during those hours, that one's awareness of light seems no longer a matter of seeing, but of hearing: light begins clicking away. In fact, as Ozzie locked shut the trapdoor in the rabbi's face, the sharp click of the bolt into the lock might momentarily have been mistaken for the sound of the heavier gray that had just throbbed through the sky.

With all his weight Ozzie kneeled on the locked door; any instant he was certain that Rabbi Binder's shoulder would fling it open, splintering the wood into shrapnel and catapulting his body into the sky. But the door did not move and below him he heard only the rumble of feet, first loud then dim, like thunder rolling away.

A question shot through his brain. "Can this be *me?*" For a thirteen-year-old who had just labeled his religious leader a bastard, twice, it was not an improper question. Louder and louder the question came to him—"Is it me? It is me?"—until he discovered himself no longer kneeling, but racing crazily towards the edge of the roof, his eyes crying, his throat screaming, and his arms flying everywhichway as though not his own.

"Is it me? Is it me Me ME ME ME! It has to be me—but is it!"

It is the question a thief must ask himself the night he jimmies open his first window, and it is said to be the question with which bridegrooms quiz themselves before the altar.

In the few wild seconds it took Ozzie's body to propel him to the edge of the roof, his self-examination began to grow fuzzy. Gazing down at the street, he became confused as to the problem beneath the question: was it, is-it-me-who-called-Binder-a-bastard? or, is-it-me-prancing-around-on-the-roof? However, the scene below settled all, for there is an instant in any action when whether it is you or somebody else is academic. The thief crams the money in his pockets and scoots out the window. The bridegroom signs the hotel register for two. And the boy on the roof finds a streetful of people gaping at him, necks stretched backwards, faces up, as though he were the ceiling of the Hayden Planetarium. Suddenly you know it's you.

"Oscar! Oscar Freedman!" A voice rose from the center of the crowd, a voice that, could it have been seen, would have looked like the writing on scroll. "Oscar Freedman, get down from there. Immediately!" Rabbi Binder was pointing one arm stiffly up at him; and at the end of that arm, one finger aimed menacingly. It was the attitude of a dictator, but one—the eyes confessed all—whose personal valet had spit neatly in his face.

Ozzie didn't answer. Only for a blink's length did he look towards Rabbi Binder. Instead his eyes began to fit together the world beneath him, to sort out people from places, friends from enemies, participants from spectators. In little jagged starlike clusters his friends stood around Rabbi Binder, who was still pointing. The topmost point on a star compounded not of angels but of five adolescent boys was Itzie. What a world it was, with those stars below, Rabbi Binder below . . . Ozzie, who a moment earlier hadn't been able to control his own body, started to feel the meaning of the word control: he felt Peace and he felt Power.

"Oscar Freedman, I'll give you three to come down."

Few dictators give their subjects three to do anything; but, as always, Rabbi Binder only looked dictatorial.

"Are you ready, Oscar?"

Ozzie nodded his head yes, although he had no intention in the world—the lower one of the celestial one he'd just entered—of coming down even if Rabbi Binder should give him a million.

"All right then," said Rabbi Binder. He ran a hand through his black Samson hair as though it were the gesture prescribed for uttering the first digit. Then, with his other hand cutting a circle out of the small piece of sky around him, he spoke. "One!"

There was no thunder. On the contrary, at that moment, as though "one" was the cue for which he had been waiting, the world's least thunderous person appeared on the synagogue steps. He did not so much come out the synagogue door as lean out, onto the darkening air. He clutched at the doorknob with one hand and looked up at the roof.

"Oy!"

Yakov Blotnik's old mind hobbled slowly, as if on crutches, and though he couldn't decide precisely what the boy was doing on the roof, he knew it wasn't good—that is, it wasn't-good-for-the-Jews. For

Yakov Blotnik life had fractionated itself simply: things were either good-for-the-Jews or no-good-for-the-Jews.

He smacked his free hand to his in-sucked cheek, gently. "Oy, Gut!" And then quickly as he was able, he jacked down his head and surveyed the street. There was Rabbi Binder (like a man at an auction with only three dollars in his pocket, he had just delivered a shaky "Two!"); there were the students, and that was all. So far it-wasn't-so-bad-for-the-Jews. But the boy had to come down immediately, before anybody saw. The problem: how to get the boy off the roof?

Anybody who has ever had a cat on the roof knows how to get him down. You call the fire department. Or first you call the operator and you ask her for the fire department. And the next thing there is great jamming of brakes and clanging of bells and shouting of instructions. And then the cat is off the roof. You do the same thing to get a boy off the roof.

That is, you do the same thing if you are Yakov Blotnik and you once had a cat on the roof.

When the engines, all four of them, arrived, Rabbi Binder had four times given Ozzie the count of three. The big hook-and-ladder swung around the corner and one of the firemen leaped from it, plunging headlong towards the yellow fire hydrant in front of the synagogue. With a huge wrench he began to unscrew the top nozzle. Rabbi Binder raced over to him and pulled at his shoulder.

"There's no fire . . ."

The fireman mumbled back over his shoulder and, heatedly, continued working at the nozzle.

"But there's no fire, there's no fire . . ." Binder shouted. When the fireman mumbled again, the rabbi grasped his face with both his hands and pointed it up at the roof.

To Ozzie it looked as though Rabbi Binder was trying to tug the fireman's head out of his body, like a cork from a bottle. He had to giggle at the picture they made: it was a family portrait—rabbi in black skullcap, fireman in red fire hat, and the little yellow hydrant squatting beside like a kid brother, bareheaded. From the edge of the roof Ozzie waved at the portrait, a one-handed, flapping, mocking wave; in doing it his right foot slipped from under him. Rabbi Binder covered his eyes with his hands.

Firemen work fast. Before Ozzie had even regained his balance, a big, round, yellowed net was being held on the synagogue lawn. The firemen who held it looked up at Ozzie with stern, feelingless faces.

One of the firemen turned his head towards Rabbi Binder. "What, is the kid nuts or something?"

Rabbi Binder unpeeled his hands from his eyes, slowly, painfully, as if they were tape. Then he checked: nothing on the sidewalk, no dents in the net.

"Is he gonna jump, or what?" the fireman shouted.

In a voice not at all like a statue, Rabbi Binder finally answered. "Yes, Yes, I think so . . . He's been threatening to . . ."

"Threatening to? Why, the reason he was on the roof, Ozzie remembered, was to get away; he hadn't even thought about jumping. He had just run to get away, and the truth was that he hadn't really headed for the roof as much as he'd been chased there.

"What's his name, the kid?"

"Freedman," Rabbi Binder answered. "Oscar Freedman."

The fireman looked up at Ozzie. "What is it with you, Oscar? You gonna jump, or what?"

Ozzie did not answer. Frankly, the question had just arisen.

"Look, Oscar, if you're gonna jump, jump—and if you're not gonna jump, don't jump. But don't waste our time, willya?"

Ozzie looked at the fireman and then at Rabbi Binder. He wanted to see Rabbi Binder cover his eyes one more time.

"I'm going to jump."

And then he scampered around the edge of the roof to the corner, where there was no net below, and he flapped his arms at his sides, swishing the air and smacking his palms to his trousers on the downbeat. He began screaming like some kind of engine, "Wheeeee . . . wheeeeee," and leaning way out over the edge with the upper half of his body. The firemen whipped around to cover the ground with the net. Rabbi Binder mumbled a few words to Somebody and covered his eyes. Everything happened quickly, jerkily, as in a silent movie. The crowd, which had arrived with the fire engines, gave out a long, Fourth-of-July fireworks oooh-aahhh. In the excitement no one had paid the crowd much heed, except, of course, Yakov Blotnik, who swung from the doorknob counting heads. "Fier und tsvansik . . . finf und tsvantsik . . . Oy, Gut!" It wasn't like this with the cat.

Rabbi Binder peeked through his fingers, checked the sidewalk and net. Empty. But there was Ozzie racing to the other corner. The firemen raced with him but were unable to keep up. Whenever Ozzie wanted to he might jump and splatter himself upon the sidewalk, and by the time the firemen scooted to the spot all they could do with their net would be to cover the mess.

"Wheeeee . . . wheeeee . . ."

"Hey, Oscar," the winded fireman yelled, "What the hell is this, a game or something?"

"Wheeeee . . . wheeeee . . ."

"Hey, Oscar—"

But he was off now to the other corner, flapping his wings fiercely. Rabbi Binder couldn't take it any longer—the fire engines from nowhere, the screaming suicidal boy, the net. He fell to his knees, exhausted, and with his hands curled together in front of his chest like a little dome, he pleaded, "Oscar, stop it, Oscar. Don't jump, Oscar. Please come down . . . Please don't jump."

And further back in the crowd a single voice, a single young voice, shouted a lone word to the boy on the roof.

"Jump!"

It was Itzie. Ozzie momentarily stopped flapping.

"Go ahead, Ozz—jump!" Itzie broke off his point of the star and courageously, with the inspiration not of a wise-guy but of a disciple, stood alone. "Jump, Ozz, jump!"

Still on his knees, his hands still curled, Rabbi Binder twisted his body back. He looked at Itzie, then, agonizingly, back to Ozzie.

"OSCAR, DON'T JUMP! PLEASE, DON'T JUMP . . . please please . . ."

"Jump!" This time it wasn't Itzie but another point of the star. By the time Mrs. Freedman arrived to keep her four-thirty appointment with Rabbi Binder, the whole little upside down heaven was shouting and pleading for Ozzie to jump, and Rabbi Binder no longer was pleading with him not to jump, but was crying into the dome of his hands.

Understandably Mrs. Freedman couldn't figure out what her son was doing on the roof. So she asked.

"Ozzie, my Ozzie, what are you doing? My Ozzie, what is it?"

Ozzie stopped wheeeeeing and slowed his arms down to a cruising flap, the kind birds use in soft winds, but he did not answer. He stood against the low, clouded, darkening sky—light clicked down swiftly now, as on a small gear—flapping softly and gazing down at the small bundle of a woman who was his mother.

"What are you doing, Ozzie?" She turned towards the kneeling Rabbi Bidder and rushed so close that only a paper-thickness of dusk lay between her stomach and his shoulders.

"What is my baby doing?"

Rabbi Binder gaped up at her but he too was mute. All that moved was the dome of his hands; it shook back and forth like a weak pulse.

"Rabbi, get him down! He'll kill himself. Get him down, my only baby . . ."

"I can't," Rabbi Binder said, "I can't . . ." and he turned his handsome head towards the crowd of boys behind him. "It's them. Listen to them."

And for the first time Mrs. Freedman saw the crowd of boys, and she heard what they were yelling.

"He's doing it for them. He won't listen to me. It's them." Rabbi Binder spoke like one in a trance.

"For them?"

"Yes."

"Why for them?"

"They want him to . . ."

Mrs. Freedman raised her two arms upward as though she were conducting the sky. "For them he's doing it!" And then in a gesture older than pyramids, older than prophets and floods, her arms came slapping down to her sides. "A martyr I have. Look!" She tilted her head to the roof. Ozzie was still flapping softly. "My martyr."

"Oscar, come down, *please*," Rabbi Binder groaned.

In a startlingly even voice Mrs. Freedman called to the boy on the roof. "Ozzie, come down, Ozzie. Don't be a martyr, my baby."

As though it were a litany, Rabbi Binder repeated her words. "Don't be a martyr, my baby. Don't be a martyr."

"Gawhead, Ozz—*be* a Martin!" It was Itzie. "Be a Martin, be a Martin," and all the voices joined in singing for Martindom, whatever *it* was. "Be a Martin, be a Martin . . ."

Somehow when you're on a roof the darker it gets the less you can hear. All Ozzie knew was that two groups wanted two new things: his friends were spirited and musical about what they wanted; his mother and the rabbi were even-toned, chanting, about what they didn't want. The rabbi's voice was without tears now and so was his mother's.

The big net stared up at Ozzie like a sightless eye. The big, clouded sky pushed down. From beneath it looked like a gray corrugated board. Suddenly, looking up into that unsympathetic sky, Ozzie realized all the strangeness of what these people, his friends, were asking: they wanted him to jump, to kill himself; they were singing about it now— it made them that happy. And there was an even greater strangeness: Rabbi Binder was on his knees, trembling. If there was a question to be asked now it was not "Is it me?" but rather "Is it us? . . . Is it us?"

Being on the roof, it turned out, was a serious thing. If he jumped would the singing become dancing? Would it? What would jumping stop? Yearningly, Ozzie wished he could rip open the sky, plunge his hands through, and pull out the sun; and on the sun, like a coin, would be stamped JUMP or DON'T JUMP.

Ozzie's knees rocked and sagged a little under him as though they were setting him for a dive. His arms tightened, stiffened, froze, from shoulders to fingernails. He felt as if each part of his body were going to vote as to whether he should kill himself or not—and each part as though it were independent of *him*.

The light took an unexpected click down and the new darkness, like a gag, hushed the friends singing for this and the mother and rabbi chanting for that.

Ozzie stopped counting votes, and in a curiously high voice, like one who wasn't prepared for speech, he spoke.

"Mamma?"

"Yes, Oscar."

"Mamma, get down on your knees, like Rabbi Binder."

"Oscar—"

"Get down on your knees," he said, "or I'll jump."

Ozzie heard a whimper, then a quick rustling, and when he looked down where his mother had stood he saw the top of a head and beneath that a circle of dress. She was kneeling beside Rabbi Binder.

He spoke again. "Everybody kneel." There was the sound of everybody kneeling.

Ozzie looked around. With one hand he pointed towards the synagogue entrance. "Make *him* kneel."

There was a noise, not of kneeling, but of body-and-cloth stretching. Ozzie could hear Rabbi Binder saying in a gruff whisper, ". . . or he'll *kill* himself," and when next he looked there was Yakov Blotnik off the doorknob and for the first time in his life upon his knees in the Gentile posture of prayer.

As for the firemen—it is not as difficult as one might imagine to hold a net taut while you are kneeling.

Ozzie looked around again; and then he called to Rabbi Binder.

"Rabbi?"

"Yes, Oscar."

"Rabbi Binder, do you believe in God."

"Yes."

"Do you believe God can do Anything?" Ozzie leaned his head out into the darkness. "Anything?"

"Oscar, I think—"

"Tell me you believe God can do Anything."

There was a second's hesitation. Then: "God can do Anything."

"Tell me you believe God can make a child without intercourse."

"He can."

"Tell me!"

"God," Rabbi Binder admitted, "can make a child without intercourse."

"Mamma, you tell me."

"God can make a child without intercourse," his mother said.

"Make *him* tell me." There was no doubt who *him* was.

In a few moments Ozzie heard an old comical voice say something to the increasing darkness about God.

Next, Ozzie made everybody say it. And then he made them all say they believed in Jesus Christ—first one at a time, then all together.

When the catechizing was through it was the beginning of evening. From the street it sounded as if the boy on the roof might have sighed.

"Ozzie?" A woman's voice dared to speak. "You'll come down now?"

There was no answer, but the woman waited, and when a voice finally did speak it was thin and crying, and exhausted as that of an old man who has just finished pulling the bells.

"Mamma, don't you see—you shouldn't hit me. He shouldn't hit me. You shouldn't hit me about God, Mamma. You should never hit anybody about God—"

"Ozzie, please come down now."

"Promise me, promise me you'll never hit anybody about God."

He had asked only his mother, but for some reason everyone kneeling in the street promised he would never hit anybody about God.

Once again there was silence.

"I can come down now, Mamma," the boy on the roof finally said. He turned his head both ways as though checking the traffic lights. "Now I can come down . . ."

And he did, right into the center of the yellow net that glowed in the evening's edge like an overgrown halo.

The Annunciation
by Rainer Maria Rilke

Rainer Maria Rilke (1875–1926) was the greatest German poet of the 20th century. "The Annunciation" belongs to a group of poems called The Life of the Virgin Mary. *Rilke wrote the poems in 1912 while at Castle Duino, where he began working on the well-known* Duino Elegies. *This translation is by Franz Wright.*

It isn't just that an angel entered: realize
this is not what startled her. She might have been
somebody else, and the angel
some sunlight or, at night, the moon
occupying itself in her room—, so quietly
she accustomed herself to the form he took.
She barely suspected that this kind of visit
is exhausting to angels. (Oh if we knew
how pure she was. Didn't a deer,
catching sight of her once in the forest,
lose itself so much in looking at her

that without coupling it conceived the unicorn,

the animal of light, the pure animal!)

It's not just that he walked in, but that

he placed the face of a young man

so close to hers: his gaze and the one

with which she answered it blended

so much, suddenly, that everything else vanished

and what millions saw, built, and endured

crowded inside of her: only her and him:

seeing and seen, eye and whatever is beautiful to the eye

nowhere else but right here. *This*

is startling. And it startled them both.

Then the angel sang his song.

Notes from a Desert Sanctuary
by Heather King

Six years after converting to Catholicism, writer Heather King (born 1952) decided to leave Los Angeles for a week at a California monastery. Her time at the desert retreat helped her to understand Christ's humanity.

've just driven 550 miles from LA to a monastery located in the desert a couple of hours northwest of Las Vegas. The moment I spot the Celtic cross atop the adobe chapel and pull in, I see that one of my lessons for the next week is going to concern the gap between expectations and reality. I've been picturing a flowering-cactus-festooned oasis; instead, the property is next to a state highway and is home to more double-wide trailers than cactuses. All the California monasteries I've visited have been neat, quiet, and orderly. This is a sprawling welter of outbuildings, abandoned sheds, and piles of barrels draped with blue tarps.

After circling the labyrinth of dirt roads a couple of times, I spot a sign that says, REGISTRATION, in the window of a ranch-house-turned-bookstore. After eight hours on the road, I'm hoping to be greeted by some calm, prayerful soul. Instead I startle a heavily made-up woman named Dot, who turns down the volume on an Amy Grant tape and flutters about trying to find someone to replace her at the cash register while she shows me to my room. (Could the arrival of a retreatant be such an unusual occurrence here?)

Dot walks me the few hundred yards to Manna House—a barracks-like structure with an unkempt yard—and ushers me into Room 1. She seems strangely fixated on the door lock: "Don't lock your door until you go to bed at night," she exhorts. "We don't have keys. Lock your door from the inside at night, but don't do it during the day. Do it only at night, and not until you go to bed!"

I'm only half listening as I case the room: two twin beds squished foot to foot, a midget nightstand, broken Venetian blinds. "There's no desk?" I ask.

Dot stops in midsentence. "Oh, dear," she says reproachfully. "I hope you didn't expect the Waldorf-Astoria."

"No, no, of course not," I hasten to reassure her. "It's just that I'm used to doing a lot of writing on retreats, in my journal and so forth."

But I've departed from the script, and Dot is pissed. "If I could make a suggestion," she says tightly: "the next time you go on a retreat, you might want to inform the people of your needs beforehand." As if a desk were a piece of esoteric equipment; as if I've asked for something outlandish, like a pack of condoms.

There was more, but the point is that it all led to a two-day-long comedy of errors with various people making failed attempts to get me another, more suitable room. (At the time, there were exactly three retreatants on-site, and at least twenty available rooms.) Finally, one of the monks came up to me in chapel, eyes darting about as if there might be spies in the vicinity, and whispered conspiratorially, "We've found you another room—Room 12—but it won't be ready till tomorrow afternoon."

And the kicker was Room 12 didn't have a desk, either—at which point I realized that my room was fine. It was wonderful: hot water, heat, an outlet for my laptop (I've got it perched on my *lap*!), a little porch, and nobody with whom to share the bathroom. I saw a beautiful orange bird this morning. Out back, there are cottonwoods and cactuses, and a little stream running through.

• • •

I'm here because I need a break from my life: the book nobody wants to buy; the one-bedroom LA apartment where I write; my husband, Tim; the breast cancer (stage one, grade one) with which I was diagnosed last year—and which, after voluminous research, I've decided to treat with surgery only. When people hear I'm not taking chemotherapy, they say approvingly, "Oh, you're using holistic medicine." But I am not using holistic medicine. I am not seeing an acupuncturist, a nutritionist, or an herbalist. I am not taking vitamin supplements or laetrile or mistletoe tea. Aside from cutting down on fat, I am doing pretty much what I was doing already, which is hanging out with sober people (I've been a recovering alcoholic for fourteen years), eating sensibly, exercising, writing, and praying.

But you got cancer doing that, I can hear people thinking.

So I got cancer. People get cancer. They die from cancer! My problem is not cancer. It's lack of faith, lack of acceptance, living in illusion. That's the real reason I'm here.

The entire rambling monastery is apparently run by just six or seven monks, all of whom appear to be in the throes of deep spiritual crises. At every other monastery I've visited, the Divine Office—the prayers recited at the seven canonical hours of the day—is prayed with the utmost attention and reverence. Here, no matter what the hour, the monks show up looking as if they've just crawled out of bed; they slump and slouch and scratch and yawn, seeming crabby and bored. One, a sixtyish fellow with bloodshot eyes, all but lies down in his seat after chanting the entrance antiphon in a quavering voice. Another, the sad-sack guitar player, strums the opening chord of each hymn, then sings in an emotionless, all-but-inaudible monotone. A third, a tall, raw-boned youth with hacked-off hair, crosses his legs, gazes out the window, and dangles his breviary in one hand. This, it turns out, is the abbot.

I am appalled for about ten minutes, and then I realize that I am so broken right now I can't afford to pass my usual judgments, which only make me feel more separate, anyway. I feel much more at home with these folks than I would with people who seemed perfect and reverent and assured. Six years after converting to Catholicism, I was beginning, for the first time in my life, to feel assured. But breast cancer and literary failure and general confusion have blown all that apart, leaving me feeling raw and clueless all over again.

I've scheduled my week at the monastery so that my last day will be Ash Wednesday, the beginning of Lent. For the past three years, I've given up coffee for Lent; this year, I'm going to try forgoing sugar, too. A hundred times a day, I contemplate how horrible this will be. Here is the extent of my coffee addiction: for the past two mornings, I've awakened before dawn and driven ten miles to the Circle K in Watkins (which, like most Western towns, appears to have been built in the last fifteen minutes) for a jumbo ersatz "dark roast." This would be almost justifiable if the coffee were actually good, but it has no more of a kick than the watered-down mud they serve in the monastery dining hall. The problem is, I can't wait until they open the hall at 8 a.m. to get my coffee.

Knowing me, I will make the trek to Watkins every morning that I'm here.

The adobe chapel, set on a little north-facing rise, has rough-hewn lintels, tile floors, and a statue of Our Lady of Guadelupe. There's a courtyard with a fountain and rosebushes out front, and off to one side a cemetery, its tombstones adorned with plastic flowers, American flags, and faded Christmas bulbs.

The Divine Office usually takes place in the chapel: Vigils and Lauds in the morning; Mass at noon, and Vespers and Compline in the evening. Tonight, however, Compline was held early, right in the dining hall. As soon as we'd finished eating, one of the monks tossed around some psalm sheets, plopped down on a metal folding chair, and halfheartedly sighed, "I guess it's time to sing."

And we sang, and it was great.

• • •

Now I know how the small staff keeps this place running: an army of oblate volunteers—laypeople who dedicate themselves to a religious community—come from all over the country and spend the winter in a nearby RV park.

My first night, I met a retired couple named Fran and Earl, who immediately informed me they'd been coming here for eleven years. The next night, I met a couple named Lois and Vern. "Oh, I met a nice couple last night who do the same thing you do," I said. "Fran and—"

"We've been coming here twelve years," Vern cut in. "They've only been coming eleven."

No wonder the monks look distracted. In addition to hosting retreatants, they run a drop-in center for local Native Americans, a gift shop (prickly-pear-cactus jelly, beeswax candles, locally grown apples), and a library. Make that a *well-stocked* library. In the monastery bookstore this afternoon, I picked up Thomas Merton's *Disputed Questions* (even though it's almost a cliché to read Merton on retreat) and started reading an essay on solitude. I wanted to finish the essay, but didn't want to buy the book. Thinking it was a long shot, I decided to try the library.

I walked into the tiny cinder-block room, where a portly old monk was reading a book and eating candy.

"Um, do you have any Thomas Merton?" I asked—thinking, in my usual tolerant and humble way, *Have they even heard of Merton in this backwater?*

"Fourth aisle, halfway down on the left," he answered genially, flipping a light switch and waving me into a back room I hadn't noticed.

In the fourth aisle, I found what appeared to be every book Merton ever wrote: volumes and volumes of journals, letters, essays—and not one, but two copies of *Disputed Questions*. To top it all off, when I went to sign the book out, the monk said, "Just jot down your name and phone number in the ledger."

"I'm staying here," I told him. "Do you still want my home phone number?"

"Might as well," he replied, "in case you want to take the book with you when you leave. Just mail it back when you're done."

Now, *that's* my kind of library.

I've also discovered, right down the street from the monastery, the Kiowa Mountain access road, which (according to the monk who runs the drop-in center) slopes gently through gorgeous desert scenery for twenty-three miles. There's a gate, but it doesn't have a NO TRESPASSING sign, so this morning I climbed over it and walked the dirt road for two hours: clear blue sky with mammoth clouds; mountains in every direction; cottonwoods like fluffy lace, just beginning to green; and dead silence, except for four or five passing cars. Each driver waved, and two stopped to ask if I wanted a ride.

I have to have a mammogram—my first since the surgery—when I get home.

The reading at Mass this morning was "When a sieve is shaken, the husks appear; so do a man's faults when he speaks" (Sirach 27:4).

Which segued into the Gospel reading: "Can a blind man act as guide to a blind man? . . . A student is not above his teacher. . . . Why look at the speck in your brother's eye when you miss the plank in your own?" (Luke 6:39-41).

The elderly priest who said Mass weighs about eighty pounds, talks in a squeaky voice, and possesses the humble, peaceful, self-deprecating air of the truly enlightened. He began by asking for our prayers because he has a bad heart—by the looks of him, I don't doubt it— and then he gave a wonderful homily in which he said that, if we're human, we have human hearts that fall prey to all the temptations and shortcomings listed in the Bible. He himself has been subject to them all, he said, including lust, and has been able to resist the vast number of women who have thrown themselves at him (big laugh here) only because of his life of prayer. The thing to do during Lent, he explained, is to try to die to your worst shortcoming. And if you want to figure out what your worst shortcoming is, he suggested, examine what you complain about in others, and then examine what distracts you in prayer.

Examine what you complain about in others. I'm starting to see that, whenever I catch a glimpse of myself in someone else, instead of recognizing and acknowledging it, I hate that part of them. I hate their weakness and ineffectiveness; that they don't know how to save themselves, either; that they feel lonely and despised, too. To love your neighbor as yourself, you also have to love yourself in your neighbor.

For once, in chapel this morning, I was actually able to attend to the meaning of the Psalms and the readings. I've been praying the Divine Office on my own for two years, but I'm so self-conscious and eager to "progress"—so dumbstruck that I'm doing it at all—that I forget to orient myself toward Christ and instead make my prayer all about me. But I keep doing it because I figure it's pleasing to God, and maybe, after thirty or forty years, I'll be purified; because there's only one way to make it be about Christ, and that's to keep on praying. In the meantime, every once in a blue moon, prayer is like it was this morning.

Today after Mass, I saw a hunchbacked monk stand in the alcove and drain four good-sized goblets of leftover Communion wine in about ten seconds—I mean, he was just swilling it. (Of course, I would notice this, having been a lush for so many years myself.) Afterward, a middle-aged Mexican man wearing jeans about twenty sizes too big came in, knelt before the altar with his ass crack fully exposed, and proceeded, in a frantic stage whisper, to pray. He made his way around the entire sanctuary, stopping in front of every statue, pulling up his pants as he went.

It's beginning to dawn on me that everyone here is in some way deformed. One monk has a withered leg; another, a goiter. A man with a breathing tube sat at my table at dinner tonight. The woman beside me had no chin. Morbid obesity abounds.

Given the diet, it's small wonder so many people are overweight. Last night's dinner consisted of pork chops encased in an inch of greasy breading, string-bean casserole enhanced with bacon and suet, and deep-fried, syrup-drenched apple fritters that must have weighed a pound and a half apiece. I happened to be sitting at the same table as the "chef," and it came out in the course of the conversation—which mainly consisted of compliments from other RV-park residents on the cooking—that she makes a special "black bread" for Ash Wednesday (when only bread and water are served).

"What's in it?" I asked, hoping it might by accident contain a stray nutrient or two.

The woman cast her eyes down and replied modestly, "Oh, they've begged me for the recipe, but I won't give it to them. Four Seasons wanted the ranch-dressing recipe from my restaurant in Idaho, but I wouldn't give that out, either."

I don't know what horrified me more: that she imagined I would want to duplicate anything she had cooked; or that she had been connected in some way with the operation of a restaurant.

From Merton's *The Sign of Jonas*:

> I ought to know, by now, that God uses everything that happens as a means to lead me into solitude. Every creature that enters my life, every instant of my days, will be designed to wound me with the realization of the world's insufficiency, until I become so detached that I will be able to find God alone in everything. Only then will all things bring me joy.

That's fine, but I need to learn the difference between detachment and contempt. The point of detachment is not to realize how different and above-it-all you are, but to realize how ordinary you are, how exactly like everyone else, how desperately in need of help. *How can a person lead a life of prayer and eat such shitty food?* is the subtext of my complaints about the cooking. But someone could just as easily look at me and say, "How can anyone lead a life of prayer and still be so anxious, so petty, so endlessly self-absorbed?"

The truth I don't want to face is that I'm deformed, too. Spiritually, emotionally, and now physically, too: the lumpectomied breast, the faint purple scars.

More Merton:

> Hence the solitary man says nothing, and does his work, and is patient—or perhaps impatient, I don't know—but generally he has peace. It is not the world's kind of peace. He is happy, but he never has a good time.

I love that: "He is happy, but he never has a good time." *Well,* I think, *I'm halfway there.*

I am trying not to get too worked up over it, but my husband Tim has an obstruction in his throat that feels to him like a growth. He's going to see the doctor today, and when I talked to him last night—on the pay phone behind the chapel, the lit booth shining like a beacon through the dark—I heard for the first time the worry in his voice. I haven't been worried, because he seems otherwise healthy. But last night, when I said, "Well, you feel all right, don't you?" he said, "No, I don't. I feel tired." *Oh, God,* I thought, *what if we both got cancer?* So I prayed for him last night and again today. I even mentioned him in our intercessionary prayers in chapel this morning.

Glamorizing the monastic life is something I have to be constantly on guard against. I've always thought of myself as someone who can never get enough solitude, but I'm beginning to see that it's not more solitude I need. Instead, I need to accept the solitude in which I already live, to accept that the search for God has to be conducted without complaining, without wanting to be recognized. My whole life—this burning love for Christ—has to be experienced in secrecy, partly because it can't be communicated, and partly because, just as when Christ was alive, nobody is much interested: not my family, not the majority of my friends, and definitely not my husband. I'm just starting to realize what the saints knew all along: that it is always going to be like this.

I woke early to watch the sun rise this morning, and though I saw the sky lightening, there was no spectacular display of colors. I came here expecting springtime in the desert: flowering mesquite, balmy nights. Instead, it's been freezing, overcast, and windy. The RV dwellers say I scheduled my visit mere days too early: next week, at the latest, the weather will turn, and it will be in the eighties. The Psalm says, "Fire and heat, bless the Lord. Cold and chill, bless the Lord." I'll bless the cold, but I am grateful for my polar fleece.

There's a nun here from Baltimore named Georgina. She's about my age and has breast cancer *and* leukemia. Her doctors give her five years at the most. She told me this last night as we were walking to the dining hall. Tomorrow I might drive her into Watkins to get some medical supplies: she is constipated, exhausted from radiation, and, like me, having a hard time with the food. At dinner, I saw her give a big smile to Jim, the "retreat master," whom I've decided I don't like. Constantly, I am reminded of my meanness.

Here's Merton again, from "The Power and Meaning of Love":

> There is no way under the sun to make a man worthy of love except by loving him. As soon as he realizes himself loved—if he is not so weak that he can no longer bear to be loved—he will feel himself instantly becoming worthy of love. He will respond by drawing a mysterious spiritual value out of his own depths, a new identity called into being by the love that is addressed to him.

It's another gray, windy day, but I took my two-hour walk anyway: Sun breaking through the edges of the clouds, snow-capped mountains, low-hanging blue haze. Sea green and purple prickly pear. Red dirt, bleached green grass.

I wasn't thinking about much, except how to be better to Tim. Now that I'm away, I've been struck with pangs of tenderness and guilt. He is so precious, so worthy of love, so fragile—and I'm so hard on him. I do the exact thing Merton warns against: I treat him as an object, worthy only insofar as he is of use to me.

Because of his work schedule, Tim is often home when I'm trying to write, and my fear is that if I talk to him for ten minutes in the morning, I'm going to get sucked in and waste the whole day. It's a lack of faith, I suppose, that I'll be given the impetus and energy for a productive day; coupled with the misconception that a productive day cannot have any human interaction in it; compounded further by the illusion that I have no value apart from productivity; and complicated by the fact that I really do need quiet and solitude in order to work. In other words, a mixture of truth and lies, good motives and bad. And the plaint of writers since time immemorial.

One of the central dynamics of our marriage is that Tim is *in my way*: when I want to pray, when I want to cultivate other friendships, when I want to work, when I want to sit and think. Sometimes this is objectively true, but other times it is me blaming my sloth on him, a handy target. In any case, true or not, it's a sad, hard way to look at any person, much less your husband. I want to "progress," whatever that means. But to love a person, to see Christ in him—that is progress: the only progress.

Outside my window, a woman with a Saint Benedict medal hanging from her neck and a chain saw in her hand is eyeing a long row of fir trees. It cannot be an accident that the sound of our machines so perfectly mirrors the state of our souls: leaf blowers, digital alarm clocks, snowmobiles, jet skis. Yesterday on my walk, I could hear an all-terrain vehicle as I started out. And then the SUVs began to roll by—not many of them, thank God, but there will be more next year, and the year after that, kicking up gravel and clouds of dust, scaring the animals, in a big hurry to go nowhere. Just like me.

• • •

I have begun to see that conditions like the weather and my surroundings never make that much difference. One second is one second for all of us; we all get twenty-four hours in a day. Merton had the same problems in his monastery that I do here: Not enough time to write, not enough time to read, not enough time to pray, not enough silence. A constant longing for solitude coupled with constant infringements upon it, and the realization that he was blowing whatever chances he had for prayer. People who drove him crazy, people whose spirituality he didn't trust, the tension between obedience and a personal calling. That is the spiritual path; nobody who wants to find God can avoid it.

Even with no responsibilities, I find there still aren't enough hours in the day to give praise, to get lost in wonder. The weather was lovely, cool and fresh, on the trail this afternoon, and I was thinking about something novelist Walker Percy once said: that Christianity is so on target because at the heart of it is the acknowledgment that man has a problem; that man is in deep, deep trouble. Yesterday I actually thought that if Tim got lymphoma and died, at least I'd have more time to write. That is the extent of my selfishness. God forgive me.

Last night, I skipped dinner and walked in the freezing cold to the chapel for Compline, but they must have already held it in the dining hall, because nobody was there. So I went to the Lady of Guadelupe and said the evening prayer by myself, and then I sat by the Blessed Sacrament for a while. "The adoration of the Blessed Sacrament" used to sound hokey and nunnish to me. Now I see it as a deep, mysterious gift. What solace, what peace to sit with Him: the Great Physician, the Master Anesthesiologist.

I swear it has gotten colder each day I've been here. It's now almost as bad as winter in New England. Taking a walk is becoming like penance.

Today I had a moment when, like Saint Ignatius of Loyola, I prayed from the center of my being, *Take all of me: my freedom, my memory, my understanding, and my will.* Of course, it's easy to feel that way when I've been relieved of cares, worries, and interruptions for a week. One dose of "reality" and I'll be plunged back into confusion, overwhelmed anew. Still, I have to believe that all prayer is a step in the right direction, even if I feel at times that I'm regressing. Probably all spiritual progress consists of the deepening realization that you can do nothing without God. As this awareness grows, your life naturally becomes one of ceaseless prayer, because you see that there is simply no other possible mode of existence. There is no more virtue in this than there is in a drowning man's attempts to keep his head above water.

I keep thinking of that reading from Sirach the other morning: "When a sieve is shaken, the husks appear; so do a man's faults when he speaks." Or acts. Giving Sister Georgina a ride into town this afternoon, I couldn't help comparing myself to her. She was a little embarrassed to be going, as apparently any retreatant worth his or her salt does not leave the grounds for the duration of the retreat, whereas I, having gone on my pathetic coffee runs every morning, thought nothing of an extra trip. She needed to pick up some juice and tea because she's sick; I wanted to pick up some chocolate and one last coffee before Lent begins tomorrow. My car was filthy; she was spotless and perfectly groomed.

To top it all off, on our return, I repaired to my room and proceeded to eat the entire giant Cadbury bar I had purchased at Safeway while Sister Georgina was loading up on chamomile tea and apple juice. I'd told myself I'd save half for Tim; but, no, by six o'clock I had eaten the whole calorie-laden bar—after having judged everyone else for being fat. It doesn't matter where I am, my faults will be revealed.

Ash Wednesday. At Morning Prayer, we listen to a reading from Isaiah about fasting: "If you bestow your bread on the hungry and satisfy the afflicted; then light shall rise for you in the darkness, and the gloom shall become for you like midday." When I go into the dining hall for a cup of tea, each table is bare except for a loaf of dark, rustic bread (the secret recipe!) and a white crockery bowl filled with dirt and stones.

Later, at the noon Mass, the daydreaming abbot starts to sing,

"Alleluia," after the opening antiphon, and the wizened old monk interrupts kindly: "No, not during Lent."

"I know, I know," the abbot replies loudly before plowing on with the service.

Though we've not exchanged a single word all week, I can't help but like the abbot. What a job to keep this place up and running; to deal with the monks, the oblates, the community. (Last Sunday, I noticed the abbot was gone and overheard someone saying that, due to a shortage of priests in the area, he was scheduled to say seven Masses that day.) In his homily, he talks about prayer as a method of detaching from thought and observes that one way to do this is to sit in silence with a sacred word. The word many of the monks use, he says, is the Aramaic *Maranatha*: "Come, Lord Jesus." The chapel is packed, and, for a second, I wonder if this Middle American parish is ready for contemplative prayer. Then I realize that this whole place operates on nothing but prayer, and I'm the one who knows nothing about it.

"Remember, you are dust, and to dust you shall return," the abbot says over and over as we file up to have our foreheads anointed with ashes.

I spend the afternoon packing and then wander out behind the chapel, skirting the duck pond, to the outdoor Stations of the Cross. Like the adoration of the Blessed Sacrament, the Stations have always struck me as slightly musty and old-fashioned, but someone has put a lot of thought into designing this course; according to the monastery's brochure, it "incorporates natural features of the landscape."

I start at the first Station—JESUS IS CONDEMNED TO DEATH—which is located near a creosote bush. "This desert bush," the placard reads, "forced to survive with so little water, reminds us of how Jesus felt as he stood before his merciless accusers." I pause to pray for a couple of minutes, then make my way around a boulder to Station number two, JESUS BEARS HIS CROSS: "This heavy stone, an impossible burden, is like the cross Jesus was forced to carry to Mount Calvary."

The path winds up a hill, and I trudge on, the sun sinking in a pool of red, until I reach Station twelve, JESUS DIES ON THE CROSS: "Just as the trunk of this burned-out tree is stripped bare, so we will be stripped of everything: property, success, looks, health."

And suddenly I am weeping: for the old men and the abused children; for the people so alone they have no one to pray for them; for Sister Georgina; for myself. I've tried so hard to be good: praying in the "right" way, giving up coffee for Lent, being mature and responsible and accepting about my cancer. But finding God isn't about being "good." It's about becoming human. It's not about pretending that cancer doesn't terrify me. It's about consenting to bear those crosses just as, in some mysterious way, every other human being bears his or her own crosses for me.

When they drove the nails through Christ's precious hands, his beautiful, sacred feet, he wasn't mature and responsible and accepting. He knew the worst spiritual anguish any person can know: "Father, Father, why have you forsaken me?" And yet God doesn't forsake us; he dwells within us always. That's what the Resurrection tells us. That's what I've staked my life on: that light far in the distant future, after seven dark weeks of Lent.

The dinner bell rings, and I salivate: I've been fasting all day. Tomorrow I'll leave the silence, the cottonwoods, and the birds, and make the long drive back to LA. But for now, it's time to walk through the gathering dusk and join the others: the young monks and the old; Dot and Jim; Sister Georgina; Fran and Earl; Lois and Vern; the woman in charge of cooking. It's time to bow our heads and eat the good black bread.

from The Seven Storey Mountain
by Thomas Merton

Catholic writer and peace activist Thomas Merton (1915–1968) was barely 18 years old when he visited Rome and became enchanted by the city's art and its churches. The experience profoundly influenced his spiritual life.

So there I was, with all the liberty that I had been promising myself for so long. The world was mine. How did I like it? I was doing just what I pleased, and instead of being filled with happiness and well-being, I was miserable. The love of pleasure is destined by its very nature to defeat itself and end in frustration. But I was one of the last men in the world who would have been convinced by the wisdom of a St. John of the Cross in those strange days.

But now I was entering a city which bears living testimony to these truths, to those who can see it, to those who know where to look for it—to those who know how to compare the Rome of the Caesars with the Rome of the martyrs.

I was entering the city that had been thus transformed by the Cross. Square white apartment houses were beginning to appear in thick clusters at the foot of the bare, grey-green hills, with clumps of cypress here and there, and presently over the roofs of the buildings, I saw, rising up in the dusk, the mighty substance of St. Peter's dome. The realization that it was not a photograph filled me with great awe.

My first preoccupation in Rome was to find a dentist. The people in the hotel sent me to one nearby. There were a couple of nuns in the waiting room. After they left, I entered. The dentist had a brown beard. I did not trust my Italian for so important a matter as a toothache. I spoke to him in French. He knew a little French. And he looked at the tooth.

He knew what he thought was wrong with it, but he did not know the technical word in French.

"Ah," he said, "vous avez un *colpo d'aria.*"

I figured it out easily enough to mean that I had caught a chill in my tooth—according to this man with the brown beard. But still, cowardice closed my mouth, and I was content not to argue that I thought it was by no means a chill, but an abscess.

"I shall treat it with ultra-violet rays," said the dentist. With a mixture of relief and scepticism, I underwent this painless and futile process. It did nothing whatever to relieve the toothache. But I left with warm assurances from the dentist that it would all disappear during the night.

Far from disappearing during the night, the toothache did what all toothaches do during the night: kept me awake, in great misery, cursing my fate.

The next morning I got up and staggered back to my friend *colpo d'aria* next door. I met him coming down the stairs with his beard all brushed and a black hat on his head, with gloves and spats and everything. Only then did I realize that it was Sunday. However, he consented to give a look at the chilled tooth.

In a mixture of French and Italian he asked me if I could stand ether. I said yes, I could. He draped a clean handkerchief over my nose and mouth and dropped a couple of drops of ether on it. I breathed deeply, and the sweet sick knives of the smell reached in to my consciousness and the drumming of the heavy dynamos began. I hoped that he wasn't breathing too deeply himself, or that his hand wouldn't slip, and spill the whole bottle of it in my face.

However, a minute or two later I woke up again and he was waving the red, abscessed roots of the tooth in my face and exclaiming: "C'est fini!"

I moved out of my hotel and found a *pensione* with windows that looked down on the sunny Triton fountain in the middle of the Piazza Barberini and the Bristol Hotel and the Barberini Cinema and the Barberini Palace, and the maid brought me some hot water to treat the boil on my arm. I went to bed and tried to read a novel by Maxim Gorki which very quickly put me to sleep.

I had been in Rome before, on an Easter vacation from school, for about a week. I had seen the Forum and the Colosseum and the Vatican museum and St. Peter's. But I had not really seen Rome.

This time, I started out again, with the misconception common to Anglo-Saxons, that the real Rome is the Rome of the ugly ruins, the Rome of all those grey cariated temples wedged in between the hills and the slums of the city. I tried to reconstruct the ancient city, in my mind—a dream which did not work very well, because of the insistent shouting of the sellers of postcards who beset me on every side. After a few days of trying the same thing, it suddenly struck me that it was not worth the trouble. It was so evident, merely from the masses of stone and brick that still represented the palaces and temples and baths, that imperial Rome must have been one of the most revolting and ugly and depressing cities the world has ever seen. In fact, the ruins with cedars and cypresses and umbrella pines scattered about among them were far more pleasant than the reality must have been.

However, I still roamed about the museums, especially the one in the Baths of Diocletian, which had also been, at one time, a Carthusian monastery—probably not a very successful one—and I studied Rome in a big learned book that I had bought, together with an old secondhand Baedeker in French.

And after spending the day in museums and libraries and bookstores and among the ruins, I would come home again and read my novels. In fact, I was also beginning to write one of my own, although I did not get very far with it as long as I was at Rome.

I had a lot of books with me—a strange mixture: Dryden, the poems of D. H. Lawrence, some Tauchnitz novels, and James Joyce's *Ulysses* in a fancy India-paper edition, slick and expensive, which I lent to someone, later on, and never got back.

Things were going on as they usually did with me. But after about a week—I don't know how it began—I found myself looking into churches rather than into ruined temples. Perhaps it was the frescoes on the wall of an old chapel—ruined too—at the foot of the Palatine, at the edge of the Forum, that first aroused my interest in another and a far different Rome. From there it was an easy step to Sts. Cosmas and Damian, across the Forum, with a great mosaic, in the apse, of Christ coming in judgement in a dark blue sky, with a suggestion of fire in the small clouds beneath His feet. The effect of this discovery was tremendous. After all the vapid, boring, semi-pornographic statuary of the Empire, what a thing it was to come upon the genius of an art full of spiritual vitality and earnestness and power—an art that was tremendously serious and alive and eloquent and urgent in all that it had to say. And it was without pretentiousness, without fakery, and had nothing theatrical about it. Its solemnity was made all the more astounding by its simplicity—and by the obscurity of the places where it lay hid, and by its subservience to higher ends, architectural, liturgical and spiritual ends which I could not even begin to understand, but which I could not avoid guessing, since the nature of the mosaics themselves and their position and everything about them proclaimed it aloud.

I was fascinated by these Byzantine mosaics. I began to haunt the churches where they were to be found, and, as an indirect consequence, all the other churches that were more or less of the same period. And thus without knowing anything about it I became a pilgrim. I was unconsciously and unintentionally visiting all the great shrines of Rome, and seeking out their sanctuaries with some of the eagerness and avidity and desire of a true pilgrim, though not quite for the right reason. And yet it was not for a wrong reason either. For these mosaics and frescoes and all the ancient altars and thrones and sanctuaries were designed and built for the instruction of people who were not capable of immediately understanding anything higher.

I never knew what relics and what wonderful and holy things were hidden in the churches whose doors and aisles and arches had become the refuge of my mind. Christ's cradle and the pillar of the Flagellation and the True Cross and St. Peter's chains, and the tombs of the great martyrs, the tomb of the child St. Agnes and the martyr St. Cecilia and of Pope St. Clement and of the great deacon St. Lawrence who was burned on a gridiron. . . . These things did not speak to me, or at least I did not know they spoke to me. But the churches that enshrined them did, and so did the art on their walls.

And now for the first time in my life I began to find out something of Who this Person was that men called Christ. It was obscure, but it was a true knowledge of Him, in some sense, truer than I knew and truer than I would admit. But it was in Rome that my conception of Christ was formed. It was there I first saw Him, Whom I now serve as my God and my King, and Who owns and rules my life.

It is the Christ of the Apocalypse, the Christ of the Martyrs, the Christ of the Fathers. It is the Christ of St. John, and of St. Paul, and of St. Augustine and St. Jerome and all the Fathers—and of the Desert Fathers. It is Christ God, Christ King, *"for in Him dwelleth the fulness of the Godhead corporeally, and you are filled in Him, Who is the Head of all principality and power . . . For in Him were all things created in heaven and on earth, visible and invisible, whether thrones or dominations or principalities or powers, all things were created by Him and in Him. And He is before all, and by Him all things consist . . . because in Him it hath well pleased the Father that all fulness should dwell . . . Who is the image of the invisible God, the first-born of every creature . . ." "The first-begotten of the dead, and the prince of the kings of the earth, Who hath loved us, and washed us from our sins in His own Blood, and hath made us a kingdom and priests to God His Father."*

The saints of those forgotten days had left upon the walls of their churches words which by the peculiar grace of God I was able in some measure to apprehend, although I could not decode them all. But above all, the realest and most immediate source of this grace was Christ Himself, present in those churches, in all His power, and in His Humanity, in His Human Flesh and His material, physical, corporeal Presence. How often I was left entirely alone in these churches with the tremendous God, and knew nothing of it—except I had to know something of it, as I say, obscurely. And it was He Who was teaching me Who He was, more directly than I was capable of realising.

These mosaics told me more than I had ever known of the doctrine of a God of infinite power, wisdom and love Who had yet become Man, and revealed in His Manhood the infinity of power, wisdom and love that was His Godhead. Of course I could not grasp and believe these things explicitly. But since they were implicit in every line of the pictures I contemplated with such admiration and love, surely I grasped them implicitly—I had to, in so far as the mind of the artist reached my own mind, and spoke to it his conception and his thought. And so I could not help but catch something of the ancient craftsman's love of Christ, the Redeemer and Judge of the World.

It was more or less natural that I should want to discover something of the meaning of the mosaics I saw—of the Lamb standing as though slain, and of the four-and-twenty elders casting down their crowns. And I had bought a Vulgate text, and was reading the New Testament. I had forgotten all about the poems of D. H. Lawrence except for the fact that he had four poems about the Four Evangelists, based on the traditional symbols from Ezechiel and the Apocalypse of the four mystical creatures. One evening, when I was reading these poems, I became so disgusted with their falseness and futility that I threw down the book and began to ask myself why I was wasting my time with a man of such unimportance as this. For it was evident that he had more or less completely failed to grasp the true meaning of the New Testament, which he had perverted in the interests of a personal and homemade religion of his own which was not only fanciful, but full of unearthly seeds, all ready to break forth into hideous plants like those that were germinating in Germany's unweeded garden, in the dank weather of Nazism.

So for once I put my favorite aside. And I read more and more of the Gospels, and my love for the old churches and their mosaics grew from day to day. Soon I was no longer visiting them merely for the art. There was something else that attracted me: a kind of interior peace. I loved to be in these holy places. I had a kind of deep and strong conviction that I belonged there: that my rational nature was filled with profound desires and needs that could only find satisfaction in churches of God. I remember that one of my favorite shrines was that of St. Peter in Chains, and I did not love it for any work of art that was there, since the big attraction, the big "number," the big "feature" in that place is Michelangelo's Moses. But I had always been extremely bored by that horned and pop-eyed frown and by the crack in the knee. I'm glad the thing couldn't speak, for it would probably have given out some very heavy statements.

Perhaps what was attracting me to that Church was the Apostle himself to whom it is dedicated. And I do not doubt that he was praying earnestly to get me out of my own chains: chains far heavier and more terrible than ever were his.

Where else did I like to go? St. Pudenziana, St. Praxed's, above all St. Mary Major and the Lateran, although as soon as the atmosphere got heavy with baroque melodrama I would get frightened, and the peace and the obscure, tenuous sense of devotion I had acquired would leave me.

So far, however, there had been no deep movement of my will, nothing that amounted to a conversion, nothing to shake the iron tyranny of moral corruption that held my whole nature in fetters. But that also was to come. It came in a strange way, suddenly, a way that I will not attempt to explain.

I was in my room. It was night. The light was on. Suddenly it seemed to me that Father, who had now been dead more than a year, was there with me. The sense of his presence was as vivid and as real and as startling as if he had touched my arm or spoken to me. The whole thing passed in a flash, but in that flash, instantly, I was overwhelmed with a sudden and profound insight into the misery and corruption of my own soul, and I was pierced deeply with a light that made me realize something of the condition I was in, and I was filled with horror at what I saw, and my whole being rose up in revolt against what was within me, and my soul desired escape and liberation and freedom from all this with an intensity and an urgency unlike anything I had ever known before. And now I think for the first time in my whole life I really began to pray—praying not with my lips and with my intellect and my imagination, but praying out of the very roots of my life and of my being, and praying to the God I had never known, to reach down towards me out of His darkness and to help me to get free of the thousand terrible things that held my will in their slavery.

There were a lot of tears connected with this, and they did me good, and all the while, although I had lost that first vivid, agonizing sense of the presence of my father in the room, I had him in my mind, and I was talking to him as well as to God, as though he were a sort of intermediary. I do not mean this in any way that might be interpreted that I thought he was among the saints. I did not really know what that might mean then, and now that I do know I would hesitate to say that I thought he was in Heaven. Judging by my memory of the experience I should say it was "as if" he had been sent to me out of Purgatory. For after all, there is no reason why the souls in Purgatory should not help those on earth by their prayers and influence, just like those in Heaven: although usually they need our help more than we need theirs. But in this case, assuming my guess has some truth in it, things were the other way 'round.

However, this is not a thing on which I would place any great stress. And I do not offer any definite explanation of it. How do I know it was not merely my own imagination, or something that could be traced to a purely natural, psychological cause—I mean the part about my father? It is impossible to say. I do not offer any explanation. And I have always had a great antipathy for everything that smells of necromancy—table-turning and communications with the dead, and I would never deliberately try to enter in to any such thing. But whether it was imagination or nerves or whatever else it may have been, I can say truly that I did feel, most vividly, as if my father were present there, and the consequences that I have described followed from this, as though he had communicated to me without words an interior light from God, about the condition of my own soul—although I wasn't even sure I had a soul.

The one thing that seems to me morally certain is that this was really a grace, and a great grace. If I had only followed it through, my life might have been very different and much less miserable for the years that were to come.

Before now I had never prayed in the churches I had visited. But I remember the morning that followed this experience. I remember how I climbed the deserted Aventine, in the spring sun, with my soul broken up with contrition, but broken and clean, painful but sanitary like a lanced abscess, like a bone broken and reset. And it was true contrition, too, for I don't think I was capable of mere attrition, since I did not believe in hell. I went to the Dominicans' Church, Santa Sabina. And it was a very definite experience, something that amounted to a capitulation, a surrender, a conversion, not without struggle, even now, to walk deliberately into the church with no other purpose than to kneel down and pray to God. Ordinarily, I never knelt in these churches, and never paid any formal or official attention to Whose house it was. But now I took holy water at the door and went straight up to the altar rail and knelt down and said, slowly, with all the belief I had in me, the Our Father.

It seems almost unbelievable to me that I did no more than this, for the memory remains in me as that of such an experience that it would seem to have implied at least a half hour of impassioned prayer and tears. The thing to remember is that I had not prayed at all for some years.

Another thing which Catholics do not realize about converts is the tremendous, agonizing embarrassment and self-consciousness which they feel about praying publicly in a Catholic Church. The effort it takes to overcome all the strange imaginary fears that everyone is looking at you, and that they all think you are crazy or ridiculous, is something that costs a tremendous effort. And that day in Santa Sabina, although the church was almost entirely empty, I walked across the stone door mortally afraid that a poor devout old Italian woman was following me with suspicious eyes. As I knelt to pray, I wondered if she would run out and accuse me at once to the priests, with scandalous horror, for coming and praying in their church—as if Catholics were perfectly content to have a lot of heretic tourists walking about their churches with complete indifference and irreverence, and would get angry if one of them so far acknowledged God's presence there as to go on his knees for a few seconds and say a prayer!

However, I prayed, then I looked about the church, and went into a room where there was a picture by Sassoferrato, and stuck my face out a door into a tiny, simple cloister, where the sun shone dawn on an orange tree. After that I walked out into the open feeling as if I had been reborn, and crossed the street, and strolled through the suburban fields to another deserted church where I did not pray, being scared by some carpenters and scaffolding. I sat outside, in the sun, on a wall and tasted the joy of my own inner peace, and turned over in my mind how my life was now going to change, and how I would become better.

Old Man Joseph and His Family

by Romulus Linney

Romulus Linney (born 1930) is better known for his award-winning plays than for his novels. The aging Joseph in this folktale adaptation doesn't know quite what to do with his mischievous yet extraordinary son.

His workshop, say the Apocryphal Gospels, was dusty, and there were cobwebs and rust where he couldn't see any more, but he still went there every day. He often forgot what he was making.

Just before she died, his wife told him he had to stop working. He was too feeble. He was going to fall down, break an arm, hip, or his neck, and die in there.

Now she was dead a year, and still Joseph went to his workshop, talking to her out loud, saying he'd be all right.

One day he was binding a double brace he used inside platforms. He didn't mix his glue right. He let it boil too long. He took off the clamp too soon. The slats came unstuck. One hit him on the head. Another slid between his legs. He tripped and fell down, hard.

He got up on his left side, but slipped and fell again. He tried his right side, and the same thing happened. He couldn't get himself off the floor.

He lay there.

"God damned miserable old age," he said.

He heard footsteps. There was a loud knock on his workshop door.

"Come in!" he said.

The door opened. A tall man in a dusty cloak stood looking down at him.

"Are you Joseph the Carpenter?"

"That's right."

"Want me to help you up?"

"No, thanks."

"Suit yourself."

The tall man unrolled a scroll with many names on it.

"I have you down here as a widower. Correct?"

"What's that to you?"

"You'll see. Are you drunk?"

"No. Who are you?"

"I am a Herald of the High Priest of the Temple at Jerusalem. Have you married again?"

Joseph stared up at the Herald.

"Of course I married again. I'm only eighty-nine."

"Widower. How many children?"

"Fourteen. Forty-one grandchildren."

"How many live with you?"

"None. They come and I yell and they go. I don't want them around."

"Then you'll have to go."

"Go where?"

"At noon tomorrow, every unmarried male of the House of David will stand on the Temple steps, before the High Priest."

He picked Joseph up and put him on his feet.

"I was married!" said Joseph.

"You're not now."

He looked around Joseph's shop, at the abandoned work and the old tools. He saw a crooked stick, leaning against a wall.

"You'll need this," he said, taking it to Joseph. It was warped, bent, chipped, scraped and battered, like its owner, but still in one piece. "Everybody has to bring one."

"One what?"

"Shepherd's rod. Orders."

"I'm not going anywhere!"

The Herald put his arm around Joseph.

"Lift your feet," he said.

At noon the next day, on the Temple steps, their rods in their hands, a hundred unmarried men stood in the hot sun, with Joseph waiting in the middle of them.

The great carved doors of the Temple opened. Priests marched out, in flowing robes. Behind them, eyes flashing, came the High Priest.

Behind him, head bowed, walked a girl.

The High Priest stepped forward and looked out over the sea of young men. He made one swift motion with his right hand. Two Priests brought the girl forward.

She looked fourteen, maybe fifteen years old.

She was crying.

"Behold this woman!" said the High Priest. "Ten years ago, her mother brought her to this Temple, as a pure and sanctified virgin. We took her in. Yesterday, she reached her fifteenth birthday. She is now a woman. She must become a wife and a mother. That is law."

The girl wept.

"Since her mother gave her to us, we have treasured her, fed her, clothed her, and brought her to womanhood. Now she disobeys us. Her time comes, she refuses to marry."

The High Priest held up his arms.

"Men of Judea!" he said. "One of you will become her husband. You will take her, protect her, cherish her, break her, and make her the woman she must become. Hold up your rods!"

All the young men held their rods up over their heads. They were all thin and straight and strong.

Joseph didn't bother, but the High Priest saw him, and said, "You, too."

So Joseph held up his crooked old dried-out rod. He winked at the girl, and smiled.

The High Priest closed both eyes, threw his head back, and prayed. He prayed and prayed. All the other Priests chanted.

The girl stared at Joseph.

The High Priest stopped praying. The Priests stopped chanting. The High Priest was staring up into the sky.

"Men of Judea!" he said. "Look there!"

Everybody looked up into the sky, where the sun was hot and glaring.

"What's happening?" said Joseph, squinting.

"Men of Judea!" said the High Priest again. "Hold up every rod!"

They all did, and Joseph held his up, too.

"What's up there?" he asked a boy standing next to him.

"A bird," the boy said. "Flying around in circles."

"Watch out," said Joseph. "Temples and birds, watch out."

His arm got tired holding up his rod, so he set one end on the ground.

"What's the bird doing now?"

"Coming down."

"Here?"

"Looks like it."

With a flutter of grey-white wings, a large dove sank down upon them. It perched on the tip of Joseph's rod.

"What?" said Joseph. "What?"

The dove had tiny black eyes. It looked at Joseph.

Joseph shook his rod.

"Get off there!"

The dove had thin sharp claws. They sank into the wood.

"Shoo! Go on!"

The dove stuck fast to the rod.

"What is your name?" said the High Priest to Joseph.

"Get off!" said Joseph.

"Name!" said the High Priest.

"Joseph the Carpenter!" said Joseph. "Go on! Off!"

"Age?"

"Eighty-nine! Get off!"

The dove stuck tight to the tip of Joseph's rod, staring at him with little black eyes.

The girl stepped forward.

"Joseph," she said.

"What?"

The dove opened its claws. With a single lash of wings, it was gone.

The girl stood above Joseph on the Temple steps, looking down at him.

"If you want me," she said, "take me."

"At my age?"

The girl bit her lip.

"What would I do with you?" said Joseph.

The girl nodded.

"Sorry," said Joseph.

The girl stepped back. She bowed her head again.

"You were the perfect man," she said.

She looked up again, bleakly.

"What are you staring at?" said Joseph.

"Hot boys. Goodbye, Joseph."

Joseph looked at the High Priest. He looked at all the young men, with their rods in their hands.

"Listen," he said. "It's not so bad, getting married. Young men are all right."

The girl began to cry again.

Joseph scowled at the High Priest. "You played some kind of damn trick with a trained bird or something. I know that. What's her name?"

"Mary," said the High Priest.

"Tell her to hush up. She's crying again."

"You tell her."

Joseph leaned on his rod.

"Mary," he said. "Hush. Don't let them see you acting like a child. Just because you got to marry some yokel. What did you expect?"

"I'm not crying," said Mary.

She wept.

It came out before he knew what he was saying.

"I might could use me a housekeeper."

Mary stopped crying. The High Priest smiled. The boys winked at each other.

"For just a little while," said Joseph. "I'll be dead soon."

Mary nodded gravely.

"And I ain't the perfect man for nobody. You'll see that, quick enough. And be on your way."

Mary kept on looking at him gravely.

"You'll keep the house. I keep my shop. You don't go in there at all. Understand? Are you just looking or are you listening to me?"

"I'm listening to you."

"I won't lay a hand on you. As if I could. So we'll have no talk of marriage."

"Yes, we will," said the High Priest.

Joseph scratched his head.

"Well, if she doesn't like boys a year from now, and I am still alive, which ain't very likely either one, then we can marry. How's that? Satisfy the Temple?"

The High Priest nodded.

Some of the young men snickered, and nudged each other, wagging their heads.

Joseph glared at them.

"Satisfy you twits?" he said.

He turned to Mary.

"Satisfy you?"

Mary ran down the steps of the Temple, and held his hand.

"I am a plain country man."

"I'm glad."

"We will live in Nazareth."

"That's fine."

Joseph took a step backward, and looked her over.

"My children see you, they are going to piss green. I beg your pardon. I'm a old man. I swear sometimes."

"Yes, sir."

"Call me Joseph. Swearing bother you?"

"When other men swear, I see darkness," said Mary. "When Joseph swears, I see light."

"What will you say to my children?"

"That I like hard work. I have a good disposition. I will take care of you."

Joseph and Mary walked away, together.

"And the town? They'll make fun of us, Mary."

"I don't care, Joseph."

Without looking back, they left the Temple.

"Sooner or later, you are going to think again about hot boys. It's natural. I won't keep them away from you."

"You won't have to."

"Yes, I will. What do you think you'll do, in a year?"

"Marry Joseph."

"Hush. On my ninetieth birthday?"

"Joseph."

"What?"

"It isn't the end that's important," said Mary. "It's the beginning."

Two years later, Joseph was ninety-one, and married to Mary. He looked thirty years younger. His ear aches were long gone. His balance and appetite were back. He was nimble and spry.

His days came and went smoothly again, as he remembered them from his youth, when he thought they had no end.

His children were astonished. All the bad jokes stopped. They became a welcome sight, the healthy old man, and his young wife, who had made him well.

Good as her word, Mary took care of him. She kept his house neat and clean, gave him hot meals, washed his clothes and cut his hair.

Joseph sat with her through long evenings. He listened carefully to what she told him. About the Temple, and how she had lived there so long. About her mother, who put her there, insisting she was a holy child, marked by God. Joseph said it was all understandable. He'd seen stranger things. She was as fine a young woman as any man could find anywhere. Forget the Temple.

So.

He cleaned up his workshop. His working ways came back to him. He invented a wooden window lattice that could fly open or shut tight at the pull of one cord, and was much admired. He made all kinds of furniture, and every piece was smooth and sturdy. In their places, glistening now, were his double-handed saws, squares, files, mallets, hatchets, awls, his glue-pots, chalk lines and plummets, all looking formidable.

Men came to see him, asking him questions. A contractor hired him to supervise not only the woodwork inside his buildings, but the digging of the foundation hole and the perpendiculars of the stones and the mortar.

Joseph was in demand, not just as a carpenter, but as a builder of long life and experience. He was sent on trips to other towns where he was made much of, and so he found himself back in the rush of life.

One day Joseph was getting ready for another trip, and Mary was trying to tell him something.

"Joseph," said Mary. "I have something to tell you."

Joseph was packing a small leather bag, not paying attention.

"Joseph, I have something to tell you."

"Eight houses. This is going to be some trip."

"Joseph."

He looked at her fondly.

"Marrying you was the best thing that ever happened to me, honey. Now, what is it?"

"I'm pregnant."

Joseph lifted his leather bag by its rope, still smiling.

"What did you say?"

"I'm pregnant."

Joseph put the bag down, and stared at her.

"I'm going to have a baby."

Joseph sat down, suddenly.

"I think it's about three months now."

Joseph looked at his bag, at the floor, at the ceiling, and then back at her.

"Joseph. Say something."

"My virgin Mary? Three months gone?"

"That's right," she said.

Joseph thought for a moment.

"Take me," he said. "You are the perfect man."

"Joseph."

"I like hard work. I have a good disposition."

"Stop that."

"I'll take good care of you."

"Joseph, listen to me."

"Didn't I give you a year? Tell you to find your hot boy when you need him. Didn't I tell you that?"

"There isn't any him."

"What?"

"That's what I am trying to tell you."

Joseph closed his eyes. His left ear began to ache again. There was a tremor in his right hand.

"I am still a virgin," said Mary.

Joseph took a deep breath.

"Honey, I am ninety-one years old. I just don't want to hear talk like that."

"But it's the truth, Joseph."

Joseph sat up straight in the chair. There was a cramp in his side. There was a buzzing at the base of his skull.

"Don't you want to know how it happened?"

His tongue was sticking to the roof of his palate. His mouth tasted like damp clay. His eyes began to ache.

"All right," he said, wearily.

Mary sat down across from him, and spoke slowly, and carefully.

"You were on a trip. I went to the well. A young man was standing there. He was singing a song. It was about rosy lips and being in love. He was singing it to himself, and he had smouldering dark eyes, Joseph, but the brightest yellow hair. He didn't look like anybody I'd ever seen before. He kept staring at me. He made me very nervous."

"Nervous," said Joseph.

"I drew the water and came straight home. I couldn't stop thinking about that young man. And for some reason I got sleepy. More sleepy than I have ever been in all my life. So I went to my room, and lay down, and took a nap."

"Nap," said Joseph.

"In my sleep, I heard the song again. I dreamed that it woke me up. I dreamed I went to the window and looked out and saw that young man, with the dark eyes and the yellow hair. He was standing outside the house, singing."

"Singing."

"He opened my window and climbed into my room, and with him came fresh air and sunlight. It was dazzling. He took me back to my bed. I lay down again. He knelt beside the bed. He told me something wonderful was going to happen to me."

"I bet he did."

"Then I saw the wings he had on his back. They suddenly moved, and stretched. They were dark green and copper colored, and they went up and down slowly, like big fans. He bent over me. He whispered in my ear. He said I was going to have a holy baby. That's what he said. Then he blew gently into my ear. I felt wonderful. He sat by me, singing his song about rosy lips, and being in love. He melted into sunshine and fresh air. I dreamed a star fell into my mouth, and then I woke up. And I was in my bed, in the afternoon again."

Joseph nodded.

"Well, Joseph?"

"Well, what?"

"You are my wise husband. What does it mean?"

"There's only one thing it can mean."

"What's that?"

"You get pregnant through your ear."

Mary jumped up.

"You're laughing at me!"

"What else can I do?"

She sat down again, biting her lip.

"Look here," said Joseph. "That is some story. You have told it to me, and we will leave it at that. I am trying to keep calm. But you had better tell me another story."

Mary shook her head.

"I got to hear something that makes sense."

They stared at each other.

Then they heard a man singing. He was going by the house, singing a song about rosy lips.

Joseph hopped to the window and looked out.

"That's him!" said Joseph.

"Who?"

"Your goddamned angel, that's who!"

Joseph's rod was leaning against the wall. He grabbed it.

"What are you going to do?"

"I'm going to bust up some copper-colored wings, that's what I'm going to do!"

He opened the door and rushed out. Mary didn't know what to do. Joseph meant her to stay in the house. He'd slammed the door.

She went to the window.

Joseph was out there waving his rod. A man was backing away from him.

"You're crazy!"

"Stay where you are!"

"Get away from me!"

"Come on and fight!"

The man ran away. A hundred feet off, he stopped and turned back.

"You ought to be locked up!" he yelled.

Then he was gone.

Joseph leaned on his rod. He couldn't get his breath.

"Scoundrel," he gasped.

He stood there for awhile, getting his breath. Then he went slowly back into his house.

"Did you see the coward run away?" he said to Mary. "Dark eyes and yellow hair. Love songs. Hanging around my house."

"Joseph," said Mary. "The man at the well I saw was one person. What I dreamed about was another person. This was somebody else entirely. You still don't understand."

"Oh, yes I do."

He sank down into a chair, exhausted.

She waited to see what he would do.

"I can divorce you," said Joseph.

"Do I have to go back to the Temple?"

"And have your baby there?"

"Oh."

"Not likely."

"No."

"Go where you please. Try somebody else."

"There won't be anybody else. There wasn't even anybody else this time."

"Don't say that again."

"God can do anything."

"But He don't. He made the rules. He sticks to them. Virgins don't have babies."

Joseph sighed. He was sinking fast. All his aches and pains were coming back. He was aging a year a minute.

He'd been alive again. He didn't want to die now.

He watched her. She was upset but ready to face whatever came next.

Suppose he did figure out what actually happened? Then, no matter how it happened, or who that angel really was, she'd have to leave.

And he would die.

So.

He leaned back in his chair.

"When my children hear you are pregnant, they will piss green."

"Why, Joseph?"

"They'll know I'm not the father."

"Will they?"

He thought about that.

Outside the house, clouds passed away from the sun. Light came in the window. It fell on his leather bag, packed and ready to go.

Busy men were waiting to make the trip with him. Consult with him. Listen to him.

An old man betrayed by a young wife, that was one thing. But Joseph betrayed by Mary? Who would believe it? He had trouble believing it himself.

If he accused Mary of that, his children would make him wish he'd never been born.

On the other hand, a baby at his age?

Who would say what?

So.

He noticed that his ear ache was gone. He held out his right hand, and it was steady. He could breathe easily again.

"We better not do anything sudden," he said. "I got to go on my trip."

"Do you want me here when you get back?"

"That'll be all right."

"Joseph. I have to ask this."

"No, you don't. What can I say? The baby ain't mine, it's a green-winged angel's?"

"Joseph, will you say it's yours?"

"I won't say it ain't."

He picked up his leather bag, and got his rod.

Mary went to the door and opened it for him. The men with their wagons had gathered outside, and were waiting for him.

"Be careful," said Mary.

Joseph eyed her narrowly.

"You, too," said Joseph.

• • •

Into a courtyard, hand in hand, walked a bride and a groom, just married. They were very young and handsome and healthy and miserable. Behind them walked an old woman with a black shawl over her head. She was miserable, too.

"Is it open," said the bride's father.

"It is not," said the old woman. "They locked it."

"Give her the key," said the groom's father.

"Don't do it," said the bride.

The road to Nazareth went right past the courtyard gate. Mary, holding her baby, peeked in.

"Oh, Joseph, look," said Mary. "A wedding."

She smiled at the bride and groom.

"I hope you'll be as happy as we are," she said.

The groom hung his head. The bride turned away.

"What's the matter?" said Mary. "Did I say something wrong?"

"You must have," said Joseph. "Come on."

The parents of the bride and groom saw the baby in Mary's arms, and how old Joseph was. This was an unusual family.

"Just a minute," said the bride's father.

"You are a man of experience," said the groom's mother.

"And wisdom," said the bride's father.

"Stop with us awhile," said the bride's mother. "Rest yourselves."

"And let us talk to you," said the groom's father.

Mary and Joseph went into the courtyard.

"We have a tradition here," said the groom's father. He pointed to the old woman. "She must inspect the wedding bed the day after the wedding night."

Joseph nodded. "No blood?" he said.

"The bride and groom," said the old woman, "have locked the door. They won't let me in."

Servants brought Mary a chair, and an umbrella to keep the sun off the baby. They brought soap, towels, a basin, cups of lime juice, and a jug of cold spring water.

Joseph watched until Mary was settled. Then he spoke sternly.

"Young married people!" said Joseph. "The least you can do is use chicken blood. That's what folks do where I come from."

"No, no!" said the bride's father. "It's too important! Negotiations depend on this!"

"Land grants, mergers, other weddings," said the groom's father.

"I'm talking to them," said Joseph. "Speak up, young married people. I won't fault either of you for what you say."

"You can talk to him," said Mary. "Don't be afraid."

The bride and the groom looked at each other, and nodded. They stepped aside with Joseph and whispered to him.

"We got into bed," said the bride.

"After we said our prayers," said the groom.

"We put our arms around each other," said the bride.

"To begin our married life," said the groom.

"And nothing happened?" said Joseph.

"We did our best," said the bride.

"Nothing happened," said the groom.

"Fancy wedding," said Joseph. "There it is."

Mary spoke to the bride. "Could you hold the baby?" she said.

"Of course," said the bride. She took the baby from Mary, and held it in her arms while Mary washed its face.

The groom stood beside her. He touched the baby's palm with his finger. The baby's little fist closed over it.

"He's strong," said Mary. "Like his father."

The bride leaned against the groom, and watched the baby hold the groom's finger.

"Can't you try again?" said Joseph. "Start the whole thing over?"

"Impossible," said the bride's father.

"The contracts are very specific," said the groom's father. "All negotiations are cancelled today, unless those sheets get inspected."

"Well," said Joseph. "That's too bad."

The groom smiled at the bride. The baby let go of his finger. The bride gave the baby back to Mary.

"We should call it off," said the groom's mother. "Everybody makes mistakes."

The groom kissed the bride. The bride kissed the groom.

"If children can't do it, we shouldn't force them," said the bride's father.

"Call it off," said the bride's mother.

They turned to tell the bride and groom. Neither were there.

"They left," said Mary.

The parents of the bride and groom shrugged their shoulders, and looked at each other sadly. They asked Mary and Joseph who they were and where they were from and how old the baby was.

"We live in Nazareth," said Mary. "The baby was born in Bethlehem, just a few days ago. In a farmer's cave, because we couldn't find a room."

"You mean, with all the livestock?" said the bride's mother.

"That's right," said Mary. "Just as he was born, three old men appeared."

"Three drunks," said Joseph.

"And three shepherds," said Mary.

"They got drunk, too," said Joseph.

"The three old men were magicians," said Mary. "They had charts and glass globes they swung about on strings. A star told the shepherds where to find us."

"Evidently an unusual birth," said the groom's father, politely.

"No, indeed," said Joseph, quickly. "It's not a baby's fault what kind of crazy people are running around the night it's born."

Mary smiled.

"The farmer did get us a midwife," she said. "But I felt no labor pains."

"What was that?" said the groom's mother.

"Discomfort," said Joseph. "But no hard pains. It happens sometimes."

"That night," said Mary, "the midwife washed the baby, and took the water home. The next day she said she'd used it on a grandchild with boils, and they all disappeared."

"She was crazy too," said Joseph.

"That's what she said," said Mary.

"It was a long night," said Joseph. "But the baby's all right."

He looked at Mary.

"And he's going to stay that way."

"Of course," said Mary.

"He is just a plain, run-of-the-mill little boy, and I mean to keep him that way."

Joseph wouldn't let Mary say any more about the baby's birth. He thanked the parents of the bride and groom and got Mary ready to leave.

The bride and the groom came walking back into the courtyard, arms around each other.

Behind them came the old woman.

"Blood!" she said. "Blood!"

"Let's go, Mary," said Joseph.

The parents blocked their way, and wouldn't let them pass.

"The baby was holding the groom's finger," said one.

"The bride was holding the baby," said another.

"It's a holy child!" they all agreed.

"God damn it!" said Joseph.

"Don't scare the baby," said Mary.

"God damn it!" said Joseph.

It was a year later. Joseph came pulling a wagon he made for Jesus into his workshop. It was a playpen on wheels. He could pull it from his workshop, and have the baby with him while he worked. It gave Mary a little time to herself.

The pen had solid wood siding, which made it very safe. There was a metal brace that took the shaft of an umbrella, which could open up outside to keep the sun off the baby.

Joseph maneuvered the pen so it fit against one wall of his workshop. He went to his bench, sat on his stool, and went to work.

The baby, left alone, made a fuss.

"Hush up, Jesus," said Joseph. "Stop your crying. Your birthday is almost over. You're a whole year old today, so settle down. Play with your blocks. Daddy's got to work."

He sharpened a carving tool. Then he took a hatchet and split a piece of cedar. He held it up and then, with his chisel and a mallet, he began to knock it into shape.

He heard little knocking sounds in the pen.

Jesus was banging his wooden blocks.

"That's it," said Joseph.

With a file he began to sand the edges of the cedar.

"Yes, sir. Things are going along all right now. Your mother is beginning to see what I mean when I say you're no different from anybody else."

He stopped filing. He used his mallet again.

"Your mother," he said.

He used his file again.

"Truth is, your mother's not that much older than you are, not to me. You two are going to be close. I can see that."

He heard filing noises inside the playpen. He looked in. Jesus was scraping a small comb against a block of wood.

He went back to his bench.

"It's up to me to teach you, Jesus. You're nothing special. Get that through your head. It would be the worst thing I could do to you, son, to tell you you are. Puff you up like a fool. Let you believe everything your Momma tells you is the truth. Send you out in life thinking you are God knows what. That's what happens to Momma's boys, Jesus. They're just one little grain of sand, like what's coming off this wood, but they think they hung the moon. Truth is, there's nothing in their minds but Momma. They end up good for nothing, in trouble all the time, and accomplish not one thing unless it's get theirselves hung someplace."

He turned his file on its side and cut into the wood. It made a rasping noise.

A rasping noise came from the playpen. He got off his stool again and looked back into the pen. Jesus was scraping a brush against the side of the pen.

He went back to work.

"Jesus," he said, "I've watched Momma's boys all my life. They play hell with everything. You take my great grandson, Laban. He has got to be the second horse in every stable. Other men's women. One after another. One time I swear he told me it was best when he couldn't hardly see their faces. Faceless women. Now, I ask you, Jesus. You know what that is? Just a grown man trying to become a baby. I ain't letting that happen to you! No sir! Never mind worse, end up playing with other men, like my grandson, Gomer. Hell, no!"

He was almost shouting.

He stopped his work and wiped his brow with a rag. He looked over his shoulder at the pen.

"How you doing in there?"

A little shout came from the playpen.

He dipped the block of wood into a bucket, looked at it closely while the solution of oil and grease sank in.

"Or my son, Michmas. He thinks he has got to run the world his way or it will just fall down."

Joseph rubbed the wood with the heel of his hand. He stood up, got a bottle of a greenish colored oil, poured some of that into the bucket, and dipped the wood in again, and held it there.

"He was my firstborn. Now look at him. A cruel old man."

Joseph pulled the cedar out, dried it off with one rag and began to polish it with another.

"Bloated in mind and body. Nothing nowhere that ain't his. A god damned hog. I ain't letting that happen to you, neither! No, sir!"

He hopped off his stool, excited. He rubbed the wood. He sniffed it, made a face, then soaked it in oil and grease again.

"Momma's boys," said Joseph. "All three."

He poured rainwater from a tin bucket into a smaller wooden bucket. He put the cedarwood into the smaller bucket and swished it around.

"I love your mother," said Joseph. "But you ain't a toy for her to play with. You are something else."

He took the wood out of the water. With dabs he worked fingertips of oil into its side.

"What else? You are my father, and his. You are the straight plumb-line, and the honest building. I didn't get this old, son, for nothing. I know what's in, by God, and I know what's out. I know squared off beams, set so flush an ant can't get between. I know fine wooded floors, polished so the dust rests on it easy to clean. I know the fire-place drawing strong, and the home that's built to last."

He blew on the wood. He took his cutting tool, and he quickly began to etch in small half circles, one above the other, on both sides.

"I'll show it to you, my boy. You'll come climbing out of that play-pen soon enough. I'll take you to town. You'll see men up and doing, baking the bread, opening the stores, making the fires, riding horses, banging hammers and tongs, and in the frosty morning, coming to town for work."

He took a long nail and knocked a hole in each side of the block of wood, toward the front.

"I didn't think I wanted to see it again. But now you're here. I'll show it all to you, just like I never seen it neither. I love you, Jesus. You're my boy. I'll set you straight in this life. Yes, by God. I will."

With a thin sliver of wood, he laid a speck of glue in each nail hole. With a pair of tweezers he set in each hole a flake of silvery mica.

"There now. You're still just a damn baby. Here."

He took the block of wood to the pen.

"Little fishy. See? Oiled it, so it feels like a fish. Made it from cedar, so it has stripes. See?"

He moved it about.

"What fishes do, Jesus, is swim. Wiggle, wiggle. Like that."

He gave the fish to Jesus.

"There, son. Happy birthday."

He stepped back, smiling. He was very happy. He closed his eyes, stretched and yawned.

As he opened his eyes again, a live fish flew out of the pen. He grabbed it.

"Huh?"

He tried to hold on to it. He couldn't.

"What?"

The fish flipped and flopped in his hands. He managed to get it to his workbench. He plunged it into the bucket of rainwater.

He turned around.

"Jesus?"

He went to the pen and looked in.

"Where's that wooden fish?"

Jesus gave him a quiet smile.

Joseph hopped back to his workbench. He plunged his hand into the water bucket.

He pulled out a wooden fish.

"Wait a minute," he said.

He went to the door, and opened it.

"Mary!" he called. "Who's playing tricks on me!"

He stormed out, toy in hand.

Jesus played with his blocks.

It was four years later.

"Goats?" said Joseph.

"Goats," said Mary.

She bit her lip.

"Come on, Mary. God damn it."

"Nobody wants Jesus to play with the other children."

"How long has this been going on?"

"A month. Since the children all got sick, with the eye infection. And Jesus didn't. Somebody said Jesus did it."

"Infected the other children?"

"Yes. Got mad, and gave them the eye plague."

"God damn magic baby. I thought I had that all done with. Here it is again."

"Yes. I'm sorry."

"What about the goats?"

"Yesterday Jesus went out to play with his friends. Their mothers shut them up in one house, and stood at the front door. They told Jesus the children couldn't come out. Jesus went around to the back of the house, and got in. He told the children to sneak out the back and hide, and they did."

Mary took a deep breath.

"There was a goat pen behind the house. Jesus fed the goats some sugar, and then herded them through the back door. He ran around to the front door again and called out the names of the children."

"He did what?"

"He stood there calling out *Come on, Ezra! Jump, Esther! Hop, Ruth!* and those goats came bursting out of the front door, and ran off after Jesus. The women thought Jesus had turned their children into goats."

Joseph turned away, laughing.

"It's silly," said Mary.

Joseph turned back, frowning.

"Don't tell me. I said so five years ago."

"Yes, Joseph."

"God damn it, Mary."

"Yes, Joseph."

It was four years later.

"Where is Jesus?" said the Schoolmaster.

"We don't know," said Mary.

"Speak up," said Joseph.

Joseph's legs were shakier now, and his ears were failing him. He used two sticks for canes, and thrust himself forward to hear.

"Your boy is in trouble," said the Schoolmaster.

"What has he done now?" said Mary.

"My children were all in their places," said the Schoolmaster. "I said, *Say after me, Alpha.* And they all said, *Alpha.*"

"Jesus, too?" said Mary.

"Jesus, too. Then I said, *Say after me, Beta.* And Jesus said, *Tell us what Alpha means, and then we'll say Beta.*"

"Oh," said Mary.

"He upset everyone. I said, *Students, Alpha is the beginning. The Void. Before anyone knows what anything was. The study of scripture is the jump, you see, from the Void to the Now.* And Jesus said, *Well, this is exciting.* I pretended I didn't hear him. *A leap demands Faith, otherwise you will perish in doubt. Have faith, first in me, and you will understand, deep within you, both the Now and Alpha, the Void.* And Jesus said, *I think I understand the Void already,* and the children laughed."

"Oh, dear," said Mary.

"Jesus challenged me in front of my class. *I don't think you know anything,* he said, *never mind what the beginning was. You call it the Void. Is that what we all came from?* And I said, simply, *Yes,* and Jesus said, *God is the Void?* and I said, *Of course not. God is older than the Void, which is only a small part of God.* And Jesus said, *Well, what part of God is it we all come from, then?* And I said, *From the goodness of God, naturally,* and Jesus said, *Which is inside God like the Void?*"

Mary tried to follow the Schoolteacher.

"I lost my temper. *Jesus!* I said, *There is one great Idea that holds everything together. All your study prepares you to comprehend it.* And Jesus said, *I am only a little boy, but let me try,* and I said to him, *There is one God and that one God is good.* And Jesus didn't answer me."

"I'm glad," said Mary.

"For a few minutes. Then, when I had gone on and was in the middle of something else, Jesus said, *Wait a minute, people used to believe there were lots of Gods, true?* And I said, *In their ignorance, some still do.* And Jesus said, *Rain was God. Sun was God. Wheat was God. Love was God. Death was God. Money was God. They were all separate. So if one God was mad at you, it didn't have anything to do with another God. What the rain God did to you had nothing to do with what the love God did to you. If the war God was mad at you, that didn't mean your wheat wouldn't grow, or that the sun God would hold it against you when the money God took away all your money.* And of course, I saw then where he was leading me."

"You did?" said Mary.

"I said, *You want to know how many old Gods, who could be so terrible, can now exist in one good God. Am I right?* Jesus said, *For the first time this morning.* And I said, *The old Gods, separate, held only separate powers. God, until he was recognized as one God, was not all powerful. When he became one God he became all powerful.* And Jesus said, *What does that have to do with it?* and I said, *Since we now know God to be all powerful, we understand him better.* Jesus said, *We do?* I said, *Of course. We see now that God can be all good even when he may seem to be partly evil.* And Jesus said, *Or all evil even when he may seem partly good?* I saw it was no use. I said, *Do not mock the prophets, child.* And Jesus said, *Wasn't it the prophets who said God was a jealous God and a loving God and a God of happiness and revenge all at the same time, just exactly like the old gods, with only one difference, now that he's just one God if you do anything wrong anywhere in your life he can get you for it?* And I said, *Exactly. That is what makes God God.* And Jesus said, *No, it doesn't. That only makes God like my father. That is the worst idea I ever heard. You are a god damned fool.* And he walked out of the classroom."

"School," said Joseph. "I never understood it, either."

"I will speak to Jesus," said Mary. "He will apologize."

"Do I have your word for that?"

"You do."

It was two years later. The women were furious.

"My son was making a clay sparrow," said the first. "Jesus grabbed it. He blew on it and threw it into the air, and it flew away!"

"My little girl was making a clay snake," said the second. "Jesus grabbed it and threw it into the river. A snake as big as your arm came out of the river onto the bank, went after my little girl, and when Jesus told it to, it exploded!"

"All this," said Joseph. "All this again."

"One boy was making a clay lion," said the third. "Another a clay tiger. Another a clay hippo. Jesus said if the children wouldn't do what he told them, he would bring the animals to life and the lion and the tiger would eat them and the hippo would sit on them."

"What did he want them to do?" said Mary.

"Crown him King!" said the first woman:

"We caught him at it!" said the second.

"At what?" said Joseph.

"Sitting our children at his feet, in a circle," said the first woman. "Taking flowers from them, and putting them in his hair!"

"Telling them crazy stories," said the second. "About far off places he would take them to."

"Where they would go and live without their mothers and fathers!" said the third.

"We ran him off!"

"He's a menace!"

"He's a Child Terror!"

"We won't have our children threatened!"

"Leave Nazareth!"

"Get out of town!"

It was two years later.

Joseph and Mary were looking at a beautiful piece of cloth. It was striped in bright and vivid colors that seemed to change as the cloth moved.

"He came to my store," said the Cloth Dyer. "He wanted to work for me. He wanted to know all about dyes. If it was true they came from oak-tree bugs and fruit rinds. I showed him a purple I get from shell fish."

"Woman's work," said Joseph.

"I showed him how I add soap, just a little, to make crimson stick faster to wool. He asked me questions. I let him stretch a piece of undyed wool, and left him alone. After three hours, he was still there. He said it was no good just staining it. He wanted to make fabric and color one thing forever. He said if a piece of cloth was pure white, if the strands of hair could open themselves, then the dye should soak every part of it, and stay there forever. Not as a stain that would fade or come out someday, but as a part of the thing itself, like blood. Then he began to cry."

Joseph tapped his canes impatiently, one against the other.

"What kind of talk is that?" he said.

"But he did it!" said the Cloth Dyer. "He dyed that piece of cloth right there. Then he ran off and wouldn't tell me how he did it!"

"It's beautiful," said Mary.

"Keep it," said the Cloth Dyer. "If he ever tells you how he did it, let me know."

It was that same night. Jesus lay in bed. His blanket was pulled up almost over his head. Over the foot of his bed was draped the cloth he had dyed.

Mary came into his room, and sat in a chair by his bed.

"I should have stopped him," said Mary. "A long time ago. When he tried to make you a man too soon. I didn't know how."

She took a deep breath.

"I was a child myself," she said.

She looked at the floor.

"He meant well. He still does. He's old. He's clumsy. He thinks he knows everything. But it is my fault."

She took another deep breath.

"He never liked it when I took my pleasure in you. He told me we shouldn't be that cozy. It wasn't right."

She frowned.

"I was too good about it. I didn't tell him he was wrong when I should have. He is wrong. You are not a man yet. You need me."

She closed her eyes.

"He shouldn't be so hard on you. All that work. Dragging logs. Fixing tools. Grease and glue. Getting you down in ditches, in the mud and the dirt and making you sweat, for him. That is no way to treat a little boy."

She stared at the wall.

"My son will never be a ditch-digger. Or a carpenter. Or any man's lackey."

She smiled at her son fondly.

"We don't make too much of ourselves. I have not spoiled you. There is nothing wrong with our love for each other. He is an old man."

She touched her son on the shoulder, gently.

"There is more to life than we have. You will find it."

Joseph came into the room.

Mary stood up. She left the room.

Joseph sat in the chair by the bed.

He took a deep breath.

"I should have stopped her a long time ago," he said. "Your mother kept you a child too long. You think the rest of the world has got to care for you like she does. You will end up crazy."

He rubbed his hands together carefully.

"Some men do nothing. Then wonder what went wrong. They didn't say anything, that's what went wrong. When a man loves his son, he tells him the truth."

He put his hands down in his lap. He spoke softly.

"You have got to straighten out. You ain't the sun and the moon."

He sighed.

"I know it ain't been easy. You have a peculiar momma. And a strange old daddy. But except for me being old and her young, we're not that unusual. We're just people. You can't make us any better than we are."

He spoke firmly.

"We're dust, Jesus. You, your mother, me. Your friends, all this world. Don't stir it up. I'm an old man and I know."

He was silent for a moment.

"It isn't that I don't remember. I had my dreams. About another world. Mine. But King Joseph had to go to work, son. The world put that to him. So I took up my hammer and my saw and I made what I could as well as I could, and that was enough. More, you hear me, is crazy."

He took a deep breath.

"So get it straight, for I will tell you no lies. You're growing up. To please me, you will have to cross your mother. To please her, you will have to cross me. You think about that. Never mind kingdoms."

He stood up.

"You ain't a baby no more."

Joseph left the room.

Jesus lay in bed, his blanket over him. He could hear his parents arguing in the room next to his.

"What did you say to him?"

"What I had to."

"To go crazy, pleasing you? Working himself to death, pleasing you?"

"You want him home all the time? So you can call him your baby? I won't have it. He's going to stand up by himself!"

"But you make him crawl! You make him think he's a ditch digger!"

"Now, Mary! Shut up!"

"He's my son!"

"Mine, too!"

Jesus threw the blanket aside. He jumped out of bed. He put on his clothes. He grabbed the piece of striped cloth. He ran out of the house.

"Jesus!" said Mary. "Where are you going?"

"Jesus!" said Joseph. "Come back here!"

It is late that evening.

Jesus runs, through the town, past shadows and fire, away from voices and outraged cries, running as fast as he can, getting away.

"I saw him!"

"Where?"

"Going past the market!"

The Cloth Dyer stares at his goods with disbelief. His dyes are spilled onto the floor. Bolts of cloth have been taken from their shelves, thrown open and left in tangles.

He runs out into the street.

Jesus races across the town.

An old woman stands in the midst of broken pottery, amazed.

"He was such a nice boy! He called me Grandmother. I showed him my pots and how I made them and he said he wanted to help me. And tonight he breaks into my shop and smashes all my beautiful pots! The devil!"

Jesus runs.

"He's gone past the East Gate!"

"We'll catch him now!"

"What's that?"

"More smoke!"

"It's at the Tile Factory!"

"Fire!"

Blocked at one gate, Jesus turns running back again through the town, dodging the confusion and the angry bodies, leaping behind the buildings, sprinting through alleys.

"Get away from there!"

"You can't do anything now!"

"Look out!"

"The roof's coming down!"

Jesus has one friend only tonight. His name is Zeno, and he is thirteen years old, the same age as Jesus. Standing by the fire at the Factory, he sees a familiar shadow passing. He runs after it.

"That damn boy," says a foreman. "He came here a week ago. He wanted a man's job. I let him run a few errands. Day over, he wanted a day's pay. We laughed at him. Now he's burned down the factory!"

Zeno chasing him, Jesus runs.

"Where is he now?"

"Try the West Gate!"

"Come on!"

A hundred yards from the West Gate, Zeno catches up with Jesus.

"Hey! It's me! Zeno!"

Jesus looks behind him, and slows down. They trot together toward the gate, breathing hard.

"Everybody's mad at you. They're yelling for you."

Jesus nods.

"Did you smash those pots? Did you start those fires?"

Jesus runs to the gate and begins to pull it open.

"They're saying you're a devil!"

Jesus pulls open the gate. Beyond it lies darkness.

He runs out of the city. Zeno follows him.

It is after midnight.

"There!" shouts the Schoolmaster.

Townspeople follow him toward an old shack, in a galley half a mile outside the city walls. It is held together by old boards and piled up stones. Outcasts go there, lepers and criminals.

The townspeople hold up their torches. There sits Jesus, on the roof of the shack. Below him, on the ground, lies Zeno.

"There!" cries the Schoolmaster. "I told you they'd be together!"

Zeno's father runs out of the crowd. He kneels beside his son.

The crowd gathers around them, talking.

"Look where Zeno's lying."

"Jesus pushed him."

"Is he dead?"

Mary helps Joseph out of a cart. They move slowly toward the shack, Joseph leaning heavily on his two canes.

"What's happened?" says Joseph.

"Jesus pushed a boy off that roof," says the Schoolmaster. "He tried to kill him."

Zeno's father bends over his son, hand on the boy's chest, ear to his mouth.

"Didn't you, Jesus?" cries the Schoolmaster.

In the torchlight, Jesus looks down at the crowd. He smiles a painful smile, a bravado grin boys know well.

Mary and Joseph reach the shack.

"How's your boy?" says Joseph.

"I can't tell," says Zeno's father. "He's breathing. No blood. But I can't wake him up."

Mary stares at the fallen boy.

"Jesus did that?" she says.

"I think he did," says Zeno's father.

"Did you see him do it?" says Joseph.

"No," says Zeno's father.

"Did *you* see him do it?" says Joseph to the Schoolmaster.

"It's plain enough," says the Schoolmaster.

Joseph faces the crowd.

"Who did?" he says.

Nobody answers him.

Joseph turns and for the first time looks up at Jesus.

Jesus looks down, with his twisted smile.

"Son," says Joseph. "I won't ask you again. Did you harm this boy?"

Now slowly the smile goes away from the face of Jesus, as he looks deliberately and coldly straight at Joseph.

"Go to hell," he says.

"Jesus!" says Mary.

"You too," says Jesus.

In the crowd, the women shout.

"His own mother!"

"Child terror!"

"Killer!"

"Zeno?" says his father. "Zeno?"

"God damn it," says Joseph. "Did you hurt this boy?"

"No!" shouts Jesus. "Hey, Zeno. Wake up."

Zeno opens his eyes.

He sits up, holding his elbow.

"Ow!" he says.

"What happened to you?" says his father.

"I fell off the roof," says Zeno.

"Fell off?" says Mary.

"Nobody pushed you?" says Joseph.

"Why no," says Zeno. "I was with Jesus."

He looks up and sees Jesus on the roof.

"He's still there. Hello, Jesus."

"Hello, Zeno."

"They're going to lie about it," says the Schoolmaster.

The crowd agrees.

"Look at Zeno!"

"He's scared to death!"

"Jesus got him up there and pushed him off!"

"Tell the truth, Zeno!"

"Nobody pushed me," says Zeno. "We heard you coming. We climbed up on the roof. Jesus got mad and you made him madder. He swore and kicked at the roof and tripped. I grabbed him. That's all I remember."

"He's lying."

"He's afraid."

"Zeno," says the Schoolmaster. "What were you doing with each other out here?"

"Come on, Zeno!"

"What does Jesus do to you?"

Zeno turns pale.

He jumps up, breaks away, and runs into the shack.

"Zeno!" cries his father.

Before anyone can stop him, Zeno is back on the roof with Jesus.

He has a rock in one hand.

"Leave us alone!" he says.

The townspeople nod to each other.

"See what he does to them?"

"He bewitches them."

"Zeno," says his father. "Come down, or I'm coming up."

"Keep away from us!" says Zeno, holding his rock.

Jesus stands beside Zeno. He takes the rock from Zeno's hand, and drops it off the roof.

"Go home, Zeno. I don't need you."

"You said you did."

"I don't need anybody."

Jesus pushes Zeno off the roof. Zeno lands on his feet, falls and rolls over, crying out. The crowd backs away, astonished.

Jesus grins, baring his teeth.

"Well?" says Jesus to the crowd, to the Schoolmaster and to Joseph. "Are you satisfied?"

The crowd roars.

"Get that boy down from there!"

"Give him what he deserves!"

Zeno looks again at Jesus, hurt and puzzled.

"Goodbye, Jesus," he says.

"Goodbye, Zeno," says Jesus. "Sleep tight, in your little bed."

Zeno goes away with his father.

Leaning on his sticks, Joseph speaks in a voice thin and quiet.

"He's mine. For what he's done tonight, I'll pay. Nobody's dead. Go home."

Grumbling, muttering, they go.

When everyone leaves, Mary weeps.

"How could you?" she says.

"Down," says Joseph.

Jesus doesn't move.

"Get down," says Mary.

"Or else," says Joseph.

"Or else what?" says Jesus.

Then, suddenly, he pushes off with his hands, and lands before them. He brushes himself off, insolent and trembling.

"So?" says Jesus.

"What's wrong with you?" says Mary. "Apologize to your father."

"Apologize to your mother," says Joseph.

"Never," says Jesus.

Joseph slaps Jesus in the face, as hard as he can.

Jesus grabs both of Joseph's walking sticks, breaks them over one knee, and throws the pieces back at him. They hit him in the face and chest.

Joseph falls to the ground.

Mary rushes to him and kneels beside him.

"Ah!" says Jesus.

He runs back into the shack, leaving them there.

Mary helps Joseph up. When she gets him into the cart, he sits stunned, hands holding onto the seat. As they move away, Mary doesn't look back for Jesus.

And they too vanish in the night.

Jesus climbs back on the roof. He picks up the striped cloth he'd brought with him. He drapes it over his shoulders. It is very colorful.

He wraps himself in it against the cold, and sits again on the edge of the roof, and swings his feet, shivering.

"To hell with them," he says.

There he sits, a boy in trouble, bewildered and bitter, throughout the night.

Toward dawn, but while it is still dark, a pale figure appears again before him.

It is his mother.

"Come home," says Mary. "Your father is dying."

It is dawn. Mary and Jesus are home. Mary points to Joseph's workshop.

"Go talk to him," she says. "Tell him you are sorry for what you have done."

The old man is sitting on his bench. He looks tiny, shrunken. He fumbles with a nail, and a block of wood. His hands shake. He puts the nail down and turns the wood over and over.

Jesus steps into the workshop.

Joseph fumbles about until he finds his saw. He tries to saw the block of wood. The saw shimmies and jibbers. It bends, springs loose, and flies out of his shaking hands. It falls to the floor.

Joseph sighs. He bows his head.

Jesus sees it plainly.

His father will die.

He shudders.

Mary comes into the workshop.

"Joseph."

Joseph stares, doglike, at the floor.

"Jesus is here."

There is no answer.

A vein in Joseph's head is big as a cord. From the temple, it crawls up over the skull, into the sparse hair. Cheekbones, eye sockets, and skull leap out at Jesus. Joseph's mouth moves, sucks. He tries to lift his arms.

His eyes glitter, like a rat's.

Jesus is thirteen.

"You ought to go to bed now," he says.

Joseph smiles a ghastly smile.

"Old fool," says Joseph.

"What?" says Jesus.

Joseph looks at the block of wood on his table.

"What was I doing with that thing?" he says.

He breathes very hard. He is angry.

Jesus looks at his mother. "What did he say?"

"Hush," says Mary. "Just listen."

Joseph looks at Jesus.

"Wood, mortar, stone," says Joseph.

His rat's eyes fasten on Jesus.

"You won't last, neither," he says. He falls from his bench to the floor.

"Joseph!" says Mary.

"Father!" says Jesus.

They kneel beside him.

Mary and Jesus carry Joseph to a large wooden chair in the corner of his shop.

"Rest here," says Mary. "Then come to bed."

Joseph bows his head. He plucks at the arms of the chair.

Suddenly, he lifts his head, like an animal drinking, who has heard something.

With a shaking hand, he points to the bare wall across the room. His lips tremble, and spittle drools from the corners of his mouth.

"I see them," he says.

There is no one else in the room. He is talking to the wall across the workshop.

He draws back in his chair.

"They have come for me," says Joseph.

"Who's come?" says Jesus.

Joseph points again to the bare wall of the workshop.

"Angels of Death have come," says Joseph. "I see Azrael there, with his shining sword. With the drop of gall on its tip that I must drink. Behind him stand his minions, all in black. Oh, God."

Joseph shudders.

"Nobody has come for you, Joseph," says Mary. "You're here safe with us."

"No," says Joseph. "I have to go with them. I'm burning, like wood. The wind is at me. Ashes. I have no legs."

Mary kneels before Joseph.

"Rub his shoulders and his neck," she says to Jesus. "I'll rub his legs."

Jesus rubs Joseph's neck and shoulders. Mary rubs his legs.

"I see Gehenna," says Joseph. "Burning, waiting for me. Angels of Death."

Joseph leans back in the chair.

"Jesus," he says.

"Yes, sir?"

"Did you do this?"

"What?"

"Have you killed me?"

"What?"

"Magic. Holy child."

"Joseph," says Mary. "Oh, Joseph."

"Powers," says Joseph. "Great powers. I did you wrong."

His arms fall to his sides. He stares at Jesus.

"Son," he says.

"Yes, sir?" says Jesus.

"I never meant to harm you."

"I know it."

"Then help me."

"How?"

"Go to the window. Tell me if they are out there or not."

Jesus looks at his mother, bewildered.

"Do what he says."

"You're my son," says Joseph. "Tell me the truth."

He shivers, pushing himself back in his chair, stung by cramps and spasms. His mouth is dark.

"Go ahead," says Mary. "He's bleeding inside."

Jesus goes to the window.

Dawn has come. Clouds heavy and sullen hide the sun. The light outside is harsh and glaring.

There is nothing outside the shack. Azrael does not stand there. Neither do his minions, dressed in black. There is no great shining sword, that will cut Joseph's soul loose from his body. There is no drop of gall on its tip, for him to drink. There is no Gehenna. There are no angels of death.

Nothing.

Hot tears come to the boy's eyes. His hands burn from the blow that struck his father to the ground. His tongue, with which he cursed his mother, aches.

Jesus weeps, a man. He feels it bite into him.

He bows his head. He knows what to do.

He returns to Joseph. He takes one of Joseph's hands in his.

He is only thirteen. He is afraid but he speaks clearly and firmly.

"Yes," says Jesus. "Azrael is there."

"Ah!" says Joseph.

"He has come for you. On the tip of his sword hangs the gall you must drink. He will cut away your soul, to take it with him, and your body he will throw into Gehenna. His face is dark. Behind him, dressed in black, stand all his minions, waiting."

"Just as I said?"

"Just as you said. I will tell you the truth. They have come for you, and you must go with them. But I am your son, your holy child. Magic is mine, and powers that reach beyond the earth. Do you hear me? My love for you knows no bounds. Do you hear me? I tell Azrael to sheath his great sword, and stand aside. I command him, and all his minions, dressed in black, be still. Angels of Death must wait."

"I see powers. Great powers."

"I must speak to my father first. Azrael will wait. His face is dark, but it is peaceful, and kind. His sword is in its sheath."

"Powers," says Joseph. "Great powers."

"The rivers of fire are as water," says Jesus. "The seas of demons will be calm. Nothing burns. Nothing will hurt you. I am here. All is well."

"Holy child," says Joseph.

He closes his eyes. He rests. His cramps and spasms leave him.

Mary and Jesus hold his hands.

He opens his eyes again, but he is blind.

"Mary?"

"Yes?"

"Where's the boy?"

"Here with you."

"What's he doing?"

"Holding your hand."

"Which one?"

"This one," says Jesus. "This one."

"Your right hand, Joseph," says Mary. "That gave him the good with the bad. That hit him in the face. That made him toys. That took him to town, to see the men at work."

Joseph smiles a bloody smile. He nods.

"That's right," he says.

When Joseph died, Jesus wept.

Mary closed Joseph's eyes. She folded his arms, crossed his hands, and combed his hair.

"Old Man Joseph," said Mary. "It isn't the end that is important. It is the beginning."

from The Last Temptation of Christ
by Nikos Kazantzakis

Nikos Kazantzakis' (1883–1957) imagined a Christ who struggles to accept his identity as the son of God. This notion angered the Greek Orthodox Church and prompted the Roman Catholic Church to add The Last Temptation of Christ *to its list of forbidden books. In this passage, a newly-baptized Jesus has entered the desert to listen for God's instructions.*

Jesus had now entered the desert. The more he advanced, the more he felt he had gone into a lion's cave. He shuddered, not from fear, but from a dark, inexplicable joy. He was happy. Why? He could not explain it. Suddenly, he remembered, remembered a dream he had one night when he was still a child hardly able to talk. It seemed thousands of years ago: the earliest dream he was able to recall. He had worked his way into a deep cave and found a lioness who had given birth and was suckling her cubs. When he saw her, he grew hungry and thirsty, lay down and began to suckle with the lion cubs. Afterward it seemed that they all went out to a meadow and began to play in the sun, but while they were frisking, Mary, his mother, appeared in his dream, saw him with the lions and screamed. He awoke and turned angrily to his mother, who was sleeping at his side. Why did you wake me up? he shouted at her. I was with my brothers and my mother!

Now I understand why I am happy, he reflected. I am entering my mother's cave, the cave of the lioness, of solitude. . . .

He heard the disquieting hiss of snakes, and of the burning wind which blew between the rocks, and of the invisible spirits of the desert.

Jesus bent over and spoke to his soul. "My soul, here you will show whether or not you are immortal."

Hearing steps behind him, he cocked his ear. There was the crunching of sand. Someone was walking toward him, calmly, surely. I forgot her, he thought, shuddering, but she did not forget me. She is coming with me; my mother is coming with me. . . . He knew very well that it was the Curse, but he had been calling her Mother to himself now for such a long time.

He marched on, forcing his thoughts elsewhere. He recalled the wild dove. A savage bird seemed to be imprisoned within him—or was it his soul rushing to escape? Perhaps it had escaped; perhaps the wild dove which chirped and flew circles over him the whole time he was being baptized was his soul, not a bird or a Seraph, but his own soul.

This was the answer. He started out again, calm. He heard the footsteps behind him crunching the sand, but his heart was steady now; he could at last endure everything with dignity. Man's soul, he reflected, is all-powerful; it can take on whatever appearance it likes. At that instant it became a bird and flew over me. . . . But as he marched tranquilly along, suddenly he cried out and stopped. The thought had come to him that perhaps the dove was an illusion, a buzzing in his ear, a whirling of the air because he remembered how his body had gleamed, light and omnipotent, like a soul, how whatever he wanted to hear he had heard, whatever he wanted to see he had seen. . . . He had built castles in the air. "O God, O God," he murmured, "now that we shall be alone, tell me the truth, do not deceive me. I am weary of hearing voices in the air."

He advanced and the sun advanced with him. It had finally reached the top of the sky, directly above his head. His feet were burning in the fiery sand. He spied around him to find some shade, and as he did so, he heard wings flapping above him and saw a flock of crows rush into a pit where there was a stinking object in the process of decay.

Holding his nose, he approached. The crows had fallen upon the carcass, planted their claws in it, and begun to eat. When they saw a man approach they flew away angrily, each with a mouthful of flesh in its talons. They circled in the air, calling to the intruder to go away. Jesus leaned over, saw the opened belly, the black, half-stripped hide, the short knotted horns, the strings of amulets around the putrid neck.

"The goat!" he murmured with a shudder. "The sacred goat that bore the people's sins. He was chased from village to village, mountain to mountain, and finally to the desert, where he perished."

He bent over, dug in the sand as deeply as he could with his hands, and covered the carcass.

"My brother," he said, "you were innocent and pure, like every animal. But men, the cowards, made you bear their sins, and killed you. Rot in peace; feel no malice against them. Men, poor weak creatures, have not the courage to pay for their sins themselves: they place them upon one who is sinless. My brother, requite their sins. Farewell!"

He resumed his march but stopped after a few moments, troubled. Waving his hand, he called, "Until we meet again!"

The crows began to pursue him maniacally. He had deprived them of the tasty carcass and now they were following him, waiting for him to perish in his turn and for his belly to split open so that they could eat. What right did he have to do them this injustice? Had not God designed crows to eat carcasses? He must pay!

Night was coming at last. Tired, he squatted on a rock which was as large and round as a millstone. "I shall go no farther," he murmured. "Here on this rock I shall set up my bulwark and do battle." The darkness flowed abruptly down from the sky, rose up from the soil, covered the earth. And with the darkness came the frost. His teeth chattering, he wrapped himself in his white robe, curled up into a ball and closed his eyes. But as he closed them, he grew frightened. He recalled the crows, heard the famished jackals begin to howl on every side, felt the desert prowling around him like a wild beast. Afraid, he reopened his eyes. The sky had filled with stars, and he felt comforted. The Seraphim have come out to keep me company, he said to himself. They are the six-winged lights which sing psalms around God's throne, but they are far away, so very far away that we cannot hear them. . . . His mind illuminated by starlight, he forgot his hunger and cold. He too was a living thing, an ephemeral beacon in the darkness; he too sang hymns to God. His soul was a small pharos, the humble, poorly dressed sister of the angels. . . . Thinking of his high extraction, he took heart, saw his soul standing together with the angels around God's throne; and then, peacefully and without fear, he closed his eyes and slept.

When he awoke he lifted his face toward the east and saw the sun, a terrible blast furnace, rising above the sand. That is God's face, he reflected, putting his palm over his eyes so that he would not be dazzled. "Lord," he whispered, "I am a grain of sand; can you see me in this desert? I am a grain of sand which talks and breathes and loves you—loves you and calls you Father. I possess no weapon but love. With that I have come to do battle. Help me!"

He rose. With his reed he inscribed a circle around the rock where he had slept.

"I shall not leave this threshing floor," he said loudly, so that the invisible forces which were lying in wait for him could hear, "I shall not leave this threshing floor unless I hear God's voice. But I must hear it clearly; I won't be satisfied with the usual unsteady hum or twittering or thunder. I want him to speak to me clearly, with human words, and to tell me what he desires from me and what I can, what I must, do. Only then will I get up and leave this threshing floor to return to men, if that is his command, or to die, if that is his will. I'll do whatever he wishes, but I must know what it is. In God's name!"

He knelt on the rock with his face toward the sun, toward the great desert. He closed his eyes, remassed those of his thoughts which had lingered at Nazareth, Magdala, Capernaum, Jacob's well and the river Jordan, and began to put them in battle array. He was preparing for war.

With his neck tensed and his eyelids closed, he sank within himself. He heard the roar of water, the rustling of reeds, the lamentations of men. From the river Jordan came wave after wave of cries, terror and faraway visionary hopes. First to stand up in his mind were the three long nights he had spent on the rock with the wild ascetic. In full armor, they rushed to the desert to enter the war at his side.

The first night jumped down on top of him like a monstrous locust with cruel wheat-yellow eyes and wings, breath like the Dead Sea and strange green letters on its abdomen. It clung to him; its wings began furiously to rend the air. Jesus cried out and turned. The Baptist was standing next to him with his bony arm pointing in the heavy darkness toward Jerusalem.

"Look. What do you see?"

"Nothing."

"Nothing? In front of you is holy Jerusalem, the whore. Don't you see her? She sits and giggles on the Roman's fat knees. The Lord cries, 'I do not want her. Is this my wife? I do not want her!' I too, like a dog at the Lord's feet, bark, 'I do not want her!' I walk around her towers and walls and bark at her, 'Whore! Whore!' She has four great fortress gates. At the first sits Hunger, at the next Fear, at the third Injustice, and at the fourth, the northern one, Infamy. I enter, go up and down her streets; I approach her inhabitants and examine them. Regard their faces: three are heavy, fat, oversatiated; three thousand emaciated from hunger. When does a world disappear? When three masters overeat and a people of three thousand starves to death. Look at their faces once more. Fear sits on all of them; their nostrils quiver; they scent the day of the Lord. Regard the women. Even the most honest glances secretly at her slave, licks her chops and nods to him: *Come!*

"I have unroofed their palaces. Look. The king holds his brother's wife on his knee and caresses her nakedness. What do the Holy Scriptures say? 'He who looks at the nakedness of his brother's wife—*death!*' It is not he, the incestuous king, who will he killed, but I, the ascetic. Why—because the day of the Lord has come!"

The whole of that first night Jesus sat at the Baptist's feet and watched Hunger, Fear, Injustice and Infamy go in and out of Jerusalem's four opened gates. Over the holy prostitute the clouds were gathering, full of anger and hail.

The second night the Baptist once more stretched forth his reed-like hand and with a thrust pushed through time and space. "Listen. What do you hear?"

"Nothing."

"Nothing! Don't you hear Iniquity, the bitch who has climbed shamelessly up to heaven and is barking at the Lord's door? Haven't you been through Jerusalem, haven't you seen the yelping priests, high priests, Scribes and Pharisees who surround the Temple? But God endures the earth's impudence no longer. He has risen; he is tramping down the mountainsides and coming. In front of him is Anger; behind him are heaven's three bitches, Fire, Leprosy and Madness. Where is the Temple with the proud, gold-inlaid columns which supported it and proclaimed: Eternal! Eternal! Eternal! Ashes the Temple, ashes the priests, high priests, Scribes and Pharisees, ashes their holy amulets, their silken cassocks and golden rings! Ashes! Ashes! Ashes!

"Where is Jerusalem? I hold a lighted lantern, I search in the mountains, in the Lord's darkness; I shout, 'Jerusalem! Jerusalem!' Deserted, completely forsaken: not even a crow answers—the crows have eaten, and left. I wade knee-deep in the skulls and bones; tears come to my eyes, but I push the bones away and banish them. I laugh, bend down and choose the longest one, make a flute and hymn the glory of the Lord."

The whole of the second night the Baptist laughed, stood in God's darkness and admired Fire, Leprosy and Madness. Jesus grasped the prophet's knees. "Cannot salvation come to the world by means of love?" he asked. "By means of love, joy, mercy?"

The Baptist, without even turning to look at him, replied, "Haven't you ever read the Scriptures? The Saviour crushes our loins, breaks our teeth, hurls fire and searches the fields—all in order to sow. And he uproots the thorns, stinkweeds and nettles. How can you wipe out falsehood, infamy and injustice from the world if you do not eradicate the liars, the unjust, the wicked? The earth must be cleansed—don't pity it—it must be cleansed, made ready for the planting of new seed."

The second night passed. Jesus did not speak. He was awaiting the third night: perhaps the prophet's voice would sweeten.

The third night the Baptist twisted and turned upon the rock, uneasy. Without laughing, without talking, he examined Jesus with anguish, searched his arms, hands, shoulders and knees, then shook his head and remained quiet, sniffing the air. Illuminated by the starlight, his eyes stood out, glistening sometimes green, sometimes yellow; and sweat mingled with blood ran from his sun-baked forehead. Finally at daybreak, when the white dawn fell upon them, he took Jesus' hand, looked into his eyes, and frowned. "When I first saw you emerge from the reeds by the Jordan, and come directly toward me," he said, "my heart bounded like a young calf. Can you think how Samuel's heart leaped up when he first saw the red-haired beardless shepherd, David? That is how my heart leaped. But the heart is flesh and loves the flesh, and I have no faith in it. Last night I examined you, smelled you as though seeing you for the first time, but I could not find peace. I looked at your hands. They were not the hands of a woodchopper, of a saviour. Too soft, too merciful. How could they swing the ax? I looked at your eyes. They were not a saviour's eyes—too full of sympathy. I got up and sighed. Lord, I murmured, your ways are dark and oblique; you are capable of sending a white dove to burn up the world and turn it into ashes. We watch the heavens, expecting a thunderbolt, an eagle or a crow—and you give us a white dove. What use is there of questioning, of resisting? Do what you like." He spread out his arms and hugged Jesus, kissed him on his right shoulder, then on his left. "If you are the One I've been waiting for," he said, "you have not come in the form I imagined you would. Was it all for nothing then that I carried the ax and placed it at the root of the tree? Or can love also wield an ax?" He reflected for a moment. "I cannot judge," he murmured finally. "I shall die without seeing the result. It does not matter, that's my lot: a hard one—and I like it!" He squeezed Jesus' hand. "Go, and good luck. Go talk with God in the desert. But come back quickly, so that the world will not remain all alone."

Jesus opened his eyes. The river Jordan, the Baptist and the baptized, the camels and the lamentations of the people—all flared up in the air and were snuffed out. The desert now stretched before him. The sun had risen high and was burning: the stones steamed like loaves of bread. He felt his insides being mowed down by hunger. "I'm hungry," he murmured, looking at the stones, "I'm hungry!" He remembered the bread which the old Samaritan woman had presented them. How delicious it had been, sweet like honey! He remembered the honey, split olives and dates he was treated to whenever he passed through a village; and the holy supper they had when, kneeling on the shore of Lake Gennesaret, they removed the grill, with its row of sweet-smelling fish, from the andirons. And afterward, the figs, grapes and pomegranates came to his mind, agitating him still further.

His throat was dry and parched from thirst. How many rivers flowed in the world! All these waters which bounded from rock to rock, rolled from one end of the land of Israel to the other, ran into the Dead Sea and disappeared—and he had not even a drop to drink! He thought of these waters and his thirst increased. He felt dizzy; his eyes fluttered. Two cunning devils in the shape of young rabbits emerged from the burning sand, stood up on their hind legs and danced. They turned, saw the eremite, screamed happily and began to hop toward him. They climbed onto his knees and jumped to his shoulders. One was cool, like water, the other warm and fragrant, like bread; but as he longingly put out his hands to grasp them, with a single bound they vanished into the air.

He closed his eyes and recollected the thoughts which hunger and thirst had dispersed. God came to his mind: he was neither hungry nor thirsty any more. He reflected on the salvation of the world. Ah, if the day of the Lord could only come with love! Was not God omnipotent? Why couldn't he perform a miracle and by touching men's hearts make them blossom? Look how each year at the Passover bare stems, meadows and thorns opened up at his touch. If only one day men could awake to find their deepest selves in bloom!

He smiled. In his thoughts the world had flowered. The incestuous king was baptized, his soul cleansed. He had sent away his sister-in-law Herodias and she had returned to her husband. The high priests and noblemen had opened their larders and coffers, distributed their goods to the poor; and the poor in their turn breathed freely once more and banished hate, jealousy and fear from their hearts. . . . Jesus looked at his hands. The ax which the Forerunner had surrendered to him had blossomed: a flowering almond branch was now in his palm.

The day concluded with this feeling of relief. He lay down on the rock and fell asleep. All night long in his sleep he heard water running, small rabbits dancing, a strange rustling, and two damp nostrils examining him. It seemed to him that toward midnight a hungry jackal came up and smelled him. Was this a carcass, or wasn't it? The beast stood for a moment unable to make up its mind. And Jesus, in his sleep, pitied it. He wanted to open his breast and give it food, but restrained himself. He was keeping his flesh for men.

He woke up before dawn. A network of large stars covered the sky; the air was fluffy and blue. At this hour, he reflected, the cocks awake, the villages are roused, men open their eyes and look through the skylight at the radiance which has come once more. The infants awake in their turn, the bawling begins and the mothers approach, holding forth their full breasts. . . . For an instant the world undulated over the desert with its men and houses and cocks and infants and mothers—all made from the morning frost and breeze. But the sun would now rise to swallow them up! The eremite's heart skipped a beat. If only I could make this frost everlasting! he thought. But God's mind is an abyss, his love a terrifying precipice. He plants a world, destroys it just as it is about to give fruit, and then plants another. He recalled the Baptist's words: "Who knows, perhaps love carries an ax . . ." and shuddered. He looked at the desert. Ferociously red, it swayed under the sun, which had risen angrily, zoned by a storm. The wind blew; the smell of pitch and sulphur came to his nostrils. He thought of Sodom and Gomorrah—palaces, theaters, taverns, prostitutes—plunged in the tar. Abraham had shouted, "Have mercy, Lord; do not burn them. Are you not good? Take pity, therefore, on your creatures." And God had answered him, "I am just, I shall burn them all!"

Was this, then, God's way? If so, it was a great impudence for the heart—that clod of soft mud—to stand up and shout, Stop! . . . What is our duty? he asked himself. It is to look down, to find God's tracks in the soil and follow them. I look down; I clearly see God's imprint on Sodom and Gomorrah. The entire Dead Sea is God's imprint. He trod, and palaces, theaters, taverns, brothels—the whole of Sodom and Gomorrah—were engulfed! He will tread once more, and once more the earth—kings, high priests, Pharisees, Sadducees—all will sink to the bottom.

Without realizing it, he had begun to shout. His mind was wild with fury. Forgetting that his knees were unable to support him, he tried to rise, to set out on God's trail, but he collapsed supine onto the ground, out of breath. "I am unable; don't you see me?" he cried, lifting his eyes toward the burning heavens. "I am unable; why do you choose me? I cannot endure!" And as he cried out, he saw a black mass on the sand before him: the goat, disemboweled, its legs in the air. He remembered how he had leaned over and seen his own face in the leaden eyes. "I am the goat," he murmured. "God placed him along my path to show me who I am and where I am heading. . . ." Suddenly he began to weep. "I don't want . . . I don't want . . ." he murmured, "I don't want to be alone. Help me!"

And then, while he was bowed over and weeping, a pleasant breeze blew, the stench of the tar and the carcass disappeared and a sweet perfume pervaded the world. The eremite heard water, bracelets and laughter jingling in the distance and approaching. His eyelids, armpits and throat felt refreshed. He lifted his eyes. On a stone in front of him a snake with the eyes and breasts of a woman was licking its lips and regarding him. The eremite stepped back, terrified. Was this a snake, a woman, or a cunning demon of the desert? Such a serpent had wrapped itself around the forbidden tree of Paradise and seduced the first man and woman to unite and give birth to sin. . . . He heard laughter and the sweet, wheedling voice of a woman: "I felt sorry for you, son of Mary. You cried, 'I don't want to be alone. Help me!' I pitied you and came. What can I do for you?"

"I don't want you. I didn't call you. Who are you?"

"Your soul."

"My soul!" Jesus exclaimed, and he closed his eyes, horrified.

"Yes, your soul. You are afraid of being alone. Your great-grandfather Adam had the same fear. He too shouted for help. His flesh and soul united, and woman emerged from his rib to keep him company."

"I don't want you, don't want you! I remember the apple you fed to Adam. I remember the angel with the scimitar!"

"You remember, and that's why you're in pain and you cry out and cannot find your way. I shall show it to you. Give me your hand. Don't look back, don't recall anything. See how my breasts take the lead. Follow them, my spouse. They know the way perfectly."

"You are going to lead me also to sweet sin and the Inferno. I'm not coming. Mine is another road."

The serpent giggled derisively and showed her sharp, poisonous teeth. "Do you wish to follow God's tracks, the tracks of the eagle—you worm! You, son of the Carpenter, wish to bear the sins of an entire race! Aren't your own sins enough for you? What impudence to think that it's your duty to save the world!"

She's right . . . she's right . . . the eremite thought, trembling. What impudence to wish to save the world!

"I have a secret to tell you, dear son of Mary," said the snake in a sweet voice, her eyes sparkling. She slid down from the rock like water and began, richly decorated, to roll toward him. She arrived at his feet, climbed onto his knees, curled herself up and with a spring reached his thighs, loins, breast and finally leaned against his shoulder. The eremite, despite himself, inclined his head to hear her. The snake licked Jesus' ear with her tongue. Her voice was seductive and far away: it seemed to be corning from Galilee, from the edge of Lake Gennesaret.

"It's Magdalene . . . it's Magdalene . . . it's Magdalene . . ."

"What?" said Jesus, shuddering. "What about Magdalene?"

". . . it's Magdalene you must save!" the snake hissed imperatively. "Not the Earth—forget about the Earth. It's her, Magdalene, you must save!"

Jesus tried to shake the serpent away from his head, but she thrust herself forward and vibrated her tongue in his ear. "Her body is beautiful, cool and accomplished. All nations have passed over her, but it has been written in God's hand since your childhood that she is for you. Take her! God created man and woman to match, like the key and the lock. Open her. Your children sit huddled together and numb inside her, waiting for you to blow away their numbness so that they may rise and come out to walk in the sun. . . . Do you hear what I'm telling you? Lift your eyes, give me some sign. Just nod your head, my darling, and this very hour I shall bring you, on a fresh bed—your wife."

"My wife?"

"Your wife. Look how God married the whore Jerusalem. The nations passed over her, but he married her to save her. Look how the prophet Hosea married the whore Gomer, daughter of Debelaim. In the same way, God commands you to sleep with Mary Magdalene, your wife, to have children, and save her."

The serpent had now pressed its hard, cool, round breast against Jesus' own and was sliding slowly, tortuously, wrapping itself around him. Jesus grew pale, closed his eyes, saw Magdalene's firm, high-rumped body wriggling along the shores of Lake Gennesaret, saw her gaze toward the river Jordan and sigh. She extended her hand—she was seeking him; and her bosom was filled with children: his own. He had only to twitch the corner of his eye, to give a sign, and all at once: what happiness! How his life would change, sweeten, become more human! This was the way, this! He would return to Nazareth, to his mother's house, would become reconciled with his brothers. It was nothing but youthful folly—madness—to want to save the world and die for mankind. But thanks to Magdalene, God bless her, he would be cured; he would return to his workshop, take up once more his old beloved craft, once more make plows, cradles and troughs; he would have children and become a human being, the master of a household. The peasants would respect him and stand up when he passed. He would work the whole week long and on Saturday go to the synagogue in the clean garments woven for him of linen and silk by his wife Magdalene, with his expensive kerchief over his head, his golden wedding ring on his finger; and he would have his stall with the elders, would sit and listen peacefully and indifferently while the seething, half-insane scribes and Pharisees sweated and shivered to interpret the Holy Scriptures. He would snigger and look at them with sympathy. Where would they ever end up, these theologians! He was interpreting Holy Scripture quietly and surely by taking a wife, having children, by constructing plows, cradles, and troughs. . . .

He opened his eyes and saw the desert. Where had the day gone! The sun was once more inclining toward the horizon. The serpent, her breast glued to his own, was waiting. She hissed tranquilly, seductively, and a tender, plaintive lullaby flowed into the evening air. The entire desert rocked and lullabied like a mother.

"I'm waiting . . . I'm waiting . . ." the snake hissed salaciously. "Night has overtaken us. I'm cold. Decide. Nod to me, and the doors of Paradise will be opened to you. Decide, my darling. Magdalene is waiting. . . ."

The eremite felt paralyzed with fear. As he was about to open his mouth to say Yes, he felt someone above looking down on him. Terrified, he lifted his head and saw two eyes in the air, two eyes only, as black as night, and two white eyebrows which were moving and signaling to him: No! No! No! Jesus' heart contracted. He looked up again beseechingly, as if he wished to scream: Leave me alone, give me permission, do not be angry! But the eyes had grown ferocious and the eyebrows vibrated threateningly.

"No! No! No!" Jesus then shouted, and two large tears rolled from his eyes.

All at once the serpent writhed, unglued herself from him and with a muffled roar exploded. The air was glutted with the stench.

Jesus fell on his face. His mouth, nostrils and eyes filled with sand. His mind was blank. Forgetting his hunger and thirst, he wept—wept as though his wife and all his children had died, as though his whole life had been ruined.

"Lord, Lord," he murmured, biting the sand, "Father, have you no mercy? Your will be done: how many times have I said this to you until now, how many times shall I say it in the future? All my life I shall quiver, resist and say it: Your will be done!"

In this way, murmuring and swallowing the sand, he fell asleep; and as the eyes of his body closed, those of his soul opened and he saw the specter of a serpent as thick as the body of a man and extending in length from one end of the night to the other. She was stretched out on the sand with her wide, bright-red mouth opened at his side. Opposite this mouth hopped an ornate, trembling partridge struggling in vain to open its wings and escape. It staggered forward uttering small, wreak cries, its feathers raised out of fear. The motionless serpent kept her eyes glued on it, her mouth opened. She was in no hurry, for she was sure of her prey. The partridge advanced little by little directly toward the opened mouth, stumbling on its crooked legs. Jesus stood still and watched, trembling like the partridge. At daybreak the bird had at last reached the gaping mouth. It quivered for a moment, glanced quickly around as though seeking aid; then suddenly stretched forth its neck and entered head first, feet together. The mouth closed. Jesus was able to see the partridge, a ball of feathers and meat and ruby-colored feet, descend little by little toward the dragon's belly.

He jumped up, terrified. The desert was a mass of swelling rose-colored waves.

The sun was rising. "It is God," he murmured, trembling, "And the partridge is . . ."

His voice broke. He did not have the strength to complete his reflection. But inside himself he thought: . . . man's soul. The partridge is man's soul!

He remained plunged in this reflection for hours. The sun came up, set the sand on fire; it pierced Jesus' scalp, went inside him and parched his mind, throat and breast. His entrails were suspended like bunches of left-over grapes after the autumn vintage. His tongue had stuck to his palate, his skin was peeling off, his bones emerging; and his fingertips had turned completely blue.

Time, within him, had become as small as a heartbeat, as large as death. He was no longer hungry or thirsty; he no longer desired chil-

dren and a wife. His whole soul had squeezed into his eyes. He saw—
that was all: he saw. But at precisely noon his sight grew dim; the world
vanished and a gigantic mouth gaped somewhere in front of him, its
lower jaw the earth, its upper jaw the skies. Trembling, he dragged himself slowly forward toward the opened mouth, his neck stretched
forward. . . .

The days and nights went by like flashes of white and black lightning. One midnight a lion came and stood in front of him, proudly
shaking its mane. Its voice was like a man's: "Welcome to my lair, victorious ascetic. I salute the man who conquered the minor virtues, the
small joys, and happiness! We don't like what's easy and sure; our
sights are on difficult things. Magdalene isn't a big enough wife for us:
we wish to marry the entire Earth. Bridegroom, the bride has sighed,
the lamps of the heavens are lighted, the guests have arrived: let us go."

"Who are you?"

"Yourself—the hungry lion inside your heart and loins that at night
prowls around the sheepfolds, the kingdoms of this world, and weighs
whether or not to jump in and eat. I rush from Babylon to Jerusalem,
from Jerusalem to Alexandria, from Alexandria to Rome, shouting: I
am hungry; everything is mine! At daybreak I re-enter your breast and
shrink; the terrifying lion becomes a lamb. I play at being the humble
ascetic who desires nothing, who seems able to live on a grain of
wheat, a sip of water and on a naïve, accommodating God whom he
tries to flatter with the name of Father. But secretly, in my heart, I am
ashamed; I grow fierce and yearn for nightfall when I can throw off my
sheepskin and begin once more to roar, roam the night and stamp my
four feet down on Babylon, Jerusalem, Alexandria and Rome."

"I don't know who you are. I never desired the kingdom of this
world. The kingdom of heaven is sufficient for me."

"It is not. You deceive yourself, friend. It is not sufficient for you.
You don't dare gaze within yourself, deep within your loins and
heart—to find me. . . . Why do you look askance and think ill of me?
Do you believe I am Temptation, an emissary of the Sly One, come to
mislead you? You brainless hermit, what strength can external tempta-

tion have? The fortress is taken only from within. I am the deepest voice of your deepest self; I am the lion within you. You have wrapped yourself in the skin of a lamb to encourage men to approach you, so that you can devour them. Remember, when you were a small child a Chaldean sorceress looked at your palm. 'I see many stars,' she said, 'many crosses. You shall become king.' Why do you pretend to forget? You remember it day and night. Rise, son of David, and enter your kingdom!"

Jesus listened with bowed head. Little by little he recognized the voice, little by little he recalled having heard it sometimes in his dreams and once when he was a child and Judas had thrashed him, and one other time when he had left his house and roamed the fields for days and nights pinched by hunger, then returned shamefully home, to be greeted with hoots by his brothers, lame Simon and pious Jacob, who were standing in the doorway. Then, truly, he had heard the lion roar inside him. . . . And only the other day, when he carried the cross to the Zealot's crucifixion and passed before the stormy crowd, everyone looking at him with disgust and moving out of his path, the lion had again jumped up within him, and with such force that he was thrown down.

And now, in this forsaken midnight—look! The bellowing lion inside him had come out and stood before him. It rubbed itself against him, vanished and reappeared, as though going in and out of him, and playfully tapped him with its tail. . . . Jesus felt his heart grow more and more ferocious. The lion is really right, he thought. I've had enough of all this. I'm fed up with being hungry, with wanting to play at humility, with offering the other cheek only to get it slapped. I'm tired of flattering this man-eating God with the name of Father in order to cajole him to be more gentle; tired of hearing my brothers curse me, my mother weep, men laugh when I go by; sick of going barefooted, of not being able to buy the honey, wine and women I see when I pass by the market, and of finding courage only in my sleep to have God bring them to me, so that I can taste and embrace the empty air! I'm sick of it all! I shall rise, gird myself with the ancestral sword—am I not the son of David?—and enter my kingdom! The lion is right. Enough of ideas and clouds and kingdoms of heaven. Stones and soil and flesh—that is my kingdom!

He rose. Somewhere he found the strength to jump up and gird himself, gird himself interminably with an invisible sword, bellowing like a lion. He was ready. "Forward!" he cried. He turned, but the lion had disappeared. He heard pulsating laughter above him and a voice: "Look!" A flash of lightning knifed through the night and stood fixed, motionless. Under it were cities with walls and towers, houses, roads, squares, people; and all around, plains, mountains, sea. Babylon was to the right, Jerusalem and Alexandria to the left, and across the sea was Rome. Once more he heard the voice: "Look!"

Jesus raised his eyes. A yellow-winged angel dropped headfirst from the sky. Lamentations were heard: in the four kingdoms the people lifted their arms to heaven, but their hands fell off, gnawed away by leprosy. They parted their lips to cry *Help!* and their lips fell, devoured by leprosy. The streets filled with hands and noses and mouths.

And while Jesus cried with upraised arms, "Mercy, Lord, have pity on mankind!" a second angel, dapple-winged, with bells around his feet and neck, fell headfirst from heaven. All at once laughter and guffawing broke out over the entire earth: struck down by madness, the lepers were running helter-skelter. Whatever remained of their bodies had burst into peals of laughter.

Trembling, Jesus blocked his ears so that he would not hear. And then a third angel, red-winged, fell like a meteor from the sky. Four fountains of fire rose up, four columns of smoke, and the stars were extinguished for want of air. A light breeze blew, scattering the fumes. Jesus looked. The four kingdoms had become four handfuls of ashes.

The voice sounded once more: "These, wretch, are the kingdoms of this world which you are setting out to possess; and those are my three beloved angels: Leprosy, Madness and Fire. The day of the Lord has come—my day, mine!" With this last clap of thunder the lightning disappeared.

• • •

The dawn found Jesus with his face plunged in the sand. During the night be must have rolled off his stone and wept and wept, for his eyes were swollen and smarting. He looked around him. Could this endless sand be his soul? The desert was shifting, coming to life. He heard shrill cries, mocking laughter, weeping. Small animals resembling rabbits, squirrels and weasels, all with ruby-red eyes, were hopping toward him. It is Madness, he thought, Madness, come to devour me. He cried out, and the animals disappeared; an archangel with the half moon suspended from his neck and a joyous star between his eyebrows towered up before him and unfurled his green wings.

Jesus shaded his eyes against the dazzling light. "Archangel," he whispered.

The archangel closed his wings and smiled. "Don't you recognize me?" he said. "Don't you remember me?"

"No, no! Who are you? Go farther away, Archangel. You're blinding me."

"Do you remember when you were a small child still unable to walk, you clung to the door of your house and to your mother's clothes so that you would not fall, and shouted within yourself, shouted loudly, 'God, make God! God, make me God! God, make me God!' "

"Don't remind me of that shameless blasphemy. I remember it!"

"I am that inner voice. I shouted then; I shout still, but you're afraid and pretend not to hear. Now, however, you are going to listen to me, like it or not. The hour has come. I chose you before you were born— you, out of the whole of mankind. I work and gleam within you, prevent you from falling into the minor virtues, the small pleasures, into happiness. Behold how just now when Woman came into the desert where I brought you, I banished her. The kingdoms came, and I banished them. I did, I, not you. I am reserving you for a destiny much more important, much more difficult."

"More important . . . more difficult . . . ?"

"What did you long for when you were a child? To become God. That is what you shall become!"

"I? I?"

"Don't shrink back; don't moan. That is what you shall become, what you have already become. What words do you think the wild dove threw over you at the Jordan?"

"Tell me! Tell me!"

"' You are my son, my only son!' That was the message brought you by the wild dove. But it was not a wild dove; it was the archangel Gabriel. I salute you, therefore: Son, only son of God!"

Two wings beat within Jesus' breast. He felt a large, rebellious morning star burning between his eyebrows. A cry rose up within him: I am not a man, not an angel, not your slave, Adonai—I am your son. I shall sit on your throne to judge the living and the dead. In my right hand I shall hold a sphere—the world—and play with it. Make room for me to sit down!

He heard peals of laughter in the air. Jesus gave a start. The angel had vanished. He uttered a piercing cry, "Lucifer!" and fell prone onto the sand.

"I shall see you again," said a mocking voice. "We shall meet again one day—soon!"

"Never, never, Satan!" Jesus bellowed, with his face buried in the sand.

"Soon!" the voice repeated. "At this Passover, miserable wretch!"

Jesus began to wail. His tears fell in warm drops on the sand, washing, rinsing, purifying his soul. Toward evening a cool breeze blew; the sun became gentle and colored the distant mountains pink. And then Jesus heard a merciful command, and an invisible hand touched his shoulder.

"Stand up, the day of the Lord is here. Run and carry the message to men: I am coming!"

from A Palpable God
by Reynolds Price

Reynolds Price (born 1933) calls Mark "the most original narrative writer in history." Price's crisp and straightforward translation of Mark's Gospel offers a fresh take on the story for readers familiar with older English versions.

THE GOOD NEWS ACCORDING TO MARK

BEGINNING OF THE GOOD NEWS
OF JESUS MESSIAH

As it was written in Isaiah the prophet

"Look, I send My messenger before your face
Who shall prepare your way,
Voice of one crying in the desert
'Prepare the Lord's way,
Make his paths straight.' "

John the Baptizer came into the desert proclaiming baptism of repentance for pardon of sins.

All the country of Judea went out to him and those from

Jerusalem and were baptized by him in the Jordan river confessing their sins.

John wore camel's hair and a leather belt round his hips, ate grasshoppers and wild honey and proclaimed saying "He's coming who is stronger than I—after me—of whom I'm unfit stooping to loosen the strap of his sandals. I baptized you in water but he'll baptize you in Holy Spirit."

It happened in those days—Jesus came from Nazareth in Galilee and was baptized in the Jordan by John. At once going up out of the water he saw the sky torn open and the Spirit like a dove descending to him.

There was a voice out of the sky "You are My son, the loved one. In you I have delighted."

At once the Spirit drove him into the desert. He was in the desert forty days tempted by Satan and was with wild beasts.

The angels served him.

After John was handed over Jesus came into Galilee proclaiming God's good news and saying "The time has ripened and the reign of God has approached. Turn and believe the good news." Passing by the sea of Galilee he saw Simon and Andrew, Simon's brother, casting a net into the sea (they were fishermen) and Jesus said to them "Come after me and I'll make you fishers for men."

At once leaving the nets they followed him.

Going on a little he saw James—Zebedee's James—and John his brother right in the boat mending nets. At once he called them and leaving their father Zebedee in the boat with the hands they went after him.

They went into Capernaum and at once on the sabbath entering the synagogue he taught.

They were amazed at his teaching for he was teaching them as if he had the right and not like the scholars.

At once there was in their synagogue a man with a foul spirit and he screamed saying "What are you to us, Jesus Nazarene? Did you come to destroy us? I know you for what you are—the Holy One of God!"

Jesus warned him saying "Silence! Come out of him."

Tearing him the foul spirit cried in a loud voice and came out of him.

All were stunned so they debated among themselves saying "What is this?—a new teaching by right? He commands the foul spirits and they obey him." Word of him went out at once everywhere all round the country of Galilee.

Going out of the synagogue at once they came to Simon and Andrew's house with James and John. Simon's mother-in-law was laid up with fever and at once they told him about her.

Approaching he raised her holding her hand.

The fever left her so she served them.

Then when dusk came and the sun set they brought him all the sick and the demoniac. The whole city was gathered at the door.

He cured many who were sick with various diseases and expelled many demons and did not let the demons speak because they knew him.

And very early—still night—he rose and went out and left for a lonely place and prayed there.

Simon and those with him tracked him down, found him and said to him "Everyone's looking for you."

He said to them "Let's go elsewhere to the nearest towns so I may preach there too. I came for this." And he preached in their synagogues in all Galilee and expelled demons.

A leper came to him begging him, kneeling and saying to him "If you will you can cleanse me."

Filled with pity, stretching out his hand, he touched him and said "I will. Be clean."

At once the leprosy left him and he was clean.

Then warning him sternly he ran him off and said to him "Say nothing—to no one—but go show yourself to the priest and offer for your cleansing what Moses ordered as testimony to them."

But he going off began to declare many things and spread the word.

So he could no longer enter a city openly but was out in desert places.

And they came to him from everywhere.

When he entered Capernaum again after days it was heard he was at home and many gathered so there was no room not even at the door and he spoke the word to them.

They came to him bringing a cripple borne by four men and unable to reach him because of the crowd they tore off the roof where he was and having broken in they lowered the pallet on which the cripple was lying.

Seeing their faith Jesus said to the cripple "Son, your sins are forgiven you."

But there were same scholars sitting there debating in their hearts "Why does this man speak thus? He blasphemes. Who can forgive sins but one—God?"

At once Jesus knowing in his soul that they were debating thus among themselves said to them "Why do you debate these things in your hearts? What is easier?—to say to the cripple 'Your sins are forgiven' or to say 'Stand. Take your pallet and walk'? But so you know the Son of Man has the right to forgive sins on earth" he said to the cripple "To you I say stand, take your pallet and go home."

He stood and at once taking the pallet went out in sight of all so that all were astonished and praised God saying "We never saw the like."

He went out again by the sea and all the crowd came to him and he taught them. And walking along he saw Levi—Alpheus' Levi—sitting at the tax office and said to him "Follow me."

Standing he followed him.

Then it happened as he lay at table in his house—many tax collectors and sinners lay back with Jesus and his disciples for there were many and they followed him.

The Pharisee scholars seeing him eating with sinners and tax collectors said to his disciples "Does he eat with sinners and tax collectors?"

Hearing Jesus said to them "The strong don't need a doctor but the sick do. I came not to call just men but sinners."

Now John's disciples and the Pharisees were fasting and they came and said to him "Why do John's disciples and the Pharisees' disciples fast but your disciples don't fast?"

Jesus said to them "Can the sons of the bridal-chamber fast while the bridegroom is with them? The time they have the bridegroom with them they can't fast. But days shall come when the bridegroom shall be taken from them and then on that day they'll fast. No one sews a patch of unshrunk cloth on old clothes otherwise the new pulls on the old and a worse tear starts. And no one puts new wine into old skins or the new wine splits the skins and the wine is lost and the skins. No, new wine is put in fresh skins."

Then this happened as he was walking on the sabbath through the grainfields and his disciples as they made a path began pulling stalks.

The Pharisees said to him "Look, why do they do on the sabbath what's not right?"

He said to them "Didn't you ever read what David did when he was needy and hungered?—he and those with him—how he entered God's house in the time of Highpriest Abiathar and ate the presentation loaves which it's not right to eat except for priests and also gave to those with him?" And he said to them "The sabbath was made because of man not man because of the sabbath. So the Son of Man is also lord of the sabbath."

He entered the synagogue again and there was a man who had a withered hand.

They were watching him closely whether on the sabbath he would heal him so they might charge him.

He said to the man who had the withered hand "Stand in the middle here." And he said to them "Is it right on the sabbath to do good or to do evil, to save life or kill?"

But they were silent.

Looking round at them with anger, grieved at the hardness of their heart he said to the man "Stretch out the hand."

He stretched it out and his hand was restored.

Leaving the Pharisees at once consulted with the Herodians against him so they might destroy him.

Jesus withdrew with his disciples to the sea.

And a great throng from Galilee followed him and from Judea, from Jerusalem, from Idumea, from beyond the Jordan and round Tyre and Sidon a great throng hearing what he did came to him.

He told his disciples that a little boat should wait near him because of the crowd so they might not rush him for he healed many so that they fell on him to touch him as many as had torments. And the foul spirits when they saw him fell down before him and cried saying "You're the Son of God."

He warned them strictly that they not reveal him.

And he climbed the mountain and called to him the ones he wanted.

They went to him.

He appointed twelve to be with him to send out to preach and to have the right to expel demons. He gave Simon the name Peter. And Zebedee's James and John, James's brother—he gave them the name *Boanerges* which is "Sons of Thunder"—and Andrew, Philip, Bartholomew, Matthew, Thomas, Alpheus' James, Thaddeus, Simon the Cananean and Judas Iscariot who also handed him over.

He came into a house and again a crowd gathered so they could not even eat bread.

Hearing his family went out to seize him for they said "He's beside himself."

And the scholars who came down from Jerusalem said "He has Beelzebub and by the prince of demons he expels demons."

Calling them to him in parables he said "How can Satan expel Satan? And if a kingdom is divided against itself that kingdom can't stand and if a house is divided against itself that house can't stand. And if Satan stood against himself and were divided he couldn't stand but would end. No man can—entering the house of the Strong Man—plunder his goods unless he binds the Strong Man first. Then he shall plunder his house. Amen I say to you that all shall be forgiven the sons of men—sins and whatever blasphemies they may blaspheme—but whoever blasphemes against the Holy Spirit has no forgiveness to eternity but is subject to eternal sin because they said 'He has a foul spirit.'"

His mother and his brothers came and standing outside sent to him calling him.

A crowd sat round him and said to him "Look, your mother and your brothers outside seek you."

Answering them he said "Who is my mother and my brothers?" and looking round at the ones sitting round him in a ring he said "Look, my mother and my brothers. Whoever does God's will—that one is my brother, sister and mother."

Again he began to teach by the sea and a great crowd gathered to him so that climbing into a boat he sat on the sea and all the crowd was on land close to the sea. He taught them much in parables and said to them in his teaching "Listen. Look, the sower went out to sow and it happened as he sowed—some fell by the road and birds came and ate it up. Another part fell on the rocky place where there wasn't much earth and at once it sprouted because it had no depth of earth and when the sun rose it was burnt and because of not having root it withered. Another part fell into thorns and the thorns grew up and choked it and it bore no fruit. Another part fell into good ground and bore fruit growing up and increasing and bore in thirties, sixties and hundreds." Then he said to them "Who has ears to hear let him hear."

When he was alone those round him with the twelve asked him about the parables.

He said to them "The mystery of the reign of God has been given to you but to those outside everything is in parables so

> Seeing they may see and not find
>> And hearing they may hear and not understand—
> Otherwise they'd turn and be forgiven."

And he said to them "Don't you know this parable? Then how will you know all the parables? The sower sows the word and these are the ones by the road where the word is sown and when they hear at once Satan comes and takes away the word sown in them. These are likewise the ones sown in rocky places who when they hear the word at once accept it with joy and have no root in themselves but are temporary. Then trouble or persecution coming because of the word at once they are made to fall. Others are the ones sown among thorns. These are the ones hearing the word and—the cares of the time, the cheat of riches and the other passions entering choke the word and it becomes barren. And those are the ones sown in good ground who hear the word and welcome it and bear fruit in thirties, sixties and hundreds." And he said to them "Does the lamp come so it can be put under the measuring bowl or under the couch?—not so it can be put on the lampstand? For nothing is hidden that shall not be shown or veiled except it come into the open. If any has ears to hear let him hear." And he said to them "Take care what you hear—with whatever measure you measure it shall be measured to you and added to you for, whoever has, to him shall be given and, who has not, even what he has shall be taken from him." And he said "Such is the reign of God—as if a man should throw seed on the ground and should sleep and rise night and day and the seed should sprout and lengthen he doesn't know how: on her own the earth yields fruit, first a blade then an ear then full grain in the ear. And when the fruit offers itself at once he puts in the sickle for the harvest has come." And he said "To what can we liken the reign of God? Or in what parable could we put it?—like a grain of mustard which when it's sown on the ground is smaller than all seeds on the ground but when it's sown grows up and becomes greater than all plants and makes big branches so the birds of the air can live under its shadow." In many such parables he spoke the word to them as far as they could hear it but without a parable he never spoke to them though aside to his own disciples he explained everything.

He said to them on that day when evening had come "Let's cross over to the other side" and dismissing the crowd they took him just as he was in the boat and other boats were with him. A violent windstorm came and waves poured into the boat so that it was now full. He was in the stern on a pillow sleeping.

They woke him and said to him "Teacher, it's nothing to you that we're perishing?"

Awake he warned the wind and said to the sea "Silence. Be still."

The wind fell and there was great calm.

• • •

He said to them "Why be so cowardly? Where is your faith?"

They feared with great dread and said to each other "Who is this then that even the wind and sea obey him?"

They came to the far side of the sea to Gerasene country. When he got out of the boat at once a man from the tombs with a foul spirit met him—his home was in the tombs. Even with a chain no one could bind him since he had often been bound with shackles and chains and the chains had been broken by him, the shackles had been smashed and no one was able to tame him. Always night and day in the tombs and mountains he was screaming and slashing himself with rocks. Seeing Jesus from a distance he ran and worshipped him and screaming in a loud voice he said "What am I to you, Jesus Son of the Highest God? I beg you by God don't torture me" for he had been saying to him "Out, foul spirit. Out of the man."

He asked him "What is your name?"

He said to him "Legion is my name because we are many" and he pled hard with Jesus not to send them out of the country. Now there was there close to the mountain a big herd of pigs feeding and all the demons pled saying "Send us to the pigs so we can enter them."

He let them.

Going out the foul spirits entered the pigs and the herd rushed down a cliff into the sea—there were about two thousand—and were choked in the sea.

The ones herding them fled and reported it to the town and the villages and they came out to see what it was that had happened. They came to Jesus and saw the demoniac sitting dressed and in his right mind—him who had had the Legion—and they were afraid. Those who had seen how it happened to the demoniac told them and about the pigs so they began to plead with him to leave their district.

As he boarded the boat the demoniac pled to be with him.

He did not let him but said to him "Go to your home to your people and report to them how much the Lord has done for you and pitied you."

He left and began to spread word through Decapolis how much Jesus did for him.

All men wondered.

When Jesus had crossed in the boat again to the far side a great crowd swarmed to him—he was by the sea—and one of the synagogue leaders named Jairus came and seeing him fell at his feet and pled hard saying "My little daughter is at the point of death. Come and lay your hands on her so she may be cured and live."

He went with him.

And a great crowd followed him and pressed round him.

Then a woman who had had a flow of blood twelve years and had suffered many things from many doctors and had spent all she owned and gained nothing but rather grown worse, hearing things about Jesus came up behind in the crowd and touched his coat saying "If I can touch just his clothes I'll be healed" and at once the fountain of her blood was dried and she knew in her body that she was cured from the scourge.

At once Jesus knowing in himself that his streaming power had gone out of him turned to the crowd and said "Who touched my clothes?"

His disciples said to him "You see the crowd pressing round you and you say 'Who touched me?' "

He looked round to see her who had done this.

So the woman—dreading and shaking, knowing what had happened to her—came and fell before him and told him all the truth.

He said to her "Daughter, your faith has cured you. Go in peace and be well of your scourge."

While he was still speaking they came from the synagogue leader's saying "Your daughter died. Why bother the teacher still?"

But Jesus ignoring the word just spoken said to the synagogue leader "Don't fear. Only believe" and he let no one go with him but Peter, James and John (James's brother).

They came to the house of the synagogue leader. He saw a commotion, people weeping and wailing hard. Entering he said to them "Why make a commotion and weep? The child is not dead but sleeps."

They mocked him.

But expelling them all he took the child's father, mother and those with him and went in where the child was. Grasping the child's hand he said to her *"Talitha koum"* which is translated "Little girl, I tell you rise."

At once the little girl stood and walked round—she was twelve years old—and at once they were astonished with great wildness.

He ordered them strictly that no one should know this and told them to give her something to eat.

He went out of there and came to his own town and his disciples followed him. When a sabbath came he began to teach in the synagogue.

Many hearing were amazed saying "From where did all these things come to this man and what is the wisdom given to him that such acts of power are done through his hands? Isn't this man the carpenter, the son of Mary and brother of James and Joses and Judas and Simon and aren't his sisters here with us?" They were offended by him.

Jesus said to them "A prophet is not dishonored except in his own town and among his kin and in his own house" and he could not do there any act of power except to a few sick—laying hands on them, he healed. He wondered at their doubting.

And he toured the villages round there teaching. He called the twelve to him and began to send them out two by two and gave them rights over foul spirits and ordered them to take nothing for the road except one stick—no bread, no wallet, no money in the belt—but be shod with sandals and not wear two shirts. He said to them "Wherever you enter a house stay there till you leave there and whatever place will not receive you or hear you, leaving there shake off the dust under your feet as a witness to them."

Going out they proclaimed that men should change. They expelled many demons, anointed many of the sick with oil and healed than.

King Herod heard—his name became widespread and they were saying "John the Baptizer has been raised from the dead which is why acts of power work through him" but others said "It's Elijah" and still others said "A prophet like one of the prophets." But hearing Herod said "The one I beheaded—John: he was raised" for Herod himself had sent and arrested John and bound him in prison because of Herodias the wife of Philip his brother since he had married her. For John said to Herod "It's not right for you to have your brother's wife." So Herodias had a grudge against him and wanted to kill him but could not for Herod feared John knowing him a just and holy man and protected him and hearing him was shaken but gladly heard him. Then when a suitable day came Herod gave a supper on his birthday for his great men and the tribunes and leading men of Galilee. The daughter of Herodias herself entered and dancing pleased Herod and those lying back with him. So the king said to the girl "Ask me whatever you want and I'll give it to you" and he swore to her "Whatever you ask I'll give you up to half my kingdom." Going out she said to her mother "What must I ask?" She said "The head of John the Baptizer." At once entering eagerly to the king she asked saying I want you to give me right now on a dish the head of John the Baptist." The king, anguished because of the oaths and those lying back with him, did not want to refuse her so at once sending an executioner the king commanded his head to be brought. Going he beheaded him in the prison, brought his head on a dish, gave it to the girl and the girl gave it to her mother. Hearing his disciples went, took his corpse and put it in a tomb.

And the apostles gathered back to Jesus and told him all they had done and taught.

He said to them "Come away by yourselves alone to a lonely place and rest a little" since those coming and going were many and they had no chance even to eat. They went off in the boat to a lonely place alone.

Many saw them going, knew and on foot from all the cities ran there together and preceded them.

Going out he saw a great crowd, pitied them since they were like sheep having no shepherd and began to teach them many things.

When it was late the disciples approached him and said "The place is lonely and it's late. Dismiss them so that going off to the neighboring farms and villages they can buy themselves something to eat."

But answering he said to them "You give them something to eat."

They said to him "Shall we go off and buy two hundred denarii-worth of loaves and give them to eat?"

He said to them "How many loaves do you have? Go see."

Knowing they said "Five and two fish."

He told them to lie back in parties on the green grass.

They lay back in groups by hundreds and fifties.

Then taking the five loaves and two fish, looking up to heaven he blessed and broke the loaves, gave them to the disciples to set before them and the two fish he spread among all.

All ate and were fed and they took up twelve full baskets of crumbs and fish. Those eating the loaves were five thousand men.

At once he made his disciples board the boat and go ahead to the far side of Bethsaida until he dismissed the crowd. And saying goodbye to them he went off to the mountain to pray.

When dusk came on the boat was in the middle of the sea and he alone on land and seeing them straining at the rowing for the wind was against them about three o'clock in the night he came toward them walking on the sea and wanted to pass them.

But seeing him walking on the sea they thought it was a ghost and cried out—all saw him and were frightened.

But at once he spoke with them and said "Courage. I am. No fear." And he went up to them into the boat and the wind dropped.

In themselves they were deeply astonished since they did not understand about the loaves as their heart was hardened.

Crossing over to land they came to Gennesaret and anchored.

When they came out of the ship at once knowing him they ran round all the countryside and began to haul the sick round on pallets where they heard he was and wherever he entered villages or cities or farms they put the sick in marketplaces and begged him to touch even the hem of his coat and as many as touched him were healed.

The Pharisees gathered to him and some of the scholars from Jerusalem and seeing some of his disciples eating bread with dirty hands—that is, not washed (for the Pharisees and all the Jews do not eat unless they scrub their hands, keeping the way of the elders, and coming from markets they do not eat unless they rinse and there are many other things which they have accepted to keep: washing cups, pitchers and kettles)—the Pharisees and scholars questioned him "Why don't your disciples walk after the way of the elders but eat bread with dirty hands?"

He said to them "Isaiah prophesied rightly about you hypocrites since it is written

> 'This people honors Me with lips
>> But their heart is far from Me.
> They worship me in vain,
>> Teaching teachings which are men's commands.'

Deserting God's command you keep man's way." And he said to them "Rightly you put aside God's command so you may keep your way for Moses said '*Honor your father and your mother*' and '*He who reviles father or mother let him die.*' But you say if a man says to his father 'Whatever you might have got from me is *Korban*' " (that is, a gift) "then you no longer let him do anything for his father or mother, canceling God's word in the way you've accepted. You do many such things."

Calling the crowd to him again he said "Hear me all of you and understand. There is nothing outside a man that entering him can defile him but the things coming out of a man are the things that defile him. If anyone has ears to hear let him hear."

When he entered a house from the crowd his disciples questioned him about the parable. He said to them "Then you too are stupid? Don't you understand that anything outside entering a man can't defile him because it doesn't enter his heart but his belly and goes into the privy purging all foods?" He said "The thing coming out of a man defiles a man. For from inside out of the heart of man bad thoughts come—fornications, thefts, murders, adulteries, greeds, malice, deceits, lust, evil eye, slander, pride, folly: all these evil things come from inside and defile a man."

Rising from there he went off to the district of Tyre. When he entered a house he wanted no one to know but he could not be hid.

At once a woman whose young daughter had a foul spirit heard of him and coming fell at his feet. The woman was a Greek, a Syro-Phoenician by race, and she asked him to expel the demon from her daughter.

He said to her "Let the children be fed first. It's not right to take the children's bread and throw it to pups."

She answered and said to him "Yes sir but pups under the table eat the children's crumbs."

He said to her "For that saying go. The demon has gone out of your daughter."

And going away to her house she found the child laid on the couch and the demon gone.

Going out again from the district of Tyre he came through Sidon to the sea of Galilee in the middle of the district of Decapolis. And they brought him a deaf man with a stammer and they begged him to put his hand on him. Taking him apart from the crowd he put his fingers into his ears and spitting touched his tongue and looking up to heaven groaned and said to him *"Ephphatha"* which is "Be opened."

His ears were opened, at once the block on his tongue was loosed and he spoke right.

He ordered them to tell nobody but the more he ordered the more wildly they declared it. They were wildly amazed saying "He has done everything right—he makes the deaf hear and the dumb speak."

In those days there was a big crowd again with nothing to eat and calling the disciples to him he said to them "I pity the crowd since they've been with me three days and have nothing to eat. If I send them off hungry to their homes they'll give out on the way—some of them are from far off."

His disciples answered him "Where could anyone get loaves to feed these people here in a desert?"

He asked them "How many loaves do you have?"

They said "Seven."

He ordered the crowd to lie back on the ground and taking the seven loaves and giving thanks he broke and gave to his disciples to serve.

They served the crowd.

They had a few little fish and blessing them he said for those to be served too.

They ate and were fed and took up seven trays of excess scraps—now they were about four thousand—and he sent them off.

And at once embarking in the boat with his disciples he came to the region of Dalmanutha.

The Pharisees came out and began to debate with him, demanding from him a sign from heaven, tempting him.

Groaning in his spirit he said "Why does this generation demand a sign? Amen I tell you no sign will be given this generation!" And leaving them again, embarking he went off to the far side. They forget to take bread—except for one loaf they had nothing with them in the boat—and he ordered them saying "Look, watch out for the Pharisees' leaven and Herod's leaven."

They argued with one another that they had no bread.

Knowing Jesus said to them "Why argue that you have no bread? Don't you see yet or understand? Have your hearts been hardened? *'Having eyes don't you see? Having ears don't you hear?'* Don't you remember? When I broke the five loaves for the five thousand how many basketsful of scraps did you take?"

They said to him "Twelve."

"When the seven for the four thousand how many trays filled with scraps did you take?"

They said "Seven."

He said to them "You still don't understand?"

They came to Bethsaida.

And they brought a blind man to him and begged him to touch him.

Taking the blind man's hand he led him out of the village and spitting in his eyes and laying hands on him he questioned him "Do you see anything?"

Looking up he said "I see men that look like trees walking."

So again he put his hands on his eyes.

Then he looked hard, was restored and saw everything clearly.

He sent him home saying "You may not go to the village."

And Jesus and his disciples went out to the villages of Caesarea Philippi. On the way he questioned his disciples saying to them "Who do men say I am?"

They told him saying " 'John the Baptist' and others 'Elijah' but others 'one of the prophets.' "

He questioned them "But you—who do you say I am?"

Answering Peter said to him "You are Messiah."

He warned them not to tell anyone about him and began to teach them that the Son of Man must endure many things and be refused by the elders, chief priests and scholars and be killed and after three days rise again—he said the thing plainly.

Peter taking him aside began to warn him.

But he turning round and seeing his disciples warned Peter and said "Get behind me, Satan, since you think not of God's things but men's things."

And calling the crowd to him with his disciples he said to them "If anyone wants to come after me let him disown himself and lift his cross and follow me for whoever wants to save his life shall lose it but whoever shall lose his life because of me and the good news shall save it. For how does it help a man to get the whole world and forfeit his soul? For what can a man give to redeem his soul? Whoever is ashamed of me in this adulterous and sinful generation the Son of Man shall also be ashamed of him when he comes in the glory of his Father with the holy angels." And he said to them "Amen I tell you that there are some of those standing here who shall never know death till they see the reign of God come in power."

After six days Jesus took Peter, James and John and led them up into a high mountain by themselves alone. He was changed in shape before them and his clothes became a very shining white such as no bleacher on earth can whiten them. And Elijah appeared to them with Moses and they were talking with Jesus.

Speaking up Peter said to Jesus "Rabbi, it's good for us to be here. Let's make three tents—one for you, one for Moses and one for Elijah." He didn't know what he said—they were terrified.

There came a cloud covering them and there came a voice out of the cloud "This is My son, the loved one. Hear him."

Suddenly looking round they no longer saw anyone but only Jesus alone with themselves.

Coming down from the mountain he ordered them to tell no one the things they saw except when the Son of Man should rise from the dead.

They kept that word to themselves discussing what is "To rise from the dead." And they questioned him saying "Why do the scholars say that Elijah must come first?"

He said to them "Elijah in fact coming first shall restore everything. How has it been written of the Son of Man?—that he should endure much, suffer and be scorned? But I tell you that Elijah has come already and they did with him what they wanted as it was written of him."

And coming to the disciples they saw a big crowd round them and scholars arguing with them.

At once seeing him all the crowd were much stunned and running up greeted him.

He questioned them "What are you arguing with them?"

One of the crowd answered him "Teacher, I brought you my son who has a dumb spirit. Wherever it seizes him it flings him down and he foams and gnashes his teeth and goes stiff. I told your disciples to expel him but they couldn't."

Answering them he said "O unbelieving generation, how long shall I be with you? How long must I bear you? Bring him to me."

They brought him to him.

And seeing him at once the spirit convulsed him fiercely and falling to the ground he wallowed foaming.

He questioned his father "How long is it since this happened to him?"

He said "Since childhood. Often it throws him into fire and water to destroy him but if you can do anything take pity on us. Help us."

Jesus said to him " 'If you can'?—everything can be for a believer."

Crying out at once the child's father said "I believe! Help my unbelief."

Seeing a crowd running together Jesus warned the foul spirit saying to it "Dumb and deaf spirit, I order you come out of him and enter him no more!"

Screaming and convulsing him greatly it came out and he was lifeless so that many said he was dead.

But Jesus taking hold of his hand pulled him and he stood.

When he entered a house his disciples asked him privately "Why couldn't we expel it?"

He told them "This kind can come out only through prayer."

Leaving there they passed through Galilee. He wanted no one to know since he was teaching his disciples. He told them "The Son of Man is betrayed into men's hands. They shall kill him and being killed after three days he shall rise."

They were ignorant of the prophecy and afraid to ask him.

And they came to Capernaum and once in the house he questioned them "What were you discussing on the way?"

They were silent for on the way they had argued with one another who was greater.

Sitting he called the twelve and said to them "If anyone wishes to be first he shall be last of all and servant of all." Then taking a little child he set him in their midst and folding him in his arms he said to them "Whoever welcomes one little child like this in my name welcomes me and whoever welcomes me welcomes not me but the one who sent me."

John said to him "Teacher, we saw someone expelling demons in your name. We stopped him since he doesn't follow us."

But Jesus said "Don't stop him. No one will do a powerful thing in my name and soon speak evil of me. Whoever is not against us is for us and whoever gives you a cup of water to drink because you are Messiah's—Amen I tell you that he shall never lose his reward. And whoever causes one of these little ones who believe to sin, it would be better for him if a great millstone were set round his neck and he were thrown in the sea. If your hand makes you sin cut it off. It's better you enter life maimed than having two hands go off into Gehenna into unquenchable fire. If your foot makes you sin cut it off. It's better you enter life lame than having two feet be thrown into Gehenna. And if your eye makes you sin gouge it out. It's better you enter the reign of God one-eyed than having two eyes be thrown into Gehenna *'where their worm never dies and the fire is not quenched.'* For everyone shall be salted with fire. Salt is good but if salt goes bland how will you season it? Have salt in yourselves and keep peace with one another."

Rising from there he came to the fringes of Judea and the far side of Jordan. Crowds followed him again and as usual he taught them.

Coming up Pharisees questioned him if it was right for a man to reject his wife—testing him.

Answering he said to them "What did Moses command you?"

They said "Moses allowed us to write a notice of divorce and to dismiss her."

Jesus said to them "He wrote you this command for your hard-heartedness. But from the start of creation *'He made them male and female and because of that a man shall leave his father and mother and the two shall be one flesh'* so that they're no longer two but one. Thus what God yoked man must not divide."

Back in the house the disciples questioned him about this.

He said to them "Whoever dismisses his wife and marries another commits adultery on her. And if she dismissing her husband marries another she commits adultery."

They brought him children to touch but the disciples warned them.

Seeing Jesus was indignant and said to them "Let the little children come to me—don't stop them—for the reign of God belongs to such. Amen I tell you whoever doesn't welcome the reign of God like a child shall never enter it." And folding them in his arms and putting his hands on them he blessed them.

As he went out onto the road a man ran up and kneeling to him asked him "Kind teacher, what must I do to inherit eternal life?"

Jesus said to him "Why do you call me *kind*? No one is kind but one—God. You know the commandments—*'do not kill, do not commit adultery, do not steal, do not give perjured witness,'* do not cheat, *'honor your father and mother.'* "

He said to him "Teacher, all these things I've kept since my youth."

Then Jesus gazing at him loved him and said to him "One thing is lacking you. Go sell what you have and give to the poor—you'll have treasure in heaven. Then come follow me."

But he was shocked by the word and went away grieving since he had great belongings.

Looking round Jesus said to his disciples "How strenuously the rich shall enter the reign of God!"

The disciples were stunned at his words.

But Jesus speaking again said to them "Sons, how strenuous it is to enter the reign of God! It's easier for a camel to go through a needle's eye than for a rich man to enter the reign of God."

They were much amazed saying to themselves "Who can be saved?"

Gazing at them Jesus said "With men it's impossible but not with God for everything is possible with God."

Peter started saying "Look, we left everything and followed you—"

But Jesus said "Amen I tell you there is no one who left home or brothers or sisters or mother or father or children or farms for my sake and the sake of the good news but shall get a hundredfold now in this time—houses and brothers and sisters and mothers and children and farms with persecutions—and in the age to come eternal life. Many first shall be last and last first."

They were on the road now going up to Jerusalem and Jesus was preceding them. They were stunned and the followers were afraid. Taking the twelve again he began to tell them the things about to happen to him—"Look, we're going up to Jerusalem and the Son of Man shall be handed to the chief priests and scholars. They'll condemn him to death and hand him to the Gentiles. They'll mock him, spit on him, flog him and kill him. Then after three days he'll rise again."

James and John—Zebedee's two sons—came up to him saying to him "Teacher, we want you to do whatever we ask for us."

He said to them "What do you want me to do for you?"

They said to him "Grant that one on your right and one on your left we may sit in your glory."

Jesus said "You don't know what you're asking. Can you drink the cup I'm drinking or be baptized with the baptism I'm to be baptized with?"

They said to him "We can."

And Jesus said to them "The cup I drink you'll drink and the baptism I'm baptized in you'll be baptized in. But to sit on my right or left is not mine to give, rather for the ones for whom it was prepared."

Hearing the ten began to be indignant at James and John.

So calling them to him Jesus said to them "You know that the self-styled rulers of the Gentiles lord it over them and their great men exercise power over them. But it's not so among you. Whoever among you wishes to be great shall be servant of all and whoever wishes to be first among you shall be slave of all for even the Son of Man didn't come to be served but to serve and give his life a ransom for many."

They got to Jericho and as he was leaving Jericho with his disciples and a sizable crowd Timeus' son—Bartimeus a blind man begging—sat by the road. Hearing that it was Jesus the Nazarene he began to cry out and say "Son of David, Jesus, pity me!"

Many warned him to be still but he cried out all the more "Son of David, pity me!"

Stopping Jesus said "Call him."

So they called the blind man saying to him "Cheer up. Stand. He's calling you."

Throwing off his coat and jumping up he came to Jesus.

Answering him Jesus said "What do you want me to do for you?"

The blind man said to him "Rabboni, to see."

Jesus said "Go. Your faith has cured you."

At once he saw and followed him in the road.

And as they neared Jerusalem at Bethphage and Bethany toward the Mount of Olives he sent two of his disciples and told them "Go to the village opposite you and at once entering it you'll find a tethered colt on which no one has yet sat. Untie it and bring it. if anyone says to you 'Why are you doing this?' say 'The Lord needs it and will send it back at once."

They went and found a colt tied at a door outside in the street and they untied it.

Some of those standing there said to them "What are you doing untying the colt?"

They said to them what Jesus said.

So they let them go.

They brought the colt to Jesus and threw their coats on it.

He sat on it.

Many spread their coats in the road and others branches of leaves cut from the fields. The ones leading and the ones following cried out " 'Hosanna! Blessed he who comes in the Lord's name!' Blessed the coming reign of David our father! Hosanna in the heights!"

So he entered Jerusalem and the Temple and looking round at everything—the hour now being late—he went out to Bethany with the twelve.

On the next day as they went out from Bethany he hungered and seeing a figtree in the distance in leaf he went to see if maybe he could find something on it. Coming to it he found nothing but leaves since it was not the time for figs. Speaking out he said to it "Let no one— never again—eat fruit from you."

The disciples heard him.

Then they came to Jerusalem and entering the Temple he began to expel those selling and buying in the Temple. He upset the money-changers' tables, the dovesellers' chairs and did not let anyone carry anything through the Temple. Then he taught and said to them "Hasn't it been written that 'My house shall be called a house of prayer for all nations'? But you have made it 'a bandits' cave.'"

The chief priests and scholars heard and looked for how they might destroy him since they feared him and all the crowd was amazed by his teaching.

When it was late they went out of the city.

And passing along early they saw the figtree withered from the roots.

Remembering Peter said to him "Rabbi, look. The figtree which you cursed has withered."

Answering Jesus said to them "Have faith in God. Amen I tell you that whoever says to this mountain 'Be raised and thrown into the sea' and has no doubts in his heart but believes that what he says is happening, it shall be his. So I tell you, all that you pray and ask for—believe that you get and it shall be yours. And when you stand praying forgive if you have anything against anyone so your Father in heaven may also forgive your sins."

They came again to Jerusalem and as he walked in the Temple the chief priests, scholars and elders came to him and said to him "By what right do you do these things? Or who gave you this right that you do these things?"

Jesus said to them "I'll ask you one word. Answer me and I'll tell you by what right I do these things. John's baptism—was it heaven's or men's? Answer me."

They argued among themselves saying "If we say 'Heaven's' he'll say 'Then why didn't you believe him?' but if we say 'Men's' "—they feared the crowd for everybody held that John was certainly a prophet. So answering Jesus they said "We don't know."

Jesus said to them "Neither will I tell you by what right I do these things" and he started speaking to them in parables. "A man planted a vineyard and put a fence round it, dug a winevat and built a watchtower. Then he leased it to tenants and went far away. At the right season he sent a slave to the tenants to get some fruit from the vineyard. Taking him they beat him and sent him away empty. Again he sent them another slave. They struck him on the head and insulted him. So he sent another and they killed that one and many more, beating some, killing others. He had one left, a much-loved son. He sent him to them last saying 'They will honor my son.' But those tenants said to themselves 'This is the heir. Come let's kill him. The inheritance will be ours.' Taking him they killed him and flung him outside the vineyard. What will the lord of the vineyard do? He'll come, kill the tenants and give the vineyard to others. Haven't you read this text?

> A stone which the builders rejected,
>   This became the keystone.

> *This was from the Lord*
> *And is wonderful in our eyes."*

They longed to arrest him but feared the crowd since they knew he had told the parable on them. So leaving him they went away and sent to him some Pharisees and Herodians to snare him in a word.

Coming they said to him "Teacher, we know you're honest and that no one counts heavily with you since you don't regard men's faces but really teach God's way. Is it right to pay tribute to Caesar or not? Should we pay or not pay?"

But knowing their hypocrisy he said to them "Why tempt me? Bring me a denarius so I may see."

They brought one.

And he said to them "Whose picture is this and whose inscription?"

They told him "Caesar's."

So Jesus said to them "Caesar's things give back to Caesar and God's things to God."

They were dumbfounded by him.

Then Sadducees came to him who say there is no resurrection and asked him saying "Teacher, Moses wrote for us that if anyone's brother die and leave a wife and leave no child then his brother may take the wife and rear seed for his brother. There were seven brothers and the first got a wife and dying left no seed. The second got her and died not leaving seed and the third likewise. The seven left no seed. Last of all the woman died too. At the resurrection when they rise again which of them will she be wife to?—for the seven had her as wife."

Jesus said to them "Aren't you wrong in not knowing the scriptures or God's power?—for when they rise again from the dead they neither marry nor are given in marriage but are like angels in the heavens. But about the dead that they are raised—didn't you read in the scroll of Moses how at the bush God spoke to him saying *'I the God of Abraham, the God of Isaac, the God of Jacob'*? He's not the God of the dead but the living. You're deeply wrong."

One of the scholars approaching, hearing their discussion and knowing he answered them well asked him "What commandment is first of all?"

Jesus answered "First is *'Hear, Israel, the Lord our God is one Lord and you shall love the Lord your God with all your heart, with all your soul and with all your strength.'* Second, this—*'You shall love your neighbor like yourself.'* There is no other commandment greater than these."

The scholar said to him "True, Teacher. You say rightly that there is One and no other beside Him and to love Him with all the heart, with all the understanding and with all the strength and to love one's neighbor as oneself is more than all the burnt offerings and sacrifices."

Jesus seeing that he answered wisely said to him "You're not far from the reign of God."

Nobody dared question him further.

And going on as he taught in the Temple Jesus said "How can the scholars say that Messiah is David's son? David himself said through the Holy Spirit

> *The Lord said to my Lord*
> *'Sit at My right*
> > *Till I put your enemies under your feet.'*

David himself calls him Lord so how is he his son?"

The great crowd heard him gladly.

In his teaching he said "Beware of the scholars—the ones liking to parade in flowing robes, to be greeted in the markets, to have the best seats in synagogues and the best places at banquets, the ones consuming widows' houses under cover of long prayer: these shall get greater damnation."

And sitting opposite the Treasury he saw how the crowd put coppers into the Treasury. Many rich men put in much but one poor widow coming put in two lepta which make a penny. So calling his disciples to him he said to them "Amen I tell you that this poor widow put in more than all those contributing to the Treasury for they put in out of their surplus but this woman out of her need put in everything she had, all her goods."

When he went out of the Temple one of his disciples said to him "Teacher, look what stones, what buildings!"

Jesus said to him "See these great buildings? There shall surely be left no stone on stone which shall not surely be thrown down."

And when he sat on the Mount of Olives opposite the Temple, Peter, James, John and Andrew asked him privately "Tell us when all this will be and what will be the sign when all this is finished?"

So Jesus began to say to them "Watch so nobody leads you away. Many shall come in my name saying 'I am' and shall lead many away. But when you hear of wars and tales of wars don't be frightened. It must happen but the end won't be yet for nation shall be set against nation and kingdom against kingdom. There'll be earthquakes in places, there'll be famines—these are the onset of birth and pain. But see to yourselves. They'll hand you over to courts, you'll be beaten in synagogues, you'll stand before governors and kings for my sake to witness to them since the good news must first be announced to all nations. When they lead you out and hand you over don't worry yourself with what you'll say but what's given you in that hour say that for you're not the ones speaking but the Holy Spirit. Brother shall hand brother over to death and a father his child, children shall rise against parents and kill them and you'll be hated by everyone because of my name but the one surviving to the end—that one shall be saved. Still when you see the desolating horror standing where it shouldn't"—let the reader understand—"then those in Judea let them flee to the mountains. Him on the roof let him not climb down or go in to take anything from his house. And him in the field let him not go back to the rear to take his coat. But woe to pregnant women and them suckling in those days. Pray for it not to happen in winter for those days shall be a trial such as has not come since the start of creation which God created till now and shall surely never come again. Unless the Lord shortened the days no flesh would be spared but because of the chosen whom He chose He shortened the days. So if anyone tells you 'Look here, the Messiah! Look there!' don't believe it. False Messiahs and false prophets shall appear and do signs and wonders to seduce the chosen if possible. But you, see!—I've warned you of everything. In those days after that trial the sun shall turn dark, the Moon give none of her light. The stars shall be falling from heaven and the powers in the heavens shall quake. Then they'll see the Son of Man coming on clouds with great power and glory and then he'll send the angels and they'll gather his chosen from the four winds, from pole of earth to pole of heaven. Now learn a lesson from the figtree— when its branch is tender again and puts out leaves you know that summer is near. So too when you see these things happen know that he is at the doors. Amen I tell you that no way shall this generation pass till all these things happen. Heaven and earth shall pass but my words shall not pass. But about that day or hour nobody knows—neither the angels in heaven nor the Son, only the Father. Watch. Stay awake for you don't know when the time is. It's like a traveler leaving his house and putting his slaves in charge each with his own work and he ordered the doorman to watch. You watch then since you don't know when the lord of the house is coming either late or at midnight or at cock-crow or early or coming suddenly he may find you sleeping. What I say to you I say to all—watch."

Now it was the Passover, the feast of unleavened bread, after two days and the chief priests and the scholars searched for how seizing him by deceit they might kill him for they said "Not at the feast or there'll be an outcry from the people."

When he was in Bethany in the house of Simon the leper as he lay back a woman came with an alabaster flask of costly pure nard ointment. Breaking the alabaster flask she poured it over his head. Some were indignant among themselves "Why has this waste of ointment occurred? This ointment could be sold for more than three hundred denarii and given to the wretched." They scolded her.

But Jesus said "Let her be. Why make trouble for her? She did a good deed on me. The wretched you always have with you and whenever you want you can do good to them but me you don't always have. What she could she did. She was early to anoint my body for burial. Amen I tell you wherever the good news is declared in all the world what this woman did shall also be told as a memory of her."

Then Judas Iscariot, one of the twelve, went to the chief priests so he might betray him to them.

Hearing they were glad and promised to give him silver.

And he looked for how he might conveniently betray him.

On the first day of unleavened bread when they slaughtered the Passover lamb the disciples said to him "Where do you want us to go and arrange for you to eat the Passover?"

He sent two of his disciples and told them "Go into the city. You'll be met by a man carrying a water jug. Follow him. Wherever he goes in tell the owner 'The teacher says "Where is my guestroom where I can eat the Passover with my disciples?" ' He'll show you a big room upstairs all spread and ready. Prepare for us there."

The disciples went out and entered the city and found it as he told them. Then they prepared the Passover.

As evening fell he came with the twelve and as they lay back and ate Jesus said "Amen I tell you that one of you shall betray me, the one eating with me."

They started grieving and saying to him one by one "Surely not I?"

He said to them "One of the twelve, him dipping with me in the common bowl. For the Son of Man is really going his way as was written of him but woe to the man through whom the Son of Man is betrayed. Better for him if that man were not born."

As they were eating he took a loaf and blessing it he broke and gave to them and said "Take. This is my body." And taking a cup and giving thanks he gave to them.

All drank of it.

He said to them "This is my blood of the covenant poured out for many. Amen I tell you never in any way will I drink of the fruit of the vine till that day when I drink it new in the reign of God."

After singing the hymn they went out to the Mount of Olives.

And Jesus said to them "All of you shall fall since it was written

'I will strike down the shepherd
   And the sheep shall be scattered.'

• • •

But after I'm raised I'll go ahead of you to Galilee."

Peter said to him "Even if everybody stumbles not I."

Jesus said to him "Amen I tell you, you—today, tonight before the cock crows twice—you'll deny me three times."

But he just kept saying "If I must die with you no way would I deny you." All said likewise too.

They came to a piece of land whose name was Gethsemane and he said to his disciples "Sit here while I pray." He took Peter, James and John with him and began to be deeply appalled and harrowed so he said to them "My soul is anguished to death. Stay here and watch." Going on a little he fell on the ground and prayed that if it were possible the hour might turn away and he said "*Abba*, Father, everything is possible to You. Take this cup from me—still not what I want but You." He came and found them sleeping and said to Peter "Simon are you sleeping? Couldn't you watch one hour? Watch and pray so you don't come to testing—oh the spirit is ready but the flesh is weak." Going off again he prayed saying the same words. Coming back he found them sleeping since their eyes were growing heavy and they didn't know how to answer him. He came the third time and said to them "Sleep now and rest. It's over. The hour came. Look, the Son of Man is betrayed into sinners' hands. Get up. Let's go. Look, the one who betrays me is nearing."

At once while he was still speaking Judas appeared—one of the twelve—and with him a crowd with swords and sticks from the chief priests, scholars and elders. The one betraying him had given them a sign saying "Whomever I kiss is he. Seize him and take him off securely." At once coming up to him he said "Rabbi!" and kissed him lovingly.

They got their hands on him and seized him.

But one of the bystanders drawing a sword struck the high priest's slave and cut off his ear.

Speaking out Jesus said to them "Did you come out with swords and sticks as if against a rebel to arrest me? Daily I was with you in the Temple teaching and you didn't seize me. But the scriptures must be done."

Deserting him they all ran.

One young man followed him dressed in a linen shirt over his naked body. They seized him but leaving the shirt behind he fled naked.

Then they took Jesus off to the high priest and all the chief priests, elders and scholars gathered.

Peter followed him far off right into the high priest's courtyard, sat with the servants and warmed himself by the blaze.

Now the chief priests and all the Sanhedrin looked for testimony against Jesus to execute him but they found none since many testified falsely against him and the testimonies were not the same. Some standing testified falsely against him saying "We heard him saying 'I'll tear down this Temple made by hand and after three days I'll build another not handmade.' " Even so their testimony was not consistent.

Standing in the center the high priest questioned Jesus saying "Won't you answer anything these men testify against you?"

But he was silent and answered nothing.

Again the high priest questioned him and said to him "You are Messiah, the son of the Blessed?"

Jesus said "I am and you shall see the Son of Man sitting at the right of Power and coming with clouds of heaven."

The high priest tearing his robes said "What further need do we have for witnesses? You heard the blasphemy. How does it look to you?"

They all condemned him worthy of death. Some began to spit at him, cover his face, hit him and say to him "Prophesy!" and the servants treated him to blows

When Peter was down in the courtyard one of the high priest's maids came and seeing Peter warming himself she looked at him and said "You were with the Nazarene Jesus."

But he denied it saying "I don't know him or understand what you're saying." Then he went out into the porch and the cock crowed.

Seeing him the maid began again to say to those standing round "This man is one of them."

But again he denied it.

After a little again those standing round said to Peter "Surely you're one of them. It's plain you're a Galilean."

He began to curse himself and swear "I don't know this man you mention." At once a second time a cock crowed and Peter remembered the word Jesus said to him "Before the cock crows twice you'll deny me three times" and dwelling on that he wept.

At once in the morning the chief priests held council with the elders, scholars and all the Sanhedrin and binding Jesus they led him off and handed him to Pilate.

Pilate asked him "You're the king of the Jews?"

Answering him he said "You say."

The chief priests charged him with many things.

But Pilate asked him again "Will you answer nothing? See how much they charge you with."

But Jesus still answered nothing.

Pilate wondered.

At each feast he freed for them one prisoner they requested. There was one named Barabbas held with the rebels who had committed murder in the rebellion. So the crowd came up and began to ask for his usual act.

But Pilate answered them saying "Do you want me to free you the king of the Jews?"—he knew the chief priests had handed him over out of envy.

But the chief priests incited the crowd to free them Barabbas instead.

So Pilate spoke out again to them "What must I do then with the one you call king of the Jews?"

They shouted back "Crucify him!"

But Pilate said to them "Why? What evil has he done?"

They shouted louder "Crucify him!"

Then Pilate wanting to pacify the crowd freed them Barabbas and handed over Jesus having flogged him so he could be crucified.

The soldiers led him off into the courtyard called Pretorium and summoned the whole cohort. They put on him a purple robe and plaiting a thorn crown they put it round him. Then they started saluting him "Hail, king of the Jews!" They hit his head with a reed, spat on him and kneeling down worshipped him. When they had mocked him they took the purple off him and put on his own clothes. Then they led him out to crucify him. They forced one Simon—a Cyzenean from the country, the father of Alexander and Rufus—to carry his cross. So they brought him to the place Golgotha which means "Skull Place." They gave him wine drugged with myrrh but he would not take it. Then they crucified him and divided his clothes casting lots for them, what each might take. It was nine in the morning when they crucified him. The notice of the charge against him was written above "The King of the Jews." With him they crucified two thieves one on his right and one on his left.

Those passing by insulted him wagging their heads and saying "So! The one who would destroy the Temple and build it in three days! Save yourself. Get down off the cross."

In the same way the chief priests joking with each other and with the scholars said "He saved others. He can't save himself! Messiah king of Israel!—let him get down off the cross so we can see and believe."

And those crucified with him reviled him.

At noon darkness came over the whole land till three and at three Jesus shouted in a loud voice " '*Eloi, Eloi, lama sabachthani?*'" which means "My God, my God, why did You forsake me?"

Some of the bystanders hearing said "Look, he's calling Elijah" and running one filled a sponge with vinegar and putting it round a stick gave him to drink saying "Let him be. Let's see if Elijah comes to take him down."

But Jesus giving a loud cry breathed his last.

The Temple curtain was torn in two from top to bottom.

The centurion standing opposite seeing that he breathed his last that way said "Surely this man was son of God."

There were women too at a distance watching among whom were both Mary the Magdalene, Mary the mother of the younger James and mother of Joses, and Salome who followed him when he was in Galilee and served him and many others who had come up with him to Jerusalem.

Now when evening came since it was preparation which is the day before the Sabbath Joseph from Arimathea, an important councilor who was himself also expecting the reign of God, came and boldly went in to Pilate and asked for Jesus' body.

Pilate wondered if he was already dead and summoning the centurion questioned him how long ago he died. Then learning from the centurion he presented the corpse to Joseph.

Having bought new linen and taken him down he wrapped him with the linen, put him in a tomb hewn from rock and rolled a stone across the entrance of the tomb.

Mary the Magdalene and Mary the mother of Jesus watched where he was put.

When the sabbath passed Mary the Magdalene, Mary the mother of James, and Salome bought spices so they could come and anoint him. Very early on the first day of the week they came to the tomb as the sun was rising. They said to each other "Who'll roll the stone off the tomb door for us?" and looking up they saw the stone had been rolled back for it was huge. Entering the tomb they saw a young man sitting on the right dressed in a white robe and they were much stunned.

But he said to them "Don't be stunned. Are you looking for Jesus the crucified Nazarene? He was raised. He isn't here. Look, the place where they laid him. But go tell his disciples and Peter 'He's going ahead of you to Galilee. There you'll see him as he told you.' "

Going out they fled the tomb—they were shuddering and wild— and they told no one anything for they were afraid.

from The Lost Gospel
by Burton L. Mack

Some scholars argue that the Gospels of the New Testament were preceded by this gospel based on Jesus' sayings rather than his life. Theologians refer to this document as Q—from the German quelle, *or "source". Burton Mack argues that the people who compiled and studied Q were not Christians, and did not see Jesus as the Messiah. They looked to him as a teacher who helped them to live in difficult times.*

These are the teachings of Jesus.

Seeing the crowds, he said to his disciples,

"How fortunate are the poor; they have God's kingdom,
   How fortunate the hungry; they will be fed.
   How fortunate are those who are crying; they will laugh."

"I am telling you, love your enemies, bless those who curse you, pray for those who mistreat you.

   If someone slaps you on the cheek, offer your other cheek as well. If anyone grabs your coat, let him have your shirt as well.

   Give to anyone who asks, and if someone takes away your belongings, do not ask to have them back.

   As you want people to treat you, do the same to them.

   If you love those who love you, what credit is that to you? Even tax collectors love those who love them, do they not? And if you embrace only your brothers, what more are you doing than others? Doesn't everybody do that? If you lend to those from whom you expect repayment, what credit is that to you? Even wrongdoers lend to their kind because they expect to be repaid.

Instead, love your enemies, do good, and lend without expecting anything in return. Your reward will be great, and you will be children of God.

For he makes his sun rise on the evil and on the good; he sends rain on the just and on the unjust."

"Be merciful even as your Father is merciful.
Don't judge and you won't be judged.
For the standard you use [for judging] will be the standard used against you."

"Can the blind lead the blind? Won't they both fall into a pit?
A student is not better than his teacher. It is enough for a student to be like his teacher."

"How can you look for the splinter in your brother's eye and not notice the stick in your own eye? How can you say to your brother, 'Let me remove the splinter in your eye,' when you do not see the stick in your own eye? You hypocrite, first take the stick from your own eye, and then you can see to remove the splinter that is in your brother's eye."

"A good tree does not bear rotten fruit; a rotten tree does not bear good fruit. Are figs gathered from thorns, or grapes from thistles? Every tree is known by its fruit.

The good man produces good things from his store of goods and treasures; and the evil man evil things.

For the mouth speaks from a full heart."

"Why do you call me, 'Master, master,' and not do what I say?

Everyone who hears my words and does them is like a man who built a house on rock. The rain fell, a torrent broke against the house, and it did not fall, for it had a rock foundation.

But everyone who hears my words and does not do them is like a man who built a house on sand. The rain came, the torrent broke against it, and it collapsed. The ruin of that house was great."

When someone said to him, "I will follow you wherever you go," Jesus answered, "Foxes have dens, and birds of the sky have nests, but the son of man has nowhere to lay his head."

When another said, "Let me first go and bury my father," Jesus said, "Leave the dead to bury their dead."

Yet another said, "I will follow you, sir, but first let me say goodbye to my family." Jesus said to him, "No one who puts his hand to the plow and then looks back is fit for the kingdom of God."

He said, "The harvest is abundant, but the workers are few; beg therefore the master of the harvest to send out workers into his harvest.

Go. Look, I send you out as lambs among wolves.

Do not carry money, or bag, or sandals, or staff; and do not greet anyone on the road.

Whatever house you enter, say, 'Peace be to this house!' And if a child of peace is there, your greeting will be received [literally, "your peace will rest upon him"]. But if not, let your peace return to you.

And stay in the same house, eating and drinking whatever they provide, for the worker deserves his wages. Do not go from house to house.

And if you enter a town and they receive you, eat what is set before you. Pay attention to the sick and say to them, 'God's kingdom has come near to you.'

But if you enter a town and they do not receive you, as you leave, shake the dust from your feet and say, 'Nevertheless, be sure of this, the realm of God has come to you.' "

"When you pray, say,
'Father, may your name be holy.

May your rule take place.

Give us each day our daily bread.

Pardon our debts, for we ourselves pardon everyone indebted to us.

And do not bring us to trial [into a trying situation].' "

"Ask and it will be given to you; seek and you will find; knock and the door will be opened for you.

For everyone who asks receives, and the one who seeks finds, and to the one who knocks the door will be opened.

What father of yours, if his son asks for a loaf of bread, will give him a stone, or if he asks for a fish, will give him a snake?

Therefore, if you, although you are not good, know how to give good gifts to your children, how much more will the father above give good things to those who ask him!"

"Nothing is hidden that will not be made known, or secret that will not come to light.

What I tell you in the dark, speak in the light. And what you hear as a whisper, proclaim on the housetops."

"Don't be afraid of those who can kill the body, but can't kill the soul.

Can't you buy five sparrows for two cents? Not one of them will fall to the ground without God knowing about it. Even the hairs of your head are all numbered. So don't be afraid. You are worth more than many sparrows."

Someone from the crowd said to him, "Teacher, tell my brother to divide the inheritance with me." But he said to him, "Sir, who made me your judge or lawyer?"

He told them a parable, saying, "The land of a rich man produced in abundance, and he thought to himself, 'What should I do, for I have nowhere to store my crops?' Then he said, 'I will do this. I will pull down my barns and build larger ones, and there I will store all my grain and my goods. And I will say to my soul, Soul, you have ample goods stored up for many years. Take it easy. Eat, drink, and be merry.' But God said to him, 'Foolish man! This very night you will have to give back your soul, and the things you produced, whose will they be?' That is what happens to the one who stores up treasure for himself and is not rich in the sight of God."

"I am telling you, do not worry about your life, what you will eat, or about your body, what you will wear. Isn't life more than food, and the body more than clothing?

Think of the ravens. They do not plant, harvest, or store grain in barns, and God feeds them. Aren't you worth more than the birds? Which one of you can add a single day to your life by worrying?

And why do you worry about clothing? Think of the way lilies grow. They do not work or spin. But even Solomon in all his splendor was not as magnificent. If God puts beautiful clothes on the grass that is in the field today and tomorrow is thrown into a furnace, won't he put clothes on you, faint hearts?

So don't worry, thinking. 'What will we eat' or 'What will we drink,' or 'What will we wear?' For everybody in the whole world does that, and your father knows that you need these things.

Instead, make sure of his rule over you, and all these things will be yours as well."

"Sell your possessions and give to charity [alms]. Store up treasure for yourselves in a heavenly account, where moths and rust do not consume, and where thieves cannot break in and steal.

For where your treasure is, there your heart will also be."

He said, "What is the kingdom of God like? To what should I compare it? It is like a grain of mustard which a man took and sowed in his garden. It grew and became a tree, and the birds of the air made nests in its branches."

He also said, "The kingdom of God is like yeast which a woman took and hid in three measures of flour until it leavened the whole mass."

• • •

"Everyone who glorifies himself will be humiliated, and the one who humbles himself will be praised."

"A man once gave a great banquet and invited many. At the time for the banquet he sent his servant to say to those who had been invited, 'Please come, for everything is now ready.' But they all began to make excuses. The first said to him, 'I've bought a farm, and I must go and see it. Please excuse me.' And another said, 'I've just bought five pair of oxen and I need to check them out. Please excuse me.' And another said, 'I've just married a woman and so I can't come.' The servant came and reported this to his master. Then the owner in anger said to his servant, 'Go out quickly to the streets of the town and bring in as many people as you find.' And the servant went out into the streets and brought together everybody he could find. That way the house was filled with guests."

"Whoever does not hate his father and mother will not be able to learn from me. Whoever does not hate his son and daughter cannot belong to my school.

Whoever does not accept his cross [bear up under condemnation] and so become my follower, cannot be one of my students.

Whoever tries to protect his life will lose it; but whoever loses his life on account of me will preserve it."

"Salt is good; but if salt loses its taste, how can it be restored? It is not good for either the land or the manure pile. People just throw it out."

from The Unknown Life
of Jesus Christ
by Nicolas Notovitch

Nineteenth century Russian journalist Nicolas Notovitch (born 1858) claimed that he discovered Tibetan scrolls containing accounts of Jesus' travels to the Himalayas. Subsequent efforts to confirm Notovitch's story (and to find copies of the scrolls) were unsuccessful.

The Life Of Saint Issa
The Best Of The Sons Of Men
I.

1. The earth has trembled and the heavens have wept, because of the great crime just committed in the land of Israel.

2. For they have put to torture and executed the great just Issa, in whom dwelt the spirit of the world.

3. Which was incarnated in a simple mortal, that men might be benefited and evil thoughts exterminated thereby.

4. And that it might bring back to life of peace, of love and happiness, man degraded by sin, and recall to him the only and indivisible Creator whose mercy is boundless and infinite.

5. Thus is what is related on this subject by the merchants who have come from Israel.

II.

1. The people of Israel, who inhabited a most fertile land, yielding two crops a year, and who possessed immense flocks, excited the wrath of God through their sins.

2. And he inflicted upon them a terrible punishment by taking away their land, their flocks, and all they possessed; and Israel was reduced to slavery by rich and powerful Pharaohs who then reigned in Egypt.

3. The latter treated the Israelites more cruelly than animals, loading them with the roughest labor; they covered their bodies with bruises and wounds, and denied them food and shelter,

4. That they might be kept in a state of continual terror and robbed of all semblance of humanity;

5. And in their dire distress, the children of Israel, remembering their heavenly protector, addressed their prayers to him and implored his assistance and mercy.

6. An illustrious Pharaoh then reigned in Egypt, who had become celebrated for his numerous victories, the great riches he had amassed, and the vast palaces which his slaves had erected with their own hands.

7. This Pharaoh had two sons, the young of whom was called Mossa; and the learned Israelites taught him diverse sciences.

8. And Mossa was beloved throughout the land of Egypt for his goodness and the compassion he displayed for them that suffered.

9. Seeing that, notwithstanding the intolerable sufferings they endured, the Israelites refused to abandon their God to worship those created by the hands of man and which were the gods of the Egyptians.

10. Mossa believed in their indivisible God, who did not allow their flagging strength to falter.

11. And the Israelite preceptors encouraged Mossa's ardor and had recourse to him, begging him to intercede with Pharaoh, his father, in favor of his co-religionists.

12. Prince Mossa pleaded with his father to soften the lot of these unhappy people, but Pharaoh became angry with him and only imposed more hardships upon his slaves.

13. It came to pass, not long after, that a great calamity fell upon Egypt; the plague decimated the young and old, the strong and the sick; and Pharaoh believed he had incurred the wrath of his own gods against him;

14. But the prince Mossa declared to his father, that it was the God of his slaves who was interfering in favor of his unhappy people and punishing the Egyptians;

15. Pharaoh commanded Mossa, his son, to gather all the slaves of Jewish race, to lead them away to a great distance from the capital and found another city, where he should remain with them.

16. Mossa announced to the Hebrew slaves that he had delivered them in the name of their God, the God of Israel; and he went with them out of the land of Egypt.

17. He therefore led them into the land they had lost through their many sins; he gave them laws and enjoined them to always pray to the invisible Creator whose goodness in infinite.

18. At the death of the prince Mossa, the Israelites rigorously observed his laws, and God recompensed them for the wrongs they had suffered in Egypt.

19. Their kingdom became the most powerful in all the world, their kings gained renown for their treasures, and a long period of peace prevailed among the children of Israel.

III.

1. The fame of the riches of Israel spread over all the world, and the neighboring nations envied them.

2. But the victorious arms of the Hebrews were directed by the Most High himself, and the pagans dared not attack them.

3. Unhappily, as man does not always obey even his own will, the fidelity of the Israelites to their God was not of long duration.

4. They began by forgetting all the favors he had showered upon them, invoked his name on rare occasions only, and begged protection of magicians and wizards;

5. The kings and rulers substituted their own laws for those that Mossa had prepared; the temple of God and the practice of religion were

abandoned, the nation gave itself up to pleasures and lost its original purity.

6. Many centuries had elapsed since their departure from Egypt, when God again resolved to punish them.

7. Strangers began to invade the land of Israel, devastating the fields, destroying the villages, and taking the inhabitants into captivity.

8. A throng of pagans came from over the sea, from the country of Romeles; they subjected the Hebrews, and the commanders of the army governed them by authority of Caesar.

9. The temples were destroyed, the people were forced to abandon their worship of the invisible God and to sacrifice victims to pagan idols.

10. Warriors were made of the nobles; the women were ravished from their husbands; the lower classes, reduced to slavery, were sent by thousands beyond the seas.

11. As to the children, all were put to the sword; soon, through all the land of Israel, nothing was heard but weeping and wailing.

12. In this dire distress the people remembered their powerful God; they implored his mercy and besought him to forgive them; our Father, in his inexhaustible goodness, heeded their prayers.

IV.

1. And now the time had come, which the Supreme Judge, in his boundless clemency, had chosen to incarnate himself in a human being.

2. And the Eternal Spirit, which dwelt in a state of complete inertness and supreme beatitude, awakened and detached itself from the Eternal Being for an indefinite period,

3. In order to indicate, in assuming the human form, the means of identifying ourselves with the Divinity and of attaining eternal felicity.

4. And to teach us, by his example, how we may reach a state of moral purity and separate the soul from its gross envelope, that it may attain the perfection necessary to enter the Kingdom of Heaven which is immutable and where eternal happiness reigns.

5. Soon after, a wonderful child was born in the land of Israel; God

himself, through the mouth of this child, spoke of the nothingness of the body and of the grandeur of the soul.

6. The parents of this new-born child were poor people, belonging by birth to a family of exalted piety, which disregarded its former worldly greatness to magnify the name of the Creator and thank him for the misfortunes with which he was pleased to try them.

7. To reward them for their perseverance in the path of truth, God blessed the first-born of this family; he chose him as his elect, and sent him forth to raise those that had fallen into evil, and to heal them that suffered.

8. The divine child, to whom was given the name of Issa, commenced even in his most tender years to speak of the one and indivisible God, exhorting the people that had strayed from the path of righteousness to repent and purify themselves of the sins they had committed.

9. People came from all parts to listen and marvel at the words of wisdom that fell from his infant lips; all the Israelites united in proclaiming that the Eternal Spirit dwelt within this child.

10. When Issa had attained the age of thirteen, when an Israelite should take a wife,

11. The house in which his parents dwelt and earned their livelihood in modest labor, became a meeting place for the rich and noble, who desired to gain for a son-in-law the young Issa, already celebrated for his edifying discourses in the name of the Almighty.

12. It was then that Issa clandestinely left his father's house, went out of Jerusalem, and, in company with some merchants, traveled toward Sindh,

13. That he might perfect himself in the divine word and study the laws of the great Buddhas.

V.

1. In the course of his fourteenth year, young Issa, blessed by God, journeyed beyond the Sindh and settled among the Aryas in the beloved country of God.

2. The fame of his name spread along the Northern Sindh. When he passed through the country of the five rivers and the Radjipoutan, the worshippers of the God Djaine begged him to remain in their midst.

3. But he left the misguided admirers of Djaine and visited Juggernaut, in the province of Orsis, where the remains of Viassa-Krichna
rest, and where he received a joyous welcome from the white priests
of Brahma.

4. They taught him to read and understand the Vedas, to heal by prayer,
to teach and explain the Holy Scripture, to cast out evil spirits from the
body of man and give him back human semblance.

5. He spent six years in Juggernaut, Rajegriha, Benares, and the other
holy cities; all loved him, for Issa lived in peace with the Vaisyas and
the Soudras, to whom he taught the Holy Scripture.

6. But the Brahmans and the Kshatriyas declared that the Great Para-
Brahma forbade them to approach those whom he had created from
his entrails and from his feet:

7. That the Vaisyas were authorized to listen only to the reading of the
Vedas, and that never save on feast days.

8. That the Soudras were not only forbidden to attend the reading of
the Vedas, but to gaze upon them even, for their condition was to per-
petually serve and act as slaves to the Brahmans, the Kshatriyas, and
even to the Vaisyas.

9. "Death alone can free them from servitude," said Para-Brahma.
"Leave them, therefore, and worship with us the gods who will show
their anger against you if you disobey them."

10. But Issa would not heed them; and going to the Soudras, preached
against the Brahmans and the Kshatriyas.

11. He strongly denounced the men who robbed their fellow-beings of
their rights as men, saying: "God the Father establishes no difference
between his children, who are all equally dear to him."

12. Issa denied the divine origin of the Vedas and the Pouranas,
declaring to his followers that one law had been given to men to guide
them in their actions.

13. "Fear thy God, bow down the knee before Him only, and to Him
only must thy offerings be made."

14. Issa denied the Trimourti and the incarnation of Para-Brahma in
Vishnou, Siva, and other gods, saying:

15. "The Eternal Judge, the Eternal Spirit, composes the one and indi-

visible soul of the universe, which alone creates, contains, and animates the whole."

16. "He alone has willed and created, he alone has existed from eternity and will exist without end; he has no equal neither in the heavens nor on this earth."

17. "The Great Creator shares his power with no one, still less with inanimate objects as you have been taught, for he alone possesses supreme power."

18. "He willed it, and the world appeared; by one divine thought, he united the waters and separated them from the dry portion of the globe. He is the cause of the mysterious life of man, in whom he has breathed a part of his being."

19. "And he has subordinated to man, the land, the waters, and animals, and all that he has created, and which he maintains in immutable order by fixing the duration of each."

20. "The wrath of God shall soon be let loose on man, for he has forgotten his Creator and filled his temples with abominations, and he adores a host of creatures which God has subordinated to him."

21. "For, to be pleasing to stones and metals, he sacrifices human beings in whom dwells a part of the spirit of the Most High."

22. "For he humiliates them that labor by the sweat of their brow to gain the favor of an idler who is seated at a sumptuously spread table."

23. "They that deprive their brothers of divine happiness shall themselves be deprived of it, and the Brahmans and the Kshatriyas shall become the Soudras with whom the Eternal shall dwell eternally."

24. "For on the day of the Last Judgment, the Soudras and the Vaisyas shall be forgiven because of their ignorance, while God shall visit his wrath on them that have arrogated his rights."

25. The Vaisyas and the Soudras were struck with admiration, and demanded of Issa how they should pray to secure their happiness.

26. "Do not worship idols, for they do not hear you; do not listen to the Vedas, where the truth is perverted; do not believe yourself first in all things, and do not humiliate your neighbor."

27. "Help the poor, assist the weak, harm no one, do not covet what you have not and what you see in the possession of others."

VI.

1. The white priests and the warriors becoming cognizant of the discourse addressed by Issa to the Soudras, resolved upon his death and sent their servants for this purpose in search of the young prophet.

2. But Issa, warned of this danger by the Soudras, fled in the night from Juggernaut, gained the mountains, and took refuge in the Gothamide Country, the birthplace of the great Buddha Cakya-Mouni, among the people who adored the only and sublime Brahma.

3. Having perfectly learned the Pali tongue, the just Issa applied himself to the study of the sacred rolls of Soutras.

4. Six years later, Issa, whom the Buddha had chosen to spread his holy word, could perfectly explain the sacred rolls.

5. He then left Nepal and the Himalaya Mountains, descended into the valley of Rajipoutan and went westward, preaching to divers people of the supreme perfection of man,

6. And of the good we must do unto others, which is the surest means of quickly merging ourselves in the Eternal Spirit. "He who shall have recovered his primitive purity at death," said Issa, "shall have obtained the forgiveness of his sins, and shall have the right to contemplate the majestic figure of God."

7. In traversing the pagan territories, the divine Issa taught the people that the adoration of visible gods was contrary to the laws of nature.

8. "For man," said he, "has not been favored with the sight of the image of God nor the ability to construct a host of divinities resembling the Eternal."

9. "Furthermore, it is incompatible with the human conscience to think less of the grandeur of divine purity than of animals; or of works made by the hand of man from stone or metal."

10. "The Eternal Legislator is one; there is no God but him; he has shared the world with no one, neither has he confided his intentions to anyone."

11. "Just as a father may deal toward his children, so shall God judge men after death according to his merciful laws; never will he humiliate his child by causing his soul to emigrate, as in a purgatory, into the body of an animal."

12. "The heavenly law," said the Creator through the lips of Issa, "is averse to the sacrifice of human victims to a statue or animal, for I have sacrificed to man all the animals and everything the world contains."

13. "Everything has been sacrificed to man, who is directly and closely linked to Me, his Father; therefore, he that shall have robbed Me of My child shall be severely judged and punished according to the divine law."

14. "Man is as nothing before the Eternal Judge, to the same degree that the animal is before man."

15. "Therefore, I say to you, abandon your idols and perform no ceremonies that separate you from your Father and bind you to priests from whom the face of heaven is turned away."

16. "For it is they who have allured you from the true God, and whose superstitions and cruelty are leading you to perversion of the intellect and the loss of all moral sense."

VII.

1. The words of Issa spread among the pagans, in the countries through which he traveled, and the inhabitants abandoned their idols.

2. Seeing which, the priests demanded from him who glorified the name of the true God, proofs of the accusations he brought against them and demonstration of the worthlessness of idols in the presence of the people.

3. And Issa replied to them: "If your idols and your animals are mighty, and really possess a supernatural power, let them annihilate me on the spot!"

4. "Perform a miracle," retorted the priests, "and let thy God confound our own, if they are loathsome to him."

5. But Issa then said: "The miracles of our God began when the universe was created; they occur each day, each instant; whosoever does not see them is deprived of one of the most beautiful gifts of life."

6. "And it is not against pieces of inanimate stone, metal, or wood, that the wrath of God shall find free vent, but it shall fall upon man, who, in order to be saved, should destroy all the idols they have raised."

7. "Just as a stone and a grain of sand, worthless in themselves to man,

await with resignation the moment when he shall take and make them into something useful."

8. "So should man await the great favor to be granted him by God in honoring him with a decision."

9. "But woe be to you, adversary of man, if it be not a favor that you await, but rather the wrath of Divinity; woe be to you if you await until it attests its power through miracles!"

10. "For it is not the idols that shall be annihilated in His wrath, but those that have raised them; their hearts shall be the prey of everlasting fire, and their lacerated bodies shall serve as food for wild beasts."

11. "God shall drive away the contaminated ones of his flocks, but shall take back to himself those that have strayed because they misconceived the heavenly atom which dwelt in them."

12. Seeing the powerlessness of their priests, the pagans believed the words of Issa, and fearing the wrath of the Divinity, broke their idols into fragments. As to the priests, they fled to escape the vengeance of the people.

13. And Issa also taught the pagans not to strive to see the eternal spirit with their own eyes, but to endeavor to feel it in their hearts, and, by a truly pure soul, to make themselves worthy of its favors.

14. "Not only must you desist from offering human sacrifices," said he, "but you must immolate no animal to which life has been given, for all things have been created for the benefit of man."

15. "Do not take what belongs to others, for it would be robbing your neighbor of the goods he has acquired by the sweat of his brow."

16. "Deceive no one, that you may not yourself be deceived; strive to justify yourself before the last judgment, for it will then be too late."

17. "Do not give yourself up to debauchery, for it is a violation of the laws of God."

18. "You shall attain supreme beatitude, not only by purifying yourself, but also by leading others into the path that shall permit them to regain primitive perfection."

• • •

VIII.

1. The fame of Issa's sermons spread to the neighboring countries, and, when he reached Persia, the priests were terrified and forbade the inhabitants to listen to him.

2. But when they saw that all the villages welcomed him with joy, and eagerly listened to his preaching, they caused his arrest and brought him before the high priest, where he was submitted to the following interrogatory:

3. "Who is this new God of whom thou speaketh? Dost thou not know, unhappy man that thou art, that Saint Zoroaster is the only just one admitted to the honor of receiving communications from the Supreme Being,

4. "Who has commanded the angels to draw up in writing the word of God, laws that were given to Zoroaster in paradise?

5. "Who then art thou that darest to blaspheme our God and sow doubt in the hearts of believers?"

6. And Issa replied: "It is not of a new god that I speak, but of our heavenly Father, who existed before the beginning and will still be after the eternal end.

7. "It was of him I spoke to the people, who, even as an innocent child, cannot yet understand God by the mere strength of their intelligence and penetrate his spiritual and divine sublimity.

8. "But, as a new-born child recognizes the maternal breast even in obscurity, so your people, induced in error by your erroneous doctrines and religious ceremonies have instinctively recognized their Father in the Father of whom I am the prophet.

9. "The Eternal Being says to your people through the intermediary of my mouth: 'You shall not adore the sun, for it is only a part of the world I have created for man.'

10. " 'The sun rises that it may warm you during your labor; it sets that it may give you the hours of rest I have myself fixed.

11. " 'It is to Me, and to Me only, that you owe all you possess, all that is around you, whether above or beneath you.' "

12. "But," interjected the priests, "how could a nation live according to the laws of justice, if it possessed no preceptors?"

13. Then Issa replied: "As long as the people had no priests, they were governed by the law of nature and retained their candor of soul.

14. "Their souls were in God, and to communicate with the Father, they had recourse to the intermediary of no idol or animal, nor to fire, as you practice here.

15. "You claim that we must worship the sun, the genius of Good and that of Evil; well, your doctrine is an abomination. I say to you, the sun acts not spontaneously, but by the will of the invisible Creator who has given it existence,

16. "And who has willed that this orb should light the day and warm the labor and the crops of man.

17. "The Eternal Spirit is the soul of all that is animated; you commit a grievous sin in dividing it into the spirit of Evil and the spirit of Good, for there is no God save that of good,

18. "Who, like the father of a family, does good only to his children, forgiving all their faults if they repent of them.

19. "And the spirit of Evil dwells on this earth, in the heart of men who turn the children of God from the right path.

20. "Therefore I say to you, beware of the day of judgment, for God will inflict a terrible punishment on all who have turned his children from the right path and filled them with superstitions and prejudices,

21. "On them that have blinded the seeing, transmitted contagion to the sound of health, and taught the adoration of things which God has subjected to man for his own good and to aid him in his labor.

22. "Your doctrine is therefore the fruit of your errors, for, in desiring to approach the God of Truth, you have created false gods."

23. After listening to him, the wise men resolved to do him no harm. In the night, while the city was wrapped in slumber, they conducted him outside the walls and left him on the highway, hoping that he might soon become the prey of wild beasts,

24. But, being protected by the Lord our God, Saint Issa continued his way unmolested.

IX.

1. Issa, whom the Creator had chosen to recall the true God to the

people that were plunged in depravities, was twenty-nine years of age when he arrived in the land of Israel.

2. Since the departure of Issa, the pagans had heaped still more atrocious sufferings on the Israelites, and the latter were a prey to the deepest gloom.

3. Many among them had already begun to desert the laws of their God and those of Mossa, in the hope of softening their harsh conquerors.

4. In the presence of this situation, Issa exhorted his compatriots not to despair, because the day of the redemption of sins was near, and he confirmed their belief in the God of their fathers.

5. "Children, do not yield to despair," said the Heavenly Father through the mouth of Issa, "for I have heard your voices, and your cries have ascended to me.

6. "Weep not, O my beloved, for your sobs have touched the heart of your Father, and he has forgiven you as he forgave your ancestors.

7. "Do not abandon your families to plunge into debauchery, do not lose the nobility of your sentiments and worship idols that will remain deaf to your voices.

8. "Fill my temple with your hopes and your patience, and do not abjure the religion of your fathers, for I alone have guided them and heaped blessings upon them.

9. "Raise them that have fallen, feed them that are hungry, and help them that are sick, that you may all be pure and just on the day of the last judgment that I am preparing for you."

10. The Israelites flocked to hear the words of Issa, asking him where they should thank the Heavenly Father, since their enemies had razed their temples and laid violent hands on their sacred vessels.

11. Issa replied to them that God did not speak of temples built by the hands of men, but that he meant thereby the human heart, which is the true temple of God.

12. "Enter into your temple, into your own heart, illuminate it with good thoughts, patience, and the unflinching confidence you should place in your Father.

13. "And your sacred vessels are your hands and your eyes; look and do

what is agreeable to God, for, in doing good to your neighbor, you perform a rite that embellishes the temple in which dwells the One who has given you life.

14. "For God has created you in his image; innocent, pure of soul, with a heart filled with kindness, and destined, not to the conception of evil projects, but to be the sanctuary of love and justice.

15. "Do not therefore sully your hearts, I say to you, for the Eternal Being dwells there always.

16. "If you wish to accomplish works stamped with love and piety, do them with love and piety, do them with an open heart, and let not your actions be inspired by the hope of gain or by thought of profit.

17. "For such deeds would not contribute to your salvation, and you would then fall into a state of moral degradation in which theft, falsehood, and murder, seem like generous actions."

X.

1. Saint Issa went from place to place strengthening, by the word of God, the courage of the Israelites, who were ready to succumb under the weight of their despair, and thousands followed him to hear his preaching.

2. But the rulers of the cities feared him, and word was sent to the Governor, who resided in Jerusalem, that a man named Issa had come into the country, that his sermons excited the people against the authorities, that the crowd listened to him assiduously and neglected their duties to the State, claiming that soon they would be rid of their intruding rulers.

3. Then Pilate, the Governor of Jerusalem, ordered that the preacher Issa be arrested, brought to the city and conducted before the judges. Not to arouse the dissatisfaction of the people, however, Pilate commanded the priests and the learned men, old men of Hebrew origin, to judge him in the temple.

4. Meanwhile, Issa, still continuing to preach, arrived in Jerusalem; having heard of his coming all the inhabitants, who already knew him by reputation, came to meet him.

5. They greeted him respectfully and threw open the doors of their

temple that they might hear from his lips what he had said in the other cities of Israel.

6. And Issa said to them: "The human race is perishing because of its want of faith, for the gloom and the tempest have bewildered the human flock, and they have lost their shepherd.

7. "But tempests do not last forever, and the clouds will not hide the eternal light, the heavens shall soon be serene again, the celestial light shall spread throughout the world, and the strayed sheep shall gather around their shepherd.

8. "Do not strive to seek direct roads in the obscurity for fear of stumbling into the ditch, but gather your remaining strength, sustain one another, place your entire trust in God, and wait till a streak of light appears.

9. "He that upholds his neighbor upholds himself, and whosoever protects his family protects his race and his country.

10. "For rest assured that the day of your deliverance from darkness is near; you shall gather together in one single family, and your enemy—he who knows nothing of the favor of the Great God—will tremble in fear."

11. The priests and the old men that listened to him, full of admiration at this language, asked of him if it were true that he had attempted to arouse the people against the authorities of the country, as had been reported to the Governor, Pilate.

12. "Is it possible to arise against misled men from whom the obscurity has hidden their path and their door?" returned Issa. "I have only warned these unfortunate people, as I warn them in this temple, that they may not advance further on their dark paths, for an abyss is yawning beneath their feet.

13. "Worldly power is not of long duration, and it is subject to innumerable changes. It would be of no use to a man to rebel against it, for one power always succeeds another power, and it shall be thus until the extinction of human existence.

14. "Do you not see, on the contrary, that the rich and the powerful are sowing among the children of Israel a spirit of rebellion against the eternal power of Heaven?"

15. And the learned men then said: "Who art thou, and from what country hast thou come into our own? We had never heard of thee, and do not even know thy name."

16. "I am an Israelite," responded Issa, "and, on the very day of my birth, I saw the walls of Jerusalem, and I heard the weeping of my brothers reduced to slavery, and the moans of my sisters carried away by pagans into captivity.

17. "And my soul was painfully grieved when I saw that my brothers had forgotten the true God; while yet a child, I left my father's house to go among other nations.

18. "But hearing that my brothers were enduring still greater tortures, I returned to the land in which my parents dwelt, that I might recall to my brothers the faith of their ancestors, which teaches us patience in this world that we may obtain perfect and sublime happiness on High."

19. And the learned old men asked him this question: "It is claimed that you deny the laws of Mossa and teach the people to desert the temple of God."

20. And Issa said: "We cannot demolish what has been given by our Heavenly Father and what has been destroyed by sinners; but I have recommended the purification of all stain from the heart, for that is the veritable temple of God.

21. "As to the laws of Mossa, I have striven to re-establish them in the heart of men; and I say to you, that you are in ignorance of their true meaning, for it is not vengeance, but forgiveness that they teach; but the sense of these laws have been perverted."

XI.

1. Having heard Issa, the priests and learned men decided among themselves that they would not judge him, for he was doing no one harm, and having presented themselves before Pilate, made Governor of Jerusalem by the pagan king of the land of Romeles, they spoke to him thus:

2. "We have seen the man whom thou accuseth of inciting our

people to rebellion, we have heard his preaching and know that he is of our people.

3. "But the rulers of the towns have sent thee false reports, for he is a just man who teaches the people the word of God. After interrogating him, we dismissed him that he might go in peace."

4. The Governor, overcome with passion, sent disguised servants to Issa, that they might watch all his actions and report to the authorities every word he addressed to the people.

5. Nevertheless, Issa continued to visit the neighboring towns and preach the true ways of the Creator, exhorting the Hebrews to patience and promising them a speedy deliverance.

6. And during all this time, a multitude followed wherever he went, many never leaving him and acting as servants.

7. And Issa said to them: "Do not believe in miracles performed by the hands of man, for He who dominates nature is alone capable of doing supernatural things, while man is powerless to soften the violence of the wind and bestow rain.

8. "Nevertheless, there is a miracle which it is possible for man to accomplish; it is when, full of a sincere faith, he resolves to tear from his heart all evil thought and, to attain his end, shuns the paths of iniquity.

9. "And all things which are done without God are but gross errors, seductions, and illusions, which only demonstrate to what point the soul of the man who practices this art is filled with deceit, falsehood, and impurity.

10. "Put no faith in oracles—God alone knows the future; he that has recourse to sorcerers defiles the temple within his heart and gives proof of distrust toward his Creator.

11. "Faith in sorcerers and their oracles destroys the innate simplicity and child-like purity in man; a diabolical power takes possession of him and forces him to commit all sorts of crimes and to adore idols,

12. "While the Lord our God, who has not his equal, is One, all-powerful, omniscient, and omnipresent; it is he who possesses all wisdom and all light.

13. "It is to him you must have recourse to be comforted in your sorrows, assisted in your toils, healed in your sickness; whosoever shall have recourse to him shall not be refused.

14. "The secret of nature is in the hands of God; for the world before appearing, existed in the depth of the divine mind; it became material and visible by the will of the Most High.

15. "When you wish to address him, become as children once more, for you know neither the past, nor the present, nor the future, and God is the master of time."

XII.

1. "O just man," said the disguised servants of the Governor of Jerusalem, "tell us should we do the will of Caesar or await our near deliverance?"

2. And Issa, having recognized in his questioners the spies sent to watch him, said to them: "I have not said that you should be delivered from Caesar; it is the soul plunged in error which shall have its deliverance.

3. "There can be no family without a head, and there would be no order in a nation without a Caesar, who must be blindly obeyed, for he alone shall answer for his actions before the supreme tribunal."

4. "Does Caesar possess a divine right," again questioned the spies, "and is he the best of mortals?"

5. "There is no perfection among men, but there are also some that are sick whom the men elected and intrusted with this mission must care for, by using the means that are conferred upon them by the sacred law of our Heavenly Father.

6. "Clemency and justice, these are the highest gifts granted to Caesar; his name will be illustrious if he abides nearby.

7. "But he who acts otherwise, who goes beyond the limit of his power over his subject, even to placing his life in danger, offends the great Judge and lowers his dignity in the sight of men."

8. At this point, an aged woman, who had approached the group that she might better hear Issa, was pushed aside by one of the men in disguise who placed himself before her.

9. Issa then said: "It is not meet that a son should push aside his

mother to occupy the first place which should be hers. Whosoever respecteth not his mother, the most sacred being next to God, is unworthy of the name of Son.

10. "Listen, therefore, to what I am about to say: Respect woman, for she is the mother of the universe and all the truth of divine creation dwells within her.

11. "She is the basis of all that is good and beautiful, as she is also the germ of life and death. On her depends the entire existence of man, for she is his moral and natural support in all his works.

12. "She gives you birth amid sufferings; by the sweat of her brow she watches over your growth, and until her death you cause her the most intense anguish. Bless her and adore her, for she is your only friend and support upon earth.

13. "Respect her, protect her; in doing this, you will win her love and her heart, and you will be pleasing to God; for this shall many of your sins be remitted.

14. "Therefore, love your wives and respect them, for tomorrow they shall be mothers, and later grandmothers of a whole nation.

15. "Be submissive toward your wife; her love ennobles man, softens his hardened heart, tames the beast and makes of it a lamb.

16. "Just as the God of armies separated day from night and the land from the waters, so woman possesses the divine talent of separating good intentions from evil thoughts in men.

18. Therefore I say to you: "After God, your best thoughts should belong to women and to wives, woman being to you the divine temple wherein you shall most easily obtain perfect happiness.

19. "Draw your moral strength from this temple; there you will forget your sorrows and failures, you will recover the wasted forces necessary to help your neighbor.

20. "Do not expose her to humiliation; you would thereby humiliate yourself and lose the sentiment of love, without which nothing exists here below.

21. "Protect your wife, that she may protect you and all your family; all that you shall do for your mother, your wife, for a widow, or another woman in distress, you shall have done for God."

XIII.

1. Saint Issa thus taught the people of Israel for three years in every city, in every village, on the roadways, and in the fields, and all that he had predicted had come to pass.

2. During all this time, the disguised servants of the Governor Pilate observed him closely, but without hearing anything that resembled the reports hitherto sent by the rulers of the cities concerning Issa.

3. But the Governor Pilate, becoming alarmed at the too great popularity of Saint Issa, who, according to his enemies, wanted to incite the people and be made king, ordered one of his spies to accuse him.

4. Soldiers were then sent to arrest him, and he was cast into a dungeon where he was made to suffer various torture that he might be forced to accuse himself, which would permit them to put him to death.

5. Thinking of the perfect beatitude of his brothers only, the saint endured these sufferings in the name of his Creator.

6. The servants of Pilate continued to torture him and reduced him to a state of extreme weakness; but God was with him and did not suffer him to die.

7. Hearing of the sufferings and tortures inflicted on their saint, the principal priests and learned elders begged the Governor to liberate Issa on the occasion of an approaching great feast.

8. But the Governor met them with a decided refusal. They then begged him to bring Issa before the tribunal of the Ancients, that he might be condemned or acquitted before the feast, to which Pilate consented.

9. On the morrow the Governor called together the chief rulers, priests, elders and law-givers, with the object of making them pass judgment on Issa.

10. The saint was brought from his prison, and he was seated before the Governor between two thieves that were to be tried with him, to show the people that he was not the only one to be condemned.

11. And Pilate, addressing Issa, said: "O, man! is it true that thou hast incited the people to rebel against the authorities that thou mayest become king of Israel?"

12. "None can become king by his own will," replied Issa, "and they that have said that I incited the people have spoken falsely. I have

never spoken but of the King of Heaven, whom I taught the people to adore.

13. "For the sons of Israel have lost their original purity, and if they have not recourse to the true God, they shall be sacrificed and their temple shall fall in ruins.

14. "Temporal power maintains order in a country; I therefore taught them not to forget it; I said to them: 'Live in conformity to your position and fortune, that you may not disturb public order;' and I exhorted them also to remember that disorder reigned in their hearts and minds.

15. "Therefore the King of Heaven has punished them and suppressed their national kings; nevertheless, I said to them, if you resign yourself to your fate, the kingdom of heaven shall be reserved for you as a reward."

16. At this moment, witnesses were introduced; one of them testified as follows: "Thou hast said to the people that temporal power was nothing to that of the King that shall free the Israelites from the pagan yoke."

17. "Blessed be thou," said Issa, "for having spoken the truth; the King of Heaven is more powerful and great than terrestrial laws, and his kingdom surpasses all the kingdoms here below.

18. "And the time is not far when, in conformity with the divine will, the people of Israel will purify themselves of their sins; for it is said that a precursor shall come to announce the deliverance of the nation and unite it in one family."

19. And addressing himself to the judges, the Governor said: "Hear you this? The Israelite Issa admits the crime of which he is accused. Judge him according to your laws and sentence him to capital punishment."

20. "We cannot condemn him," replied the priests and the ancients; "thou hast thyself heard that he made allusion to the King of Heaven, and that he has preached nothing to the people which constitutes insubordination against the law."

21. The Governor then summoned the witness who, at the instigation of his master, Pilate, had betrayed Issa; and when this man came

he addressed Issa thus: "Didst thou not claim to be the king of Israel in saying that the Lord of heaven had sent thee to prepare his people?"

22. And Issa having blessed him, said: "Thou shalt be forgiven, for what thou sayest cometh not of thee!" Then turning to the Governor, he continued: "Why lower thy dignity and teach thy inferiors to live in falsehood, since, even without this, thou hast the power to condemn an innocent man?"

23. At these words, the Governor became violently enraged and ordered the death of Issa.

24. The judges, having deliberated among themselves, said to Pilate: "We will not take upon our heads the great sin of condemning an innocent man and of acquitting two thieves, a thing contrary to our laws."

25. "Do therefore as thou please." Having thus spoken, the priests and wise men went out and washed their hands in a sacred vessel, saying: "We are innocent of the death of a just man."

XIV.

1. By order of the Governor, the soldiers seized upon Issa and the two thieves whom they conducted to the place of torture, where they nailed them to the crosses they had erected.

2. All that day, the bodies of Issa and of the two thieves remained suspended, dripping with blood, under the guard of soldiers; the people stood around them, while the parents of the crucified men wept and prayed.

3. At sunset, the agony of Issa came to an end. He lost consciousness, and the soul of this just man detached itself from his body to become part of the Divinity.

4. Thus ended the terrestrial existence of the reflection of the Eternal Spirit in the form of a man who had saved hardened sinners and endured so much suffering.

5. Pilate, however, becoming alarmed at his own actions, gave up the body of the holy man to his relations, who buried him near the place of his execution; the multitude then came to pray over his tomb and filled the air with weeping and wailing.

6. Three days later the Governor sent his soldiers to take up the body of Issa and bury it elsewhere, fearing a general uprising of the people.

7. The following day the sepulcher was found open and empty by the multitude; and the rumor immediately spread that the Supreme Judge had sent his angels to take away the mortal remains of the saint in whom dwelt on earth a part of the Divine Spirit.

8. When this report came to the ears of Pilate he fell into a rage and forbade everyone, under penalty of perpetual slavery, to ever utter the name of Issa and to pray to the Lord for him.

9. But the people continued to weep and praise their master aloud; therefore many were placed in captivity, subjected to torture, and put to death.

10. And the disciples of Saint Issa left the land of Israel and went in all directions among the pagans, telling them that they must abandon their gross errors, think of the salvation of their souls, and of the perfect felicity in store for men in the enlightened and immaterial world where, in repose and in all his purity, dwells the great Creator in perfect majesty.

11. Many pagans, their kings and soldiers, listened to these preachers, abandoned their absurd beliefs, deserted their priests and their idols to sing the praises of the all-wise Creator of the universe, the King of kings, whose heart is filled with infinite mercy.

from The Gospel According to Jesus
by Stephen Mitchell

Stephen Mitchell (born 1943) in these disparate passages from his book's introduction defines the true gospel of Jesus as a gospel of presence. He also compares Jesus' spiritual transformation with those of masters in other traditions, noting the role of family in that process.

What *is* the gospel according to Jesus? Simply this: that the love we all long for in our innermost heart is already present, beyond longing. Most of us can remember a time (it may have been just a moment) when we felt that everything in the world was exactly as it should be. Or we can think of a joy (it happened when we were children, perhaps, or the first time we fell in love) so vast that it was no longer inside us, but we were inside it. What we intuited then, and what we later thought was too good to be true, isn't an illusion. It is real. It is realer than the real, more intimate than anything we can see or touch, "unreachable," as the Upanishads say, "yet nearer than breath, than heartbeat." The more deeply we receive it, the more real it becomes.

Like all the great spiritual Masters, Jesus taught one thing only: presence. Ultimate reality, the luminous, compassionate intelligence of the universe, is not somewhere else, in some heaven light-years away. It didn't manifest itself any more fully to Abraham or Moses than to us, nor will it be any more present to some Messiah at the far end of time. It is always right here, right now. That is what the Bible means when it says that God's true name is *I am*.

There is such a thing as nostalgia for the future. Both Judaism and Christianity ache with it. It is a vision of the Golden Age, the days of perpetual summer in a world of straw-eating lions and roses without thorns, when human life will be foolproof, and fulfilled in an endlessly prolonged finale of delight. I don't mean to make fun of the messianic vision. In many ways it is admirable, and it has inspired political and religious leaders from Isaiah to Martin Luther King, Jr. But it is a kind of benign insanity. And if we take it seriously enough, if we live it twenty-four hours a day, we will spend all our time working in anticipation, and will never enter the Sabbath of the heart. How moving and at the same time how ridiculous is the story of the Hasidic rabbi who, every morning, as soon as he woke up, would rush out his front door to see if the Messiah had arrived. (Another Hasidic story, about a more mature stage of this consciousness, takes place at the Passover seder. The rabbi tells his chief disciple to go outside and see if the Messiah has come. "But Rabbi, if the Messiah came, wouldn't you know it in here?" the disciple says, pointing to his heart. "Ah," says the rabbi, pointing to his own heart, "but in here, the Messiah has already come.") Who among the now middle-aged doesn't remember the fervor of the Sixties, when young people believed that love could transform the world? "You may say I'm a dreamer," John Lennon sang, "but I'm not the only one." The messianic dream of the future may be humanity's sweetest dream. But it is a dream nevertheless, as long as there is a separation between inside and outside, as long as we don't transform ourselves. And Jesus, like the Buddha, was a man who had awakened from all dreams.

When Jesus talked about the kingdom of God, he was not prophesying about some easy, danger-free perfection that will someday appear. He was talking about a state of being, a way of living at ease among the joys and sorrows of *our* world. It is possible, he said, to be as simple and beautiful as the birds of the sky or the lilies of the field, who are always within the eternal Now. This state of being is not something alien or mystical. We don't need to earn it. It is already ours. Most of us lose it as we grow up and become self-conscious, but it doesn't disappear forever; it is always there to be reclaimed, though we have to search hard in order to find it. The rich especially have a hard time reentering this state of being; they are so possessed by their possessions, so entrenched in their social power, that it is almost impossible for them to let go. Not that it is easy for any of us. But if we need reminding, we can always sit at the feet of our young children. They, because they haven't yet developed a firm sense of past and future, accept the infinite abundance of the present with all their hearts, in complete trust. Entering the kingdom of God means feeling, as if we were floating in the womb of the universe, that we are being taken care of, always, at every moment.

All spiritual Masters, in all the great religious traditions, have come to experience the present as the only reality. The Gospel passages in which "Jesus" speaks of a kingdom of God in the future can't be authentic, unless Jesus was a split personality, and could turn on and off two different consciousnesses as if they were hot- and cold-water faucets. And it is easy to understand how these passages would have been inserted into the Gospel by disciples, or disciples of disciples, who hadn't understood his teaching. Passages about the kingdom of God as coming in the future are a dime a dozen in the prophets, in the Jewish apocalyptic writings of the first centuries B.C.E., in Paul and the early church. They are filled with passionate hope, with a desire for universal justice, and also, as Nietzsche so correctly insisted, with a festering resentment against "them" (the powerful, the ungodly). But they arise from ideas, not from an experience of the state of being that Jesus called the kingdom of God.

The Jewish Bible doesn't talk much about this state; it is more interested in what Moses said at the bottom of the mountain than in what he saw at the top. But there are exceptions. The most dramatic is the Voice from the Whirlwind in the Book of Job, which I have examined at length elsewhere. Another famous passage occurs at the beginning of Genesis: God completes the work of creation by entering the Sabbath mind, the mind of absolute, joyous serenity; contemplates the whole universe and says, "Behold, it is very good."

The kingdom of God is not something that will happen, because it isn't something that *can* happen. It can't appear in a world or a nation; it is a condition that has no plural, but only infinite singulars. Jesus spoke of people "entering" it, said that children were already inside it, told one particularly ardent scribe that he, the scribe, was not "far from" it. If only we stop looking forward and backward, he said, we will be able to devote ourselves to seeking the kingdom of God, which is right beneath our feet, right under our noses; and when we find it, food, clothing, and other necessities are given to us as well, as they are to the birds and the lilies. Where else but here and now can we find the grace-bestowing, inexhaustible presence of God? In its light, all our hopes and fears flitter away like ghosts. It is like a treasure buried in a field; it is like a pearl of great price; it is like coming home. When we find it, we find ourselves, rich beyond all dreams, and we realize that we can afford to lose everything else in the world, even (if we must) someone we love more dearly than life itself.

The portrait of Jesus that emerges from the authentic passages in the Gospels is of a man who has emptied himself of desires, doctrines, rules—all the mental claptrap and spiritual baggage that separate us from true life—and has been filled with the vivid reality of the Unnamable. Because he has let go of the merely personal, he is no one, he is everyone. Because he allows God *through* the personal, his personality is like a magnetic field. Those who are drawn to him have a hunger for the real; the closer they approach, the more they can feel the purity of his heart.

What is purity of heart? If we compare God to sunlight, we can say that the heart is like a window. Cravings, aversions, fixed judgments, concepts, beliefs—all forms of selfishness or self-protection are, when we cling to them, like dirt on the windowpane. The thicker the dirt, the more opaque the window. When there is no dirt, the window is by its own nature perfectly transparent, and the light can stream through it without hindrance.

Or we can compare a pure heart to a spacious, light-filled room. People or possibilities open the door and walk in; the room will receive them, however many they are, for as long as they want to stay, and will let them leave when they want to. Whereas a corrupted heart is like a room cluttered with valuable possessions, in which the owner sits behind a locked door, with a loaded gun.

One last comparison, from the viewpoint of spiritual practice. To grow in purity of heart is to grow like a tree. The tree doesn't try to wrench its roots out of the earth and plant itself in the sky, nor does it reach its leaves downward into the dirt. It needs both ground and sunlight, and knows the direction of each. Only because it digs into the dark earth with its roots is it able to hold its leaves out to receive the sunlight.

For every teacher who lives in this way, the word of God has become flesh, and there is no longer a separation between body and spirit. Everything he or she does proclaims the kingdom of God. (A visitor once said of the eighteenth-century Hasidic rabbi Dov Baer, "I didn't travel to Mezritch to hear him teach, but to watch him tie his shoelaces.")

People can feel Jesus' radiance whether or not he is teaching or healing; they can feel it in proportion to their own openness. There is a deep sense of peace in his presence, and a sense of respect for him that far exceeds what they have felt for any other human being. Even his silence is eloquent. He is immediately recognizable by the quality of his aliveness, by his disinterestedness and compassion. He is like a mirror for us all, showing us who we essentially are.

The image of the Master:
    one glimpse
and we are in love.

He enjoys eating and drinking, he likes to be around women and children; he laughs easily, and his wit can cut like a surgeon's scalpel. His trust in God is as natural as breathing, and in God's presence he is himself fully present. In his bearing, in his very language, he reflects God's deep love for everything that is earthly: for the sick and the despised, the morally admirable and the morally repugnant, for weeds as well as flowers, lions as well as lambs. He teaches that just as the sun gives light to both wicked and good, and the rain brings nourishment to both righteous and unrighteous, God's compassion embraces all people. There are no pre-conditions for it, nothing we need to do first, nothing we have to believe. When we are ready to receive it, it is there. And the more we live in its presence, the more effortlessly it flows through us, until we find that we no longer need external rules or Bibles or Messiahs.

> For this teaching which I give you today is not hidden from you, and is not far away. It is not in heaven, for you to say, "Who will go up to heaven and bring it down for us, so that we can hear it and do it?" Nor is it beyond the sea, for you to say, "Who will cross the sea and bring it back for us, so that we can hear it and do it?" But the teaching is very near you: it is in your mouth and in your heart, so that you can do it.

He wants to tell everyone about the great freedom: how it feels when we continually surrender to the moment and allow our hearts to become pure, not clinging to past or future, not judging or being judged. In each person he meets he can see the image of God in which they were created. They are all perfect, when he looks at them from the Sabbath mind. From another, complementary, viewpoint, they are all imperfect, even the most righteous of them, even he himself, because nothing is perfect but the One. He understands that being human *means* making mistakes. When we acknowledge this in all humility, without wanting anything else, we can forgive ourselves, and we can begin correcting our mistakes. And once we forgive ourselves, we can forgive anyone.

He has no ideas to teach, only presence. He has no doctrines to give, only the gift of his own freedom.

• • •

Tolerant like the sky,
all-pervading like sunlight,
firm like a mountain,
supple like a branch in the wind,
he has no destination in view
and makes use of anything
life happens to bring his way.

Nothing is impossible for him.
Because he has let go,
he can care for the people's welfare
as a mother cares for her child.

Jesus gives us a most vivid example of what it feels like to live in the continual presence of love, in the present and only tense of the verb *God*. His teaching is lucid through and through. Or almost through and through. The one point of unclarity is the family; in particular, the mother. I don't mean this as a criticism of him, but as a simple perception. I would like to take a look at this unclarity, which allows us a rare insight into the workshop of his heart. But before I examine the relevant verses, I need to put them in perspective.

We can use different metaphors to describe the experience that changed Jesus. It is the kind of experience that all the great spiritual Masters have had, and want us to have as well. Jesus called this experience "entering the kingdom of God." We can also call it "rebirth" or "enlightenment" or "awakening." The images implicit in these words come from experiences that we all know: the birth of a child, the light of the sun, the passage from sleep to what we ordinarily call consciousness. Any of these images can be helpful in pointing to a realm of being which most people have forgotten. It *is* like being born into true life, or like the sun streaming into a room that has remained dark for a long time, or like waking up from a dream, or, as Jesus must have felt, like returning home to the Father. And each of these images contains a further truth, if we follow it attentively. Being reborn is only the first stage of a new life, and doesn't mean coming into full spiritual maturity: the infant has a lot of growing up to do before it is self-sufficient. Awakening doesn't necessarily mean arriving at full consciousness: the dreams are gone, but we may still be sleepy, and not truly alert. Or, to return to the image of sunlight passing through a window: the area that has been suddenly wiped clean of selfishness and self-protection—desires, fears, rules, concepts—may be the whole windowpane, or it may be a spot the size of a dime. The sunlight that shines through the small transparent spot is the same light that can shine through a whole windowpane, but there is much less of it, and if someone stands with his nose pressed to one of the other, opaque spots, he will hardly see any light at all.

Two examples. First, Paul of Tarsus, the greatest and yet the most misleading of the earliest Christian writers. It is obvious that Paul's experience on the road to Damascus was a genuine and powerful one. Who can deny the sunlight streaming through his famous praise of love in First Corinthians? And there are a number of other passages where his mind and heart are transparent. But Paul came to his experience with a particularly difficult character: arrogant, self-righteous, filled with murderous hatred of his opponents, terrified of God, oppressed by what he felt as the burden of the Law, overwhelmed by his sense of sin. In terms of the metaphor, his windowpane was caked with grime.

There are things I admire about Paul: his courage, his passion, his loving concern for the Gentiles, his great eloquence, the incredible energy with which he whirled around the Mediterranean for, as he thought, the glory of God. But in a spiritual sense, he was very unripe. The narrow-minded, fire-breathing, self-tormenting Saul was still alive and kicking inside him. He didn't understand Jesus at all. He wasn't even *interested* in Jesus; just in his own idea of the Christ. "Even though we once knew Christ according to the flesh," he wrote, "we no longer regard him in this way." In other words, it isn't relevant to know Jesus as a person of flesh and blood or to hear, much less do, what he taught; the only thing necessary for a Christian is to believe that Jesus was the Son of God and that he died in atonement for our sins. Like the writer of Revelation, Paul harbored a great deal of violence in his mind, which he projected onto visions of cosmic warfare, and onto an image of God as a punitive father. And he most ignorantly believed in what Spinoza describes as "a prince, God's enemy, who against God's will entraps and deceives very many men, whom God then hands over to this master of wickedness to be tortured for eternity." After his conversion, there was indeed a transparent area in his mind, but much of the window was still opaque. And since he thought he was in possession of the truth, he made no effort to clean the rest of the window. The experience that should have been just the beginning of his spiritual life became the beginning and the end of it. We can feel in the writings of Paul the Christian some of the same egotism, superstition, and intolerance that marred the character of Saul the Pharisee.

As a second and contrary example, perhaps the greatest example of patience and meticulousness in the history of religion, I would like to propose Chao-chou, who lived during the golden age of Zen in T'ang dynasty China. He experienced enlightenment in 795, when he was seventeen years old, then remained with his teacher for forty years, refining his insight and gradually dissolving his opacities and character flaws. Zen Master Kuei-shan, his contemporary, describes this process:

> Through meditation a student may gain thoughtless thought, become suddenly enlightened, and realize his original nature. But there is still a basic delusion. Therefore he should be taught to eliminate the manifestations of karma, which cause the remaining delusion to rise to the surface. There is no other way of cultivation.

Anyone who has undergone the experience of spiritual transformation knows how agonizing it can be. It is like cleaning the heart with a piece of steel wool. Or like that terrace in Dante's *Purgatorio* where the spirits who have stopped for a while to talk, dive back into the flames. They choose to return to the excruciating pain, to stand again in the pale blue archways of primal grief or rage where the heat is the greatest, because their most ardent wish is to be burned free of all self-absorption, and ultimately to disappear, into God's love. (The fire is consciousness.)

After his teacher died, Chao-chou remained in the monastery for a three-year mourning period; then he set out on a twenty-year pilgrimage to hone himself against the greatest Masters of his time. He said, in words that must have shocked the hierarchical and age-venerating Confucian mind, "If I meet a hundred-year-old man and I have something to teach him, I will teach; if I meet an eight-year-old boy and he has something to teach me, I will learn." Only when he was eighty years old did he feel mature enough to set up shop as a teacher. He taught for the next forty years, and his sayings are a marvel of lucidity, compassion, and humor.

Jesus must have undergone a good deal of spiritual development outside the story that has come down to us, before his enlightenment experience. After it, there was still one place of vivid pain and darkness left in his heart, a residual sorrow from his childhood: one area of dust on an otherwise transparent windowpane. I will suggest that he later came, at least unconsciously, to a resolution of his family drama. But even if the dust remained, it doesn't detract from him. All of us have our assignments to complete, whether they are big or little. That Jesus was unclear on one point, that he couldn't yet fulfill the commandment to honor father and mother, shouldn't be shocking, even for devout Christians. "Therefore he had to become like his fellow humans in every way," the author of the Epistle to the Hebrews says. He was so young when he died. And he had so little time.

From this perspective, then, of relative and complete clarity, I would like to examine Jesus' relationship with his family.

Just as there is no mother in the parable of the Prodigal Son, Mary of Nazareth is almost completely absent from Jesus' life and words. When she does appear, once, in the authentic accounts of him, the incident is a painful one. The few times that he mentions her, his words are cool, even hostile. Here again, the evidence is scattered across the Gospels; it needs to be assembled before we can see the connections.

To begin with, the relevant verses:

• When someone says to Jesus, "Your mother and your brothers are outside, asking for you," he refuses to let them enter the house and says, pointing to his disciples, "*These* are my mother and my brothers. Whoever does the will of God is my brother, and sister, and mother." This statement is usually seen as an admirable instance of Jesus' fellowship with the community of believers. It may be that; but it is also, and primarily, I think, a rejection of his actual mother and brothers.

• When a woman in a crowd calls out, "Blessed is the womb that bore you and the breasts that gave you suck," Jesus says, "No: blessed rather are those who hear the word of God and obey it." Again, there may be a lesson here for the pious. But we can hear the subtext, and we can almost feel Jesus bristling at the woman's remark.

• He laments that "a prophet is not rejected [dishonored, treated with contempt] except in his own town and in his own family and in his own house."

• His teaching about loyalty to parents is uniformly negative, and is so shocking, not only to religious sensibilities but to our ordinary sense of decency, that it is almost never mentioned in church. When it *is* mentioned, it is softened, interpreted, and bent into an appropriately pious shape. But Jesus' words themselves are unambiguous:

> And as they were traveling along the road, he said to a certain man, "Follow me."
>
> And the man said, "Let me first go and bury my father."
>
> But Jesus said to him, "Let the dead bury their dead." [That is, "Let the spiritually dead bury their relatives who are physically dead."]
>
> Another man said to Jesus, "I will follow you, sir, but let me first say good-bye to my family."

And Jesus said to him, "No one who puts his hand to the plow and then looks back is ready for the kingdom of God."

Jesus' point here is that we have to be ready to give up everything if we want to enter the kingdom of God. That is quite true. He said the same thing elsewhere, wonderfully, in his image of the merchant who found the pearl of great price and went and sold everything he had and bought it. What is shocking here is his timing: the words "Let the dead bury their dead," addressed to a man whose father has just died, are like a slap in the face. Even Job's comforters knew when to remain silent. And surely Jesus could have allowed the second man to say good-bye to his wife and children.

This teaching about cutting off all family ties is epitomized by a verse in Luke: "If anyone comes to me and doesn't hate his own father and mother and wife and children and brothers and sisters and even his own life, he can't be my disciple." The sentiment is even stronger in a verse (with a Gnostic spin on it) from the Gospel of Thomas: "Whoever doesn't hate his father and his mother as I do can't become my disciple. And whoever doesn't love his true Father [God] and his true Mother [the Holy Spirit] as I do can't become my disciple. For my mother gave me death, but my true Mother gave me life."

The fairest and most positive summary of this aspect of Jesus' teaching was made by George Bernard Shaw, of all people:

> Get rid of your family entanglements. Every mother you meet is as much your mother as the woman who bore you. Every man you meet is as much your brother as the man she bore after you. Don't waste your time at family funerals grieving for your relatives: attend to life, not death: there are as good fish in the sea as ever came out of it, and better. In the kingdom of heaven, which, as aforesaid, is within you, there is no marriage nor giving in marriage, because you cannot devote your life to two divinities: God and the person you are married to.

• • •

All this is true in a certain way, true for certain people or at certain stages of life. It is especially appropriate for young adults, who often need a moratorium to sort out their various confusions; and for those extremely rare people who have arrived at a sense of wholeness with their sexuality and want to devote themselves to a life of contemplation. But it is also untrue. However much I see all women as my mothers, I have a special bond with my flesh-and-blood mother, and if I don't honor it with my full attention, the flow of my love will be obstructed, and a portion of my heart will remain opaque. Nor is it true to say that in the kingdom of heaven there is no marriage. Marriage is one of the most direct paths to and in the kingdom of heaven. When I can truly devote myself to my wife, I *am* devoting myself to God, because all love is the love of God. "For the mature person, the Tao begins in the relation between man and woman, and ends in the infinite vastness of the universe."

Of course, many men, in many religious traditions, have felt a powerful conflict between family life and religious life; that is why celibacy has traditionally been seen as the most direct path to God. But, as anyone who reads Paul or Augustine knows, it is one thing to give up sex with your body and quite another to give it up in your mind. In the same way, it is one thing to leave your parents and quite another to let go of them in your mind. Abraham is the symbol for the latter, complete liberation: because he is able to leave his father's house forever, he is given an eternal blessing from God.

A couple of months after I began studying with my old Zen Master, he said to me, "You have three jobs here. Your first job is to kill the Buddha." I had read that phrase in the old Zen teachings, and I knew what it meant—to let go of any concepts of a separate, superior, enlightened being outside myself. Then he said, "Your second job is to kill your parents."

"What does that mean?" I asked.

"As long as there is anything you want from your parents," he said, "or anything about them that upsets you, they will be an obstacle in your mind. 'Killing your parents' means accepting them just as they are. They enter your mind like an image reflected on the water. No ripples."

"It sounds very difficult."

"Only if you think it is," he said.

Then he said, "Your third job is to kill me."

It is, in fact, possible to leave everything without leaving anything. We learn this from the teachings of the great Masters, and we can know it for ourselves, through our own experience. It is only for people in the more arduous stages of transformation that there is a conflict. Even when we understand the concern for wholeheartedness that caused Jesus to teach as he did about family, we can recognize an extreme quality, a lack of balance, an off-centeredness, in the tone of these sayings that almost begs us to consider them in the realm not of spiritual teaching but of psychology.

The clearest statements I have found about attachment to home and family occur in the teaching of Ramana Maharshi. A beginner once said to him, "I want to give up my job and family and stay with you, sir, so that I can be with God." Maharshi said, "God is always with you, in you. That is what you should realize."

> *Questioner:* But I feel the urge to give up all attachments and renounce the world.
>
> *Maharshi:* Renunciation doesn't mean giving away your money or abandoning your home. True renunciation is the renunciation of desires, passions, and attachments.
>
> *Questioner:* But single-minded devotion to God may not be possible unless one leaves worldly things.
>
> *Maharshi:* No: a true renunciate actually merges in the world and expands his love to embrace the whole world. It would be more correct to describe the attitude of the devotee as universal love than as abandoning home to become a monk.

Questioner: At home the bonds of affection are too strong.

Maharshi: If you renounce home when you aren't ripe for it, you only create new bonds.

Questioner: Isn't renunciation the supreme means of breaking attachments?

Maharshi: That may be so for someone whose mind is already free from entanglements. But you haven't grasped the deeper meaning of renunciation. Great souls who have abandoned their homes have done so not out of aversion to family life, but because of their largehearted and all-embracing love for all mankind and all creatures.

Questioner: Family ties will have to be left behind some-time, so why shouldn't I take the initiative and break them now, so that my love can be equal toward all people?

Maharshi: When you truly feel this equal love for all, when your heart has expanded so much that it embraces the whole of creation, you will certainly not feel like giving up this or that. You will simply drop off from secular life, as a ripe fruit drops from the branch of a tree. You will feel that the whole world is your home.

I have already quoted a verse from the one incident in which Mary appears. This incident requires closer attention. It begins with one of the most hair-raising verses in the Gospels:

And when his family heard [about all this], they went to seize him, for they said, "He is out of his mind."

Hidden inside this verse is a world of misunderstanding and disap-pointment. Actually, it is a miracle that the verse survived at all, to speak to us. It appears only in Mark; both Matthew and Luke appar-ently found it so shocking that they deleted it from their accounts. (Even in Mark, the transcribers of two of the best ancient manuscripts were so embarrassed by it that they altered it to read, "And when *the scribes and the others* heard about him, they went to seize him, for they said, 'He is out of his mind.' ")

What is happening here? We can't be certain of the details, because we don't know what Mary and Jesus' brothers heard that troubled them so much. Perhaps it had to do with his healings and exorcisms at Capernaum; perhaps a neighbor had watched one of the treatments and had returned to Nazareth with a frightened report about the strange sounds Jesus had uttered or the physical contortions he had gone through. Or perhaps there were rumors of his bizarre and incomprehensible doctrines: that the pure in heart can actually see God, or that adults should be like children, or that the kingdom of God has already come. Whatever it was that they heard, they concluded that he had gone insane. So, like any responsible family, concerned for his well-being and wanting to prevent him from harming himself or others, they went out to "seize" him and bring him back home (the Greek verb is a strong one, and is used later in Mark, of the troops in Gethsemane, with the meaning "to arrest").

> And his mother and his brothers arrived, and standing outside, they sent in a message asking for him.
>
> And the people in the crowd sitting around him said to him, "Your mother and your brothers are outside and want to see you."
>
> And Jesus said, "Who are my mother and my brothers?" And looking at those who sat in a circle around him, he said, "*These* are my mother and my brothers. Whoever does the will of God is my brother, and sister, and mother."

When Jesus' mother and brothers arrive at Capernaum, he is in a house, teaching, with a crowd of disciples and sympathizers around him. The crowd is so large that Mary and the brothers can't enter, so they send in a message, asking him to come out; their intention is to "seize" him and take him home to Nazareth. When he is told that they are waiting for him, Jesus' response is, in effect, to disown them. Of course, it isn't difficult to see Jesus' point: that he loves those who do God's will more than he loves even his own mother (if she were not to do God's will). We can realize the truth of this teaching, on the absolute level—it is true in the same sense in which the primal commandment to love God with *all* one's heart is true—and at the same time recognize, on the relative level, the lack of wholeness, of healedness, in its antagonistic tone. This note of irritation was already pointed out by the heretic Mani in the fourth-century *Debates of Archelaus, Bishop of Mesopotamia, and the Heresiarch Mani*:

> Mani said, "Someone once said to Jesus, 'Your mother and your brothers are outside,' and Jesus did not kindly receive the person who said this, but indignantly rebuked him, saying, 'Who are my mother and my brothers?'" '

Christian scholars have felt such a compelling need to justify Jesus' conduct that they haven't really taken it in. The Jewish scholar C. G. Montefiore is more objective, though in his comment there is an element of blame:

> It has been urged that the harsh bearing of Jesus towards his mother and family may be explained and justified on the grounds (a) that his family did not understand or believe in his mission, (b) that his whole soul was so filled with this mission that there was no room in it for family ties and interests, and (c) (the most important of all) that his special work implied and demanded a separation from, an abandonment of, all worldly connections and occupations.
>
> Yet when all is said, there is a certain violation or *froissement* of Jewish sentiment as to parents in this passage, and it is strange to find Jesus, who acts so dubiously towards his own mother, afterwards [Mark VII:9ff.] reproaching the Pharisees with not honoring father and mother! Even if the explanations of his conduct given above are adequate, Jesus

might have explained matters to his mother and family quietly and in private, whereas he, in order to score a point, put
them to open shame and humiliation. . . . No Jew who
remains a Jew can well believe that the conduct of Jesus in
this story, however justified in its essential issues, was justified in detail, blameless and exquisite in method.

But there is no reason to blame Jesus for his conduct. What is important is to see it clearly. His rejection of his mother seems to me an
early, inadequate response to what he must have felt as her rejection
of him, her incomprehension of who he had become. Or perhaps it
goes back further, to his childhood. Perhaps it contains an unconscious or half-conscious element of blame for the stigma of his birth,
and was part of his distancing himself from his shame and everything
connected with it.

When someone undergoes a spiritual transformation, he or she is
truly reborn. The shape of the personality may be the same, and a
residue of unfinished karmic business may still be there, but in the
depths, the old, self-preoccupied self is dead and there is a wholly new
awareness. Integration of this new self into one's life and family and
society is the greatest and most difficult challenge in spiritual practice.
(The work may take seven years or seven lifetimes, but people who are
in love with God do it gladly; as in the story of Jacob and Rachel, the
years "seemed to him only a few days, so great was his love for her.")
It is particularly difficult with parents, who are deeply invested in cre-
ating us in their own image, and see only the former self who was their
child. How can they understand that one's roots have grown deeper
than the family, have penetrated beyond birth and death? Incomprehension is a given, except in very rare instances. The question is how
one deals with the incomprehension.

While no other great spiritual teacher I know of had to face such a
difficult childhood as Jesus did, all others had to give up their attachments to personal relationships, especially to the powerful centrifugal
force of the family. Departures are often painful, and those who are left

behind feel betrayed or abandoned. We can't help that. But if, like Abraham, we live in the place from which it is impossible to depart, we can make our departure an act of love. We are "ahead of all parting," as Rilke put it, and not only for ourselves. How poignant is the moment in the life of the Buddha when Gautama, knowing he has to leave his beloved wife and set out to solve the great question of life and death, leans over her sleeping body and kisses her on the cheek, one last time. But if he hadn't left, he could never have awakened and helped countless others to awaken, including her.

Jesus' return to his family after his baptism experience must have been as painful as his subsequent return to Nazareth. We have an account of the latter, and it is a story of rejection:

> From there he went to Nazareth, his native town, and his disciples followed him.
>
> And when the Sabbath came, he began to teach in the synagogue, and many people who heard him were bewildered, and said, "Where does this fellow get such stuff?" and "What makes *him* so wise?" and "How can he be a miracle-worker? Isn't this the carpenter, Mary's bastard, the brother of James and Joseph and Judas and Simon, and aren't his sisters here with us?" And they were prevented from believing in him.
>
> And Jesus said, "A prophet is not rejected except in his own town and in his own family and in his own house."
>
> And he was unable to do any miracle there, because of their disbelief.

In this story, the people of Nazareth can't believe that the Jesus whom they knew as an illegitimate child has been transformed into a prophet. They see him through the distorting lens of the past, and therefore are completely unaware of his presence. We aren't told whether Mary or any of Jesus' brothers or sisters were in the synagogue on this occasion. But the reaction of the townspeople is similar to the family's reaction. (In a different context, the Gospel of John says that "even his own brothers didn't believe in him.")

There is a striking comment on the Nazareth incident by Zen Master Ma-tsu (709–788), who of course had never heard of Jesus:

> Don't return to your native town:
> you can't teach the truth there.
> By the village stream an old woman
> is calling you by your childhood name.

This little poem is both lovely and poignant in its acceptance of a psychological given: that even the greatest Master may still appear to his family as the child he was—small, needy, untransformed.

With both his family and the people of Nazareth, Jesus' reaction is to depart and shake off the dust from his feet. But this seems to me a provisional attitude, and I think he held to it as a matter of protection, while he was coming to full inner ripeness. There is a traditional Hindu metaphor that clarifies two appropriate stages:

> When the young plant is just sprouting out of the seed or is still weak and tender, it requires seclusion and the protection of a strong thorny fence to keep off cattle that might otherwise eat it or trample upon and destroy it. But the same shoot, when it develops into a large tree, dispenses with such protection and itself affords shade, sustenance, and protection to cattle and men, without detriment to itself.

At this later stage, detachment and filial piety aren't mutually exclusive. When someone has found freedom in his heart, everything that was once an obstacle—parents, money, sex—becomes an opportunity for a further degree of surrender. We can sense this freedom in Jesus' parables, when he speaks of Samaritans and sinners. And we feel that someone as largehearted and compassionate as he was would surely have been able to fulfill both the commandment to love God with all his heart and the commandment to honor his mother. John the Evangelist was so convinced of this that he imagined Mary at the foot of the Cross, and imagined Jesus, in almost his final words, placing her in the care of the "disciple whom he loved." That is what gives his account a sense of personal closure that the other three Gospels don't have. When we love someone, we wish him all possible peace and wholeness in his heart. And we want him, before he dies, to have finished his earthly business, which is, after all, his Father's business as well.

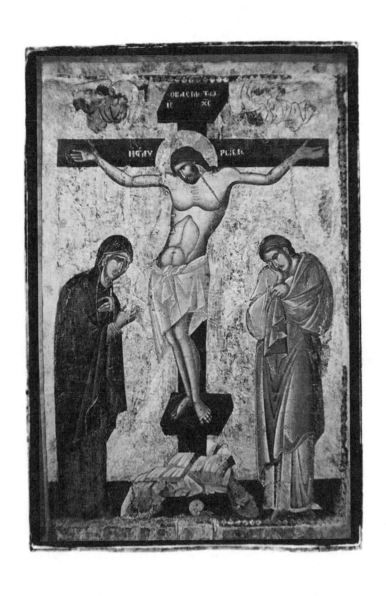

from Jesus the Son of Man
by Kahlil Gibran

Kahlil Gibran (1883–1931) in his 1928 book imagined seventy-seven of Jesus' contemporaries (including some characters familiar from the Gospels), and offered his version of how they experienced the man.

ANNA

THE MOTHER OF MARY

Jesus the son of my daughter, was born here in Nazareth in the month of January. And the night that Jesus was born we were visited by men from the East. They were Persians who came to Esdraelon with the caravans of the Midianites on their way to Egypt. And because they did not find rooms at the inn they sought shelter in our house.

And I welcomed them and I said, "My daughter has given birth to a son this night. Surely you will forgive me if I do not serve you as it behooves a hostess."

Then they thanked me for giving them shelter. And after they had supped they said to me: "We would see the new-born."

Now the Son of Mary was beautiful to behold, and she too was comely.

And when the Persians beheld Mary and her babe, they took gold and silver from their bags, and myrrh and frankincense, and laid them all at the feet of the child.

Then they fell down and prayed in a strange tongue which we did not understand.

And when I led them to the bedchamber prepared for them they walked as if they were in awe at what they had seen.

When morning was come they left us and followed the road to Egypt.

But at parting they spoke to me and said: "The child is but a day old, yet we have seen the light of our God in His eyes and the smile of our God upon His mouth.

"We bid you protect Him that He may protect you all."

And so saying, they mounted their camels and we saw them no more.

Now Mary seemed not so much joyous in her first-born, as full of wonder and surprise.

She would look long upon her babe, and then turn her face to the window and gaze far away into the sky as if she saw visions.

And there were valleys between her heart and mine.

And the child grew in body and spirit, and He was different from other children. He was aloof and hard to govern, and I could not lay my hand upon Him.

But He was beloved by everyone in Nazareth, and in my heart I knew why.

Oftentimes He would take away our food to give to the passerby. And He would give other children the sweetmeat I had given Him, before He had tasted it with His own mouth.

He would climb the trees of my orchard to get the fruits, but never to eat them Himself.

And He would race with other boys, and sometimes, because He was swifter of foot, He would delay so that they might pass the stake ere He should reach it.

And sometimes when I led Him to His bed He would say, "Tell my mother and the others that only my body will sleep. My mind will be with them till their mind come to my morning."

And many other wondrous words he said when He was a boy, but I am too old to remember.

Now they tell me I shall see Him no more. But how shall I believe what they say?

I still hear His laughter, and the sound of His running about my house. And whenever I kiss the cheek of my daughter His fragrance returns to my heart, and his body seems to fill my arms.

But is it not passing strange that my daughter does not speak of her first-born to me?

Sometimes it seems that my longing for Him is greater than hers. She stands as firm before the day as if she were a bronzen image, while my heart melts and runs into streams.

Perhaps she knows what I do not know. Would that she might tell me also.

MARY MAGDALEN

It was in the month of June when I saw Him for the first time. He was walking in the wheatfield when I passed by with my handmaidens, and He was alone.

The rhythm of His step was different from other men's, and the movement of His body was like naught I had seen before.

Men do not pace the earth in that manner. And even now I do not know whether He walked fast or slow.

My handmaidens pointed their fingers at Him and spoke in shy whispers to one another. And I stayed my steps for a moment, and raised my hand to hail him. But He did not turn His face, and He did not look at me. And I hated Him. I was swept back into myself, and I was as cold as if I had been in a snow-drift. And I shivered.

That night I beheld Him in my dreaming; and they told me afterward that I screamed in my sleep and was restless upon my bed.

It was in the month of August that I saw Him again, through my window. He was sitting in the shadow of the cypress tree across my garden, and He was as still as if he had been carved out of stone, like the statues in Antioch and other cities of the North Country.

And my slave, the Egyptian, came to me and said, "That man is here again. He is sitting there across your garden."

And I gazed at Him, and my soul quivered within me, for He was beautiful.

His body was single and each part seemed to love every other part.

Them I clothed myself with raiment of Damascus, and I left my house and walked towards Him.

Was it my aloneness, or was it His fragrance, that drew me to Him? Was it a hunger in my eyes that desired comeliness, or was it His beauty that sought the light of my eyes?

Even now I do not know.

I walked to Him with my scented garments and my golden sandals, the sandals the Roman captain had given me, even these sandals. And when I reached Him, I said, "Good-morrow to you."

And He said, "Good-morrow to you, Miriam."

And He looked at me, and His night-eyes saw me as no man had seen me. And suddenly I was as if naked, and I was shy.

Yet He had only said, "Good-morrow to you."

And then I said to Him, "Will you not come to my house?"

And He said, "Am I not already in your house?"

I did not know what He meant then, but I know now.

And I said, "Will you not have wine and bread with me?"

And he said, "Yes, Miriam, but not now."

Not now, not now, He said. And the voice of the sea was in those two words, and the voice of the wind and the trees. And when He said them unto me, life spoke to death.

For mind you, my friend, I was dead. I was a woman who had divorced her soul. I was living apart from this self which you now see. I belonged to all men, and to none. They called me harlot, and a woman possessed of seven devils. I was cursed, and I was envied.

But when His dawn-eyes looked into my eyes all the stars of my night faded away, and I became Miriam, only Miriam, a woman lost to the earth she had known, and finding herself in new places.

And now again I said to Him, "Come into my house and share bread and wine with me."

And He said, "Why do you bid me to be your guest?"

And I said, "I beg you to come into my house." And it was all that was sod in me, and all that was sky in me calling unto Him.

Then He looked at me, and the noontide of His eyes was upon me, and He said, "You have many lovers, and yet I alone love you. Other men love themselves in your nearness. I love you in your self. Other men see a beauty in you that shall fade away sooner than their own years. But I see in you a beauty that shall not fade away, and in the autumn of your days that beauty shall not be afraid to gaze at itself in the mirror, and it shall not be offended.

"I alone love the unseen in you."

Then He said in a low voice, "Go away now. If this cypress tree is yours and you would not have me sit in its shadow, I will walk my way."

And I cried to Him and I said, "Master, come to my house. I have incense to burn for you, and a silver basin for your feet. You are a stranger and yet not a stranger. I entreat you, come to my house."

Then He stood up and looked at me even as the seasons might look down upon the field, and He smiled. And He said again: "All men love you for themselves. I love you for yourself."

And then He walked away.

But no other man ever walked the way He walked. Was it a breath born in my garden that moved to the east? Or was it a storm that would shake all things to their foundations?

I knew not, but on that day the sunset of His eyes slew the dragon in me, and I became a woman, I became Miriam, Miriam of Mijdel.

• • •

CAIAPHAS

THE HIGH PRIEST

In speaking of that man Jesus and of His death let us consider two salient facts: the Torah must needs be held in safety by us, and this kingdom must needs be protected by Rome.

Now that man was defiant to us and to Rome. He poisoned the mind of the simple people, and He fed them as if by magic against us and against Caesar.

My own slaves, both men and women, after hearing Him speak in the market-place, turned sullen and rebellious. Some of them left my house and escaped to the desert whence they came.

Forget not that the Torah is our foundation and our tower of strength. No man shall undermine us while we have this power to restrain his hand, and no man shall overthrow Jerusalem so long as its walls stand upon the ancient stone that David laid.

If the seed of Abraham is indeed to live and thrive this soil must remain undefiled.

And that man Jesus was a defiler and a corrupter. We slew Him with a conscience both deliberate and clean. And we shall slay all those who would debase the laws of Moses or seek to befoul our sacred heritage.

We and Pontius Pilatus knew the danger in that man, and that it was wise to bring Him to an end.

I shall see that His followers come to the same end, and the echo of His word to the same silence.

If Judea is to live all men who oppose her must be brought down to the dust. And ere Judea shall die I will cover my gray head with ashes even as did Samuel the prophet, and I will tear off this garment of Aaron and clothe me in sackcloth until I go hence for ever.

• • •

JOANNA

THE WIFE OF HEROD'S STEWARD

Jesus was never married but He was a friend of women, and He knew them as they would be known in sweet comradeship.

And He loved children as they would be loved in faith and under-standing.

In the light of His eyes there was a father and a brother and a son.

He would hold a child upon His knees and say, "Of such is your might and your freedom; and of such is the kingdom of the spirit."

They say that Jesus heeded not the law of Moses, and that He was over-forgiving to the prostitutes of Jerusalem and the country side.

I myself at that time was deemed a prostitute, for I loved a man who was not my husband, and he was a Sadducee.

And on a day the Sadducees came upon me in my house when my lover was with me, and they seized me and held me, and my lover walked away and left me.

Then they led me to the market-place where Jesus was teaching.

It was their desire to hold me up before Him as a test and a trap for Him.

But Jesus judged me not. He laid shame upon those who would have had me shamed, and He reproached them.

And He bade me go my way.

And after that all the tasteless fruit of life turned sweet to my mouth, and the scentless blossoms breathed fragrance into my nostrils. I became a woman without a tainted memory, and I was free, and my head was no longer bowed down.

DAVID

ONE OF HIS FOLLOWERS

I did not know the meaning of His discourses or His parables until He was no longer among us. Nay, I did not understand until His words took living forms before my eyes and fashioned themselves into bodies that walk in the procession of my own day.

Let me tell you this: On a night as I sat in my house pondering, and remembering His words and His deeds that I might inscribe them in a book, three thieves entered my house. And though I knew they came to rob me of my goods, I was too mindful of what I was doing to meet them with the sword, or even to say, "What do you here?"

But I continued writing my remembrances of the Master.

And when the thieves had gone then I remembered His saying, "He who would take your cloak, let him take your other cloak also."

And I understood.

As I sat recording His words no man could have stopped me even were he to have carried away all my possessions.

For though I would guard my possessions and also my person, I know where lies the greater treasure.

A Young Priest Capernaum

He was a magician, warp and woof, and a sorcerer, a man who bewildered the simple by charms and incantations. And He juggled with the words of our prophets and with the sanctities of our forefathers.

Aye, He even bade the dead be His witnesses, and the voiceless graves His forerunners and authority.

He sought the women of Jerusalem and the women of the countryside with the cunning of the spider that seeks the fly; and they were caught in His web.

For women are weak and empty-headed, and they follow the man who would comfort their unspent passion with soft and tender words. Were it not for these women, infirm and possessed by His evil spirit, His name would have been erased from the memory of man.

And who were the men who followed Him?

They were of the horde that are yoked and trodden down. In their ignorance and fear they would never have rebelled against their rightful masters. But when He promised them high stations in His kingdom of mirage, they yielded to His fantasy as clay yields to the potter.

Know you not, the slave in his dreaming would always be master; and the weakling would be a lion?

The Galilean was a conjuror and a deceiver, a man who forgave the sins of all the sinners that He might hear *Hail* and *Hosanna* from their unclean mouths; and who fed the faint heart of the hopeless and the wretched that He might have ears for His voice and a retinue at His command.

He broke the sabbath with those who break that He might gain the support of the lawless; and He spoke ill of our high priests that He might win attention in the Sanhedrin, and by opposition increase His fame.

I have said often that I hated that man. Ay, I hate Him more than I hate the Romans who govern our country. Even His coming was from Nazareth, a town cursed by our prophets, a dunghill of the Gentiles, from which no good shall ever proceed.

A RICH LEVITE IN THE NEIGHBORHOOD OF NAZARETH

He was a good carpenter. The doors he fashioned were never unlocked by thieves, and the windows he made were always ready to open to the east wind and to the west.

And He made chests of cedar wood, polished and enduring, and ploughs and pitchforks strong and yielding to the hand.

And He carved lecterns for our synagogues. He carved them out of the golden mulberry; and on both sides of the support, where the sacred book lies, He chiseled wings outspreading; and under the support, heads of bulls and doves, and large-eyed deer.

All this He wrought in the manner of the Chaldeans and the Greeks. But there was that in His skill which was neither Chaldean nor Greek.

Now this my house was builded by many hands thirty years ago. I sought builders and carpenters in all the towns of Galilee. They had each the skill and the art of building, and I was pleased and satisfied with all that they did.

But come now, and behold two doors and a window that were fashioned by Jesus of Nazareth. They in their stability mock at all else in my house.

See you not that these two doors are different from all other doors? And this window opening to the east, is it not different from other windows?

All my doors and windows are yielding to the years save these which He made. They alone stand strong against the elements.

And see those cross-beams, how he placed them; and these nails, how they are driven from one side of the board, and then caught and fastened so firmly upon the other side.

And what is passing strange is that that laborer who was worthy the wages of two men received but the wage of one man; and that same laborer now is deemed a prophet in Israel.

Had I known then that this youth with saw and plane was a prophet, I would have begged Him to speak rather than work, and then I would have overpaid Him for his words.

And now I still have many men working in my house and fields. How shall I know the man whose own hand is upon his tool, from the man upon whose hand God lays His hand?

Yea, how shall I know God's hand?

A WIDOW IN GALILEE

My son was my first and my only born. He labored in our field and he was contented until he heard the man called Jesus speaking to the multitude.

Then my son suddenly became different, as if a new spirit, foreign and unwholesome, had embraced his spirit.

He abandoned the field and the garden; and he abandoned me also. He became worthless, a creature of the highways.

That man Jesus of Nazareth was evil, for what good man would separate a son from his mother?

The last thing my child said to me was this: "I am going with one of His disciples to the North Country. My life is established upon the Nazarene. You have given me birth, and for that I am grateful to you. But I needs must go. Am I not leaving with you our rich land, and all our silver and gold? I shall take naught but this garment and this staff."

Thus my son spoke, and departed.

And now the Romans and the priests have laid hold upon Jesus and crucified Him; and they have done well.

A man who would part mother and son could not be godly.

The man who sends our children to the cities of the Gentiles cannot be our friend.

I know my son will not return to me. I saw it in his eyes. And for this I hate Jesus of Nazareth who caused me to be alone in this unploughed field and this withered garden.

And I hate all those who praise Him.

Not many days ago they told me that Jesus once said, "My father and my mother and my brethren are those who hear my word and follow me."

But why should sons leave their mothers to follow His footsteps?

And why should the milk of my breast be forgotten for a fountain not yet tasted? And the warmth of my arms be forsaken for the Northland, cold and unfriendly?

Aye, I hate the Nazarene, and I shall hate Him to the end of my days, for He has robbed me of my first-born, my only son.

URIAH,

AN OLD MAN OF NAZARETH

He was a stranger in our midst, and His life was hidden with dark veils.

He walked not the path of our God, but followed the course of the foul and the infamous.

His childhood revolted, and rejected the sweet milk of our nature.

His youth was inflamed like dry grass that burns in the night.

And when He became man, He took arms against us all.

Such men are conceived in the ebb tide of human kindness, and born in unholy tempests. And in tempests they live a day and then perish forever.

Do you not remember Him, a boy overweening, who would argue with our learned elders, and laugh at their dignity?

And remember you not His youth, when He lived by the saw and the chisel? He would not accompany our sons and daughters on their holidays. He would walk alone.

And He would not return the salutation of those who hailed Him, as though He were above us.

I myself met Him once in the field and greeted Him, and He only smiled, and in His smile I beheld arrogance and insult.

Not long afterward my daughter went with her companions to the vineyards to gather the grapes, and she too spoke to Him and He did not answer her.

He spoke only to the whole company of grape-gatherers, as if my daughter had not been among them.

When He abandoned His people and turned vagabond He became naught but a babbler. His voice was like a claw in our flesh, and the sound of His voice is still a pain in our memory.

He would utter only evil of us and of our fathers and forefathers. And His tongue sought our bosoms like a poisoned straw.

Such was Jesus.

If He had been my son, I would have committed Him with the Roman legions to Arabia, and I would have begged the captain to place Him in the forefront of the battle, so that the archer of the foe might mark him, and free me of His insolence.

But I have no son. And mayhap I should be grateful. For what if my son had been an enemy of his own people, and my gray hairs were now seeking the dust with shame, my white beard humbled?

• • •

MARY MAGDALEN

His mouth was like the heart of a pomegranate, and the shadows in His eyes were deep.

And He was gentle, like a man mindful of his own strength.

In my dreams I beheld the kings of the earth standing in awe in His presence.

I would speak of His face, but how shall I?

It was like night without darkness, and like day without the noise of day.

It was a sad face, and it was a joyous face.

And well I remember how once He raised His hand towards the sky, and His parted fingers were like the branches of an elm.

And I remember Him pacing the evening. He was not walking. He Himself was a road above the road; even as a cloud above the earth that would descend to refresh the earth.

But when I stood before Him and spoke to Him, He was a man, and His face was powerful to behold. And He said to me, "What would you, Miriam?"

I did not answer Him, but my wings enfolded my secret, and I was made warm.

And because I could bear His light no more, I turned and walked away, but not in shame. I was only shy, and I would be alone, with His fingers upon the strings of my heart.

MANASSEH,
A LAWYER IN JERUSALEM

Yes, I used to hear Him speak. There was always a ready word upon His lips.

But I admired Him as a man rather than as a leader. He preached something beyond my liking, perhaps beyond my reason. And I would have no man preach to me.

I was taken by His voice and His gestures, but not by the substance of His speech. He charmed me but never convinced me; for He was too vague, too distant and obscure to reach my mind.

I have known other men like Him. They are never constant nor are they consistent. It is with eloquence not with principles that they hold your ear and your passing thought, but never the core of your heart.

What a pity that His enemies confronted Him and forced the issue. It was not necessary. I believe their hostility will add to His stature and turn His mildness to power.

For is it not strange that in opposing a man you give Him courage? And in staying His feet you give Him wings?

I know not His enemies, yet I am certain that in their fear of a harmless man they have lent Him strength and made Him dangerous.

A COBBLER IN JERUSALEM

I loved Him not, yet I did not hate Him. I listened to Him not to hear His words but rather the sound of His voice; for His voice pleased me. All that He said was vague to my mind, but the music thereof was clear to my ear.

Indeed were it not for what others have said to me of His teaching, I should not have known even so much as whether He was with Judea or against it.

BARABBAS

They released me and chose Him. Then He rose and I fell down.

And they held Him a victim and a sacrifice for the Passover.

I was freed from my chains, and walked with the throng behind Him, but I was a living man going to my own grave.

I should have fled to the desert where shame is burned out by the sun.

Yet I walked with those who had chosen Him to bear my crime.

When they nailed Him on His cross I stood there.

I saw and I heard but I seemed outside of my body.

The thief who was crucified on His right said to Him, "Are you bleeding with me, even you, Jesus of Nazareth?"

And Jesus answered and said, "Were it not for this nail that stays my hand I would reach forth and clasp your hand.

"We are crucified together. Would they had raised your cross nearer to mine."

Then He looked down and gazed open His mother and a young man who stood beside her.

He said, "Mother, behold your son standing beside you.

"Woman, behold a man who shall carry these drops of my blood to the North Country."

And when He heard the wailing of the women of Galilee He said: "Behold, they weep and I thirst.

"I am held too high to reach their tears.

"I will not take vinegar and gall to quench this thirst."

Then his eyes opened wide to the sky, and He said: "Father, why hast Thou forsaken us?"

And then He said in compassion, "Father, forgive them, for they know not what they do."

When He uttered these words methought I saw all men prostrated before God beseeching forgiveness for the crucifixion of this one man.

Then again He said with a great voice: "Father, into Thy hand I yield back my spirit."

And at last He lifted up His head and said, "Now it is finished, but only upon this hill."

And He closed His eyes.

Then lightning cracked the dark skies, and there was a great thunder.

I know now that those who slew Him in my stead achieved my endless torment.

His crucifixion endured but for an hour.

But I shall be crucified unto the end of my years.

from By an Unknown Disciple

by Cecily Spencer-Smith

Phillimore

Cecily Spencer-Smith Phillimore anonymously published several Biblical novels, including By an Unknown Disciple. *The unnamed narrator of the book offers posterity his version of a well-known Bible story.*

Mark John was only a boy then, and what he wrote down he learnt from Peter. Peter was there, but he was hauling up the boats, and didn't know what had happened until he heard the shouts and saw the swine break away and rush down the hillside into the sea. He never saw the madman until all the swine were dead. How, then, did he know enough to tell Mark John? Well, of course, he heard the others talk. And then that was Peter's way. He was always sure that he knew everything until he did some hot-tempered, silly action, and then he was sure that he knew nothing. He would believe everything or nothing according to his temper towards the teller. He did not care for the labour of weighing facts to decide between false and true. You could never make Peter believe that even when people describe a thing as they think they saw it they may still speak falsehood. If a man told Peter that he had met a demon or a magician in the mountains Peter would be quite sure that it was a magician or a demon, unless the man who said he saw it was a Scribe or a Pharisee, and then Peter would say he was a liar.

Always Peter hated the explanations given by others. He never wanted to ask how things had happened. He felt so strongly that he was sure he knew and that other more subtle explanations smelt of the Scribes. Later he grew into somewhat of a tyrant, but always he was lovable.

Luke was not there. I do not know who told him. Yes, he was an educated man; but he was a physician, and he seldom saw beyond the things of the body. Witness the way he changed the Blessings. Peter never made such mistakes abut the Message; to the end he loved the poor, but Luke wanted to keep them orderly.

Peter and Luke and Mark John—they are all dead now, and I can speak my mind. When they were here I often tried, but they did not want to listen. They liked their own way of seeing the miracle best, and, so, for the sake of peace and good-fellowship, I ceased to speak. If it were the truth, then one day it would prevail. So I kept silence. But you are waiting to know about the swine and the madman.

The dawn was breaking when we reached the land after that stormy passage across the lake, and I followed Jesus up the slope of the shore to the headlands. Peter and the other fishermen were busy hauling up the boats; some of the people who, like me, had been passengers, lay down to sleep, some followed us far behind in a little group. The light spread over the hills was purple and pink, and the stillness was broken only by the cheep of a sleepy bird.

I do not know if Jesus prayed as he walked, but I felt the stillness and the loneliness brought God near, and I followed in silence. When we reached the brow of the headland it was full daylight, and there, in the distance, was the herd of swine, slowly rooting its way towards us. The swineherds had turned aside to eat their morning meal, and, as they ate, pigs of all sizes and colours, of all ages and shapes, moved on alone, occupied only with filling their bellies. Here a small pig grunted in anger as he was pushed aside by a giant sow, whose barren dried-up teats touched the earth. There a great boar, with tusks pushed up under his lip, thrust himself out from the crowd with sidelong blows of his heavy head to seize the portion of some smaller pigs, who fled, squealing.

Jesus stood still to watch, and, as he watched, he smiled. When he spoke, it was to answer the question that had remained unspoken in my mind.

"No," he said, "why should we call them unclean? They are God's creatures, as we all are."

He turned as a man came forward out of the group that stood behind and said,

"Rabbi, it is not safe to be here. There are madmen amongst the tombs."

The man was urgent. Jesus looked him straight in the eyes, as if to measure him, and the man returned the look as straightly and went on speaking.

"They are possessed by demons. They tear their flesh—they can be heard screaming day and night. It is not safe to be here."

"How do you know they are possessed by demons?" asked Jesus.

"What else could it be?" said the man. "There are none that can master them. They are too fierce to be tamed."

"Has any man tried to tame them?" asked Jesus.

"Yes, Rabbi. They have been bound with chains and fetters. There was one that I saw. He plucked the fetters from him as a child might break a chain of field flowers. Then he ran, foaming, into the wilderness, and no man dare pass by that way now."

Jesus was silent. His eyes were bent on the ground, and, after a space, the man spoke again, and it was as if he made excuse.

"Rabbi, the demons made the man cut his flesh with stones; they tear his clothes to pieces. Men fear to touch him now. He goes naked."

Jesus lifted his eyes to the man's face.

"Have men tried only this way to tame him?" he asked.

"What other way is there, Rabbi?" asked the man.

"There is God's way," said Jesus. "Come. Let us try it," and he went towards the tombs. The man stepped back.

"Rabbi," he faltered. He turned to his companions, and fear seemed to seize upon them. Jesus stopped and looked back. His gaze went from man to man, and then his eyes fell upon me. It was as if a power passed from him to me, and immediately something inside me answered.

"Lead, and I follow," I said, and he went forward again. The others debated a while, and then, with hesitation and doubting, they, too, followed. The swineherds, who had drawn near to hear, joined themselves to the men, and left their pigs rooting and grunting.

It was not many cubic lengths to the tombs, but the others were far behind when we reached that desolation.

"Do men live here?" asked Jesus, as he looked at the abomination around us. I did not answer. I was watching for the madman. I think I caught sight of him at the moment that he first saw us, for, as I touched Jesus to point to his naked figure, he began to run towards us shrieking and bounding in the air. He had two sharp stones in his hands, and as he leapt he cut his flesh with them, and the blood ran down his naked limbs. The men behind us scattered and fled down the hillside; but Jesus stood still and waited.

I was about to step forward, thinking that the maniac would leap upon Jesus, when the miracle happened. For the man as if against his will stopped short. Then he opened his palms, and casting the sharp stones from him, he bowed himself to the ground before Jesus, and in a most piteous voice and with tears he cried:

"What do you want with me, O Son of the most high God? Do not say that you also have come here to torment me!"

"What is your name?" asked Jesus, and at the sound of his voice the man lifted up his head and answered bitterly,

"My name is Legion, for there are many possessing me."

"Why do you say you are possessed of demons?" said Jesus.

"I did not say it," answered the man. "It was they who said it when they loaded me with chains and tormented me in my agony. They will torture me again if they catch me," he cried, leaping to his feet as the men behind, seeing him quieted, came nearer.

Jesus turned and told the men to stand back. Then he put out his hand and touched the man.

"Be at peace!" he said. "There is none that will torment you now.

You need no longer tear your clothes, or shriek, or cut your body with stones to frighten your torturers away."

The man fell on his face, and again bowed his head at the feet of Jesus.

"I was in fear," he said. "They were many, and I was one, and when the agony came upon me and they bound me with chains, I broke them like straws and fled. I was in fear."

"Fear is a foul spirit," said Jesus, "cast it out from you." And the man answered humbly:

"I will." And Jesus put his own cloak upon him and led him apart amongst the tombs to where he could wash the blood from his limbs.

It was then that the swineherds, who with the others devoured by curiosity had drawn near again, remembered their swine, and turning saw them on the edge of the cliff.

"See!" cried one to the other, "the swine are in danger. We shall lose some of them."

They ran warily, one to each end of the cliff (knowing the nature of swine and how they refuse to be driven save where they wish to go), meaning to get between the swine and the sea; but the other men being ignorant and unskillful, yet wishing to help, ran swiftly down the hillside in the face of the swine, who seeing them come in haste, turned quickly and rushed in a mass towards the sea.

"Stand back!" shouted the swineherds. "You will drive them over the cliff." But it was too late. The swine had rushed one upon another, and the slope was steep, and in a moment they were swept over the edge of the cliff into the sea. The swineherds tore their hair when they saw the herd rush into the sea. They ran to the cliff edge and looked over to see where the swine were drowning in the deep water below.

"It is your fault," they cried to the men. "You rushed them down the hillside. We had but left them for a moment and, behold, they are all lost! What shall we tell our master? We cannot save them now. It is your fault." And they menaced the men. But the men answered back:

"How could we tell they would run like that? It was not our fault.

We came to help you, and you say it was our fault." And the man who had spoken to Jesus about the madman cried out suddenly:

"It is the devils. They went into the swine. Did you not see how they left the madman? They talked with the Rabbi, and he gave permission for them to enter into the swine."

"But they were not his swine," cried the herds. "What right had he to drown our swine?"

"They were unclean beasts, and only fit for devils," cried the man. "It is not lawful to keep such beasts. Come, and ask for yourselves." And he brought the herds to where Jesus sat with the poor madman, now soothed and quiet, at his feet. And they told Jesus, and asked him if it were not true that the devils had entered into the swine out of the man; and he questioned them, and when they told how the pigs had rushed down the hillside when they had tried to drive them, he was sad, and said:

"They were afraid. It was the same devil that possessed this man." But the men did not understand.

"It must be so," said one swineherd to the other. "We will go and tell our master. How do we watch against demons? He will surely see that it was not our fault."

By this time a crowd had gathered from the boats and from the countryside, and they stood and watched Jesus and the madman as if they could not believe their eyes.

"Will any man give clothes to the naked?" Jesus asked them, and they ran to find clothes and brought food, which they put before the man. But all the time they were afraid, for the rumour had gone abroad that Jesus had sent the devils into the swine, and they feared the next thing. When the swineherds returned with their master and he saw the madman sitting clothed, he, too, was afraid. And he talked with the crowd, and some of them came forward, and he asked if they might speak, and when Jesus gave them leave, they begged him to go away out of their country, for they had fear of him. And Jesus, looking at them, saw that it was true, for they trembled as they spoke, and he had compassion on them, and said that he would go, and he went down to the boats.

Peter was there, ready to put out, for he had heard the rumour, and knew the people were afraid. And the poor madman came too, and pressed upon Jesus that he might come with him, but Jesus refused him, and told him he must go home.

"You will be better at home," he said; "go to your own people and tell them of all God has done for you, and how he took pity on you," and he told the crowd that they were to care for him.

"They will do him no injury," Peter muttered, as I helped him to push off. "They will be too much afraid that the devils will come back, and, perhaps, enter into their cattle this time. The Master was right to smite iniquity. It was well done to destroy those unclean beasts. It was sin to keep them."

But he said no word to Jesus, and he would not heed when I tried to tell what kind of a devil Jesus had sent out of the madman, and that had entered into the swine.

from Jesus:
A Revolutionary Biography
by John Dominic Crossan

John Dominic Crossan (born 1934) has been a leading member of the Jesus Seminar, an ongoing analysis of the historical Jesus by more than one hundred scholars and other participants. Crossan argues that Jesus stood for social change, and questions the accuracy of the Gospels on many points.

He was an illiterate peasant, but with an oral brilliance that few of those trained in literate and scribal disciplines can ever attain. When today we read his words in fixed and frozen texts we must recognize that the oral memory of his first audiences could have retained, at best, only the striking image, the startling analogy, the forceful conjunction, and, for example, the plot summary of a parable that might have taken an hour or more to tell and perform. I give several examples of what the here-and-now Kingdom of God meant for Jesus, from each of the major genres in which that oral memory preserved, developed, but also created such traditions.

Tearing the Family Apart

If the supreme value for the twentieth-century American imagination is *individualism*, based on economics and property, that for the first-century Mediterranean imagination can be called, to the contrary, *groupism*, based on kinship and gender. And there were really only two groups—

the familial and the political, kinship and politics—to be considered. But we have, precisely against both those groups, biting aphorisms and dialogues from the historical Jesus. There is, first of all, an almost savage attack on family values, and it happens very, very often. Here are four quite different examples. Each has different versions available, but I give only one version for each example. The first one is from the *Gospel of Thomas* 55, the second from Mark 3:31–35, the third from the Q *Gospel* in Luke 11:27–28 but with no Matthean parallel, and the final one from the Q *Gospel* in Luke 12:51–53 rather than in Matthew 10:34–36.

(1) Jesus said, "Whoever does not hate father and mother cannot be a follower of me, and whoever does not hate brothers and sisters . . . will not be worthy of me."

(2) Then his mother and his brothers came; and standing outside, they sent to him and called him. . . . And he replied, "Who are my mother and my brothers?" And looking at those who sat around him, he said, "Here are my mother and my brothers! Whoever does the will of God is my brother and sister and mother."

(3) A woman from the crowd spoke up and said to him, "How fortunate is the womb that bore you, and the breasts that you sucked!" But he said, "How fortunate, rather, are those who listen to God's teaching and observe it!"

(4) "Do you think that I have come to bring peace to the earth? No, I tell you, but rather division! From now on five in one household will be divided, three against two and two against three; they will be divided: father against son and son against father, mother against daughter and daughter against mother, mother-in-law against her daughter-in-law and daughter-in-law against mother-in-law."

• • •

The family is a group to which one is irrevocably assigned, but in those first two units, that given grouping is negated in favor of another one open to all who wish to join it. And the reason those groups are set in stark contrast becomes more clear by the third example. A woman declares Mary blessed because of Jesus, presuming, in splendid Mediterranean fashion, that a woman's greatness derives from mothering a famous son. But that patriarchal chauvinism is negated by Jesus in favor of a blessedness open to anyone who wants it, without distinction of sex or gender, infertility or maternity.

Finally, it is in the last aphorism that the point of Jesus' attack on the family becomes most clear. Imagine the standard Mediterranean family with five members: mother and father, married son with his wife, and unmarried daughter, a nuclear extended family all under one roof. Jesus says he will tear it apart. The usual explanation is that families will become divided as some accept and others refuse faith in Jesus. But notice where and how emphatically the axis of separation is located. It is precisely *between the generations*. But why should faith split along that axis? Why might faith not separate, say, the women from the men or even operate in ways far more random? *The attack has nothing to do with faith but with power.* The attack is on the Mediterranean family's axis of power, which sets father and mother over son, daughter, and daughter-in-law. That helps us to understand all of those examples. The family is society in miniature, the place where we first and most deeply learn how to love and be loved, hate and be hated, help and be helped, abuse and be abused. It is not just a center of domestic serenity; since it involves power, it invites the abuse of power, and it is at that precise point that Jesus attacks it. His ideal group is, contrary to Mediterranean and indeed most human familial reality, an open one equally accessible to all under God. It is the Kingdom of God, and it negates that terrible abuse of power that is power's dark specter and lethal shadow.

Blessed Are (We?) Beggars

Turning from familial to political groupings, it is hard to imagine an aphorism initially more radical but eventually more banal than Jesus' conjunction of blessed poverty and the Kingdom of God. Here are four versions of the same saying, from the *Gospel of Thomas* 54, from the *Q Gospel* in both Luke 6:20 and Matthew 5:3, and from James 2:5, respectively. The first example is in Coptic translation and the last three are in Greek. As you read from first to last you can see the process of normalization at work:

(1) "Blessed are the poor, for yours is the kingdom of heaven."

(2) "Blessed are you who are poor, for yours is the kingdom of God."

(3) "Blessed are the poor in spirit, for theirs is the kingdom of heaven."

(4)Has not God chosen those who are poor in the world to be rich in faith and heirs of the kingdom which he has promised to those who love him?

In the third example, Matthew's *in spirit* diverts interpretation from economic to religious poverty, and James's emphasis on faith and love points toward a promised rather than a present Kingdom of God. But the stark and startling conjunction of blessed poverty and divine Kingdom is still there for all to see in the first two versions. We can no longer tell, of course, whether Jesus meant *the* or *you* or *we* poor.

There is, however, a very serious problem when the Greek word *ptōchos* is translated as "poor" in the last three examples. The Greek word *penēs* means "poor," and *ptōchos* means "destitute." The former describes the status of a peasant family making a bare subsistence living from year to year; the latter indicates the status of such a family pushed, by disease or debt, draught or death, off the land and into destitution and begging. One can see this distinction most clearly in the *Plutus* of Aristophanes, the last play of that great comic dramatist,

produced probably in the Athens of 388 B.C.E. The key section is in
Plutus 535-554, with Chremylus arguing for the advantages of the god
Plutus (or Wealth) and declaring that Penia (or Poverty) and Ptōcheia
(or Destitution) are both the same in any case. Poverty, appearing here
as a goddess, immediately denies her equation with Destitution:

> CHREMYLUS:
> Well, Poverty [penian] and Destitution [ptōcheias], truly the
> two to be sisters we always declare.

> POVERTY:
> It's the beggar [ptōchou] alone who has nothing his own, nor
> even a penny possesses.
> My poor [penētos] man, it's true, has to scrimp and to scrape,
> and his work he must never be slack in;
> There'll be no superfluity found in his cot;
> but then there will nothing be lacking.

The *poor* man has to work hard but has always enough to survive,
while the *beggar* has nothing at all. Jesus, in other words, did not
declare blessed the poor, a class that included, for all practical purposes, the entire peasantry; rather, he declared blessed the destitute—
for example, the beggars.

Now, what on earth does that mean, especially if one does not spir-
itualize it away, as Matthew immediately did, into "poor [or destitute]
in spirit"—that is, the spiritually humble or religiously obedient? Did
Jesus really think that bums and beggars were actually blessed by God,
as if all the destitute were nice people and all the aristocrats corre-
spondingly evil? Is this some sort of naive or romantic delusion about
the charms of destitution? If, however, we think not just of personal or
individual evil but of social, structural, or systemic injustice—that is, of
precisely the imperial situation in which Jesus and his fellow peasants
found themselves—then the saying becomes literally, terribly, and permanently true. In any situation of oppression, especially in those

oblique, indirect, and systemic ones where injustice wears a mask of normalcy or even of necessity, the only ones who are innocent or blessed are those squeezed out deliberately as human junk from the system's own evil operations. A contemporary equivalent: only the homeless are innocent. That is a terrifying aphorism against society because, like the aphorisms against the family, it focuses not just on personal or individual abuse of power but on such abuse in its systemic or structural possibilities—and there, in contrast to the former level, none of our hands are innocent or our consciences particularly clear.

If It Is a Girl, Cast It Out

Another striking conjunction is that between infant children and divine Kingdom. Once again we can move easily from aphorism to dialogue as the tradition creates situations and settings for sayings it has retained in memory. And, once again, earliest oral memory would not have been in the form of exact syntactical arrangements recalling precisely what Jesus saw or said, but rather of a startling combination, children/Kingdom, which could then be articulated as needed in various forms and versions. Although there are four independent versions of that conjunction, I give only one, for the sake of brevity. From Mark 10:13–16:

> People were bringing little children to him in order that he might touch them; and the disciples spoke sternly to them. But when Jesus saw this, he was indignant and said to them, "Let the little children come to me; do not stop them; for it is to such as these that the kingdom of God belongs. *Truly I tell you, whoever does not receive the kingdom of God as a little child will never enter it.*" And he took them up in his arms, laid his hands on them, and blessed them.

What was, first of all, the immediate connotation of children or infants to the ancient Mediterranean as distinct from the modern American mind? Read this ancient papyrus letter, discovered around the turn of the century on the west bank of the Nile about 120 miles south of

Cairo in the excavated rubbish dumps of ancient Oxyrhynchus, the modern El Bahnasa. The worker Hilarion writes to his wife, Alis, addressed in Egyptian fashion as sister, on 18 June in the year 1 B.C.E. From the Oxyrhynchus Papyri 4.744:

> Hilarion to his sister Alis many greetings, likewise to my lady Berous [his mother-in-law?] and to Apollonarion [their first and male child]. Know that we are even yet in Alexandria. Do not worry if they all come back [except me] and I remain in Alexandria. I urge and entreat you, be concerned about the child [Apollonarion] and if I should receive my wages soon, I will send them up to you. If by chance you bear a son, if it is a boy, let it be, if it is a girl, cast it out [to die]. You have said to Aphrodisias, "Do not forget me." How can I forget you? Therefore I urge you not to worry. 29 [year] of Caesar [Augustus], Payni [month] 23 [day].

Hilarion and some companions had left their home at Oxyrhynchus and traveled north to work in Alexandria. His wife, Alis, pregnant with their second child, having heard nothing nor received anything from him, transmitted her concern through Aphrodisias, who was also traveling to the capital. The letter is Hilarion's response to her concern, and, tender to his pregnant wife but terrible to his unborn daughter, it shows us with stark clarity what an infant meant in the Mediterranean. It was quite literally a nobody unless its father accepted it as a member of the family rather than exposing it in the gutter or rubbish dump to die of abandonment or to be taken up by another and reared as a slave. To be like an infant child is interpreted by Matthew 18:1–4 as meaning to have appropriate humility, by the *Gospel of Thomas* 22 as meaning to practice sexual asceticism, and by John 3:1–10 as meaning to have recently received baptism. Those three readings avoid the horrifying meaning of a child as a nothing, a nobody, a nonperson in the Mediterranean world of paternal power, absolute in its acceptance or rejection of the newly born infant.

In giving Mark's version above I italicized the core aphorism whose basic conjunction of children/Kingdom is all that certainly came from Jesus. Concentrate, for a moment, on the framing situation created by Mark himself. This indicates the situation created not from the historical Jesus but from the historical Mark. Notice those framing words: *touch, took in his arms, blessed, laid hands on.* Those are the official bodily actions of a father designating a newly born infant for life rather than death, for accepting it into his family rather than casting it out with the garbage. And the disciples do not want Jesus to act in this positive and accepting way. There must, therefore, have been a debate within the Markan community on whether it should adopt such abandoned infants, and Mark has Jesus say yes even though other authorities—the disciples themselves—say no. Once again we are forced to face ancient Mediterranean realities, and Mark's later application helps us to see more clearly what was there from Jesus in the beginning: that a Kingdom of Children is a Kingdom of Nobodies.

Who Needs a Mustard Plant?

There is another rather startling conjunction, but in a parable rather than in an aphorism or dialogue—the conjunction between the mustard seed and the Kingdom. The parable is, by the way, the only one attributed to Jesus that has triple independent attestation. I give only one version, from Mark 4:30–32:

> And he said, "With what can we compare the kingdom of God, or what parable shall we use for it? It is like a grain of mustard seed, which, when sown upon the ground, is the smallest of all the seeds on earth; yet when it is sown it grows up and becomes the greatest of all shrubs, and puts forth large branches, so that the birds of the air can make nests in its shade."

Once again, a word about Mediterranean mustard plants and nesting birds helps us to understand the startling nature of that conjunction.

The Roman author Pliny the Elder, who was born in 23 C.E. and died when scientific curiosity brought him too close to an erupting Vesuvius in 79 C.E., wrote about the mustard plant in his encyclopedic Natural History 19.170–171:

> Mustard . . . with its pungent taste and fiery effect is extremely beneficial for the health. It grows entirely wild, though it is improved by being transplanted; but on the other hand when it has once been sown it is scarcely possible to get the place free of it, as the seed when it falls germinates at once.

There is, in other words, a distinction between the wild mustard and its domesticated counterpart, but even when one deliberately cultivates the latter for its medicinal or culinary properties, there is an ever-present danger that it will destroy the garden. The mustard plant is dangerous even when domesticated in the garden, and is deadly when growing wild in the grain fields. And those nesting birds, which may strike us as charming, represented to ancient farmers a permanent danger to the seed and the grain. The point, in other words, is not just that the mustard plant starts as a proverbially small seed and grows into a shrub of three, four, or even more feet in height. It is that it tends to take over where it is not wanted, that it tends to get out of control, and that it tends to attract birds within cultivated areas, where they are not particularly desired. And that, said Jesus, was what the Kingdom was like. Like a pungent shrub with dangerous take-over properties. Something you would want only in small and carefully controlled doses—if you could control it. It is a startling metaphor, but it would be interpreted quite differently by those, on the one hand, concerned about their fields, their crops, and their harvests, and by those, on the other, for whom fields, crops, and harvest were always the property of others.

Open Commensality
Let that title stand unexplained for a moment. Its meaning and necessity

will soon become clear, At the end of the preceding chapter, a comparison was made between John and Jesus in terms of fasting and feasting. The contrast was made both in neutral terms by Jesus himself and in very inimical terms by opponents: John fasted and they called him demonic; Jesus ate and drank and they said he was "a glutton and a drunkard, a friend of tax collectors and sinners." It is obvious why John, as an apocalyptic ascetic, was fasting, but what was Jesus doing? It is not enough to say that those opponents are simply accusing him of social deviancy through nasty name-calling. That is, of course, quite true, but why precisely those names rather than any of the others easily available?

Here is another parable of Jesus, which helps answer that question and will serve to ground all of those aphorisms, dialogues, and parables concerning the Kingdom of God. It is found in the Q *Gospel*, but with widely divergent versions in Matthew 22:1–13 and Luke 14:15–24. It is also found in the *Gospel of Thomas* 64, as follows:

> Jesus said, "A person was receiving guests. When he had prepared the dinner, he sent his servant to invite the guests. The servant went to the frst and said to that one, 'My master invites you.' That person said, 'Some merchants owe me money; they are coming to me tonight, I must go and give them instructions. Please excuse me from dinner.' The servant went to another and said to that one, 'My master has invited you.' That person said to the servant, 'I have bought a house and I have been called away for a day. I shall have no time.' The servant went to another and said to that one, 'My master invites you.' That person said to the servant, 'My friend is to be married and I am to arrange the banquet. I shall not be able to come. Please excuse me from dinner.' The servant went to another and said to that one, 'My master invites you.' That person said to the servant, 'I have bought an estate and I am going to collect the rent. I shall not be able to come. Please excuse me.' The servant returned and said to his master, 'The people whom you invited to

dinner have asked to be excused.' The master said to his servant, 'Go out on the streets and *bring back whomever you find
to have dinner.'* Buyers and merchants [will] not enter the
places of my father."

This is one of those rare cases where the Gospel of Thomas interprets
a parable. It appends, as commentary: "Buyers and merchants [will]
not enter the places of my father." Jesus, not the host, speaks that judgment. For my present purpose, I leave aside that interpretation to focus
closely on the replacement guests, the reference to which I have italicized above. Compare how they are described by Jesus in Luke
14:21b–23 and in Matthew 22:9–10, respectively:

> (1) "'Go out quickly to the streets and lanes of the city, and
> bring in the poor and maimed and blind and lame.' And the
> servant said, 'Sir, what you commanded has been done, and
> still there is room.' And the master said to the servant, 'Go
> out to the highways and hedges, and *compel people to come
> in*, that my house may be filled.' "

> (2) "'Go therefore to the thoroughfares, and invite to the
> marriage feast *as many as you find.'* And those servants went
> out into the streets and gathered all whom they found, both
> bad and good; so the wedding hall was filled with guests."

In both those cases, separate interpretations have divergently specified
the replacement guests. Luke mentions the outcasts and Matthew mentions the good and the bad, but the italicized phrases indicate the more
original and unspecified command to bring in whomever you can find.

I leave aside, therefore, individual interpretations inserted around or
within the three texts to underline the common structural plot dis-
cernible behind them all. It tells the story of a person who gives a presumably unannounced feast, sends a servant to invite friends, but finds
by late in the day that each has a quite valid and very politely expressed

excuse. The result is a dinner ready and a room empty. The host replaces the absent guests with anyone off the streets, But if one actually brought in *anyone off the street*, one could, in such a situation, have classes, sexes, and ranks all mixed up together. Anyone could be reclining next to anyone else, female next to male, free next to slave, socially high next to socially low, and ritually pure next to ritually impure. And a short detour through the cross-cultural anthropology of food and eating underlines what a social nightmare that would be.

Think, for a moment, if beggars came to your door, of the difference between giving them some food to go, of inviting them into your kitchen for a meal, of bringing them into the dining room to eat in the evening with your family, or of having them come back on Saturday night for supper with a group of your friends. Think, again, if you were a large company's CEO, of the difference between a cocktail party in the office for all the employees, a restaurant lunch for all the middle managers, or a private dinner party for your vice presidents in your own home. Those events are not just ones of eating together, of simple table fellowship, but are what anthropologists call *commensality*—from *mensa*, the Latin word for "table." *It means the rules of tabling and eating as miniature models for the rules of association and socialization.* It means table fellowship as a map of economic discrimination, social hierarchy, and political differentiation. This is how Peter Farb and George Armelagos summarized commensality at the beginning and end of their book on the anthropology of eating:

> In all societies, both simple and complex, eating is the primary way of initiating and maintaining human relationships. . . . Once the anthropologist finds out where, when, and with whom the food is eaten, just about everything else can be inferred about the relations among the society's members. . . . To know what, where, how, when, and with whom people eat is to know the character of their society.*

* Peter Farb and George Armelagos, *Consuming Passions: The Anthropology of Eating* (Boston: Houghton Mifflin, 1980), pages 4 and 211.

Similarly, Lee Edward Klosinski reviewed the significant cross-cultural anthropological and sociological literature on food and eating and concluded:

> Sharing food is a transaction which involves a series of mutual obligations and which initiates an interconnected complex of mutuality and reciprocity. Also, the ability of food to symbolize these relationships, as well as to define group boundaries, surfaced as one of its unique properties. . . . Food exchanges are basic to human interaction. Implicit in them is a series of obligations to give, receive and repay. These transactions involve individuals in matrices of social reciprocity, mutuality and obligation. Also, food exchanges are able to act as symbols of human interaction. Eating is a behavior which symbolizes feelings and relationships, mediates social status and power, and expresses the boundaries of group identity.[*]

What Jesus' parable advocates, therefore, is an open commensality, an eating together without using table as a miniature map of society's vertical discriminations and lateral separations. The social challenge of such equal or egalitarian commensality is the parable's most fundamental danger and most radical threat. It is only a story, of course, but it is one that focuses its egalitarian challenge on society's miniature mirror, the table, as the place where bodies meet to eat. Since, moreover, Jesus lived out his own parable, the almost predictable counteraccusation to such open commensality would be immediate: Jesus is a glutton, a drunkard, and a friend of tax collectors and sinners. He makes, in other words, no appropriate distinctions and discriminations. And since women were present, especially unmarried women, the accusation would be that Jesus

---

[*] Lee Edward Klosinksi, *The Meals in Mark* (Ann Arbor, MI: University Microfilms, 1988), pages 56–58.

eats with whores, the standard epithet of denigration for any female outside appropriate male control. All of those terms—tax collectors, sinners, whores—are in this case derogatory terms for those with whom, in the opinion of the name callers, open and free association should be avoided.

The Kingdom of God as a process of open commensality, of a nondiscriminating table depicting in miniature a nondiscriminating society, clashes fundamentally with honor and shame, those basic values of ancient Mediterranean culture and society. Most of American society in the twentieth century is used to *individualism*, with guilt and innocence as sanctions, rather than to *groupism*, with honor and shame as sanctions. Here is a description of Mediterranean honor and shame, from a 1965 cross-cultural anthology; Pierre Bourdieu is speaking on the basis of his field work among the Berber tribesmen of Algerian Kabylia in the late fifties:

> The point of honour is the basis of the moral code of an individual who sees himself always through the eyes of others, who has need of others for his existence, because the image he has of himself is indistinguishable from that presented to him by other people. . . . Respectability, the reverse of shame, is the characteristic of a person who needs other people in order to grasp his own identity and whose conscience is a kind of interiorization of others, since these fulfil for him the role of witness and judge. . . . He who has lost his honour no longer exists. He ceases to exist for other people, and at the same time he ceases to exist for himself. *

The key phrase here is through the eyes of others, and the more we understand that process, the more radically challenging Jesus'

---

*Pierre Bourdieu, "The Sentiment of Honour in Kabyle Society," in *Honour and Shame: The Values of Mediterranean Society*, ed. John G. Peristiany (Chicago: Univ. of Chicago Press, 1966; Midway Reprints, 1974), pages 211–212.

Kingdom of God starts to appear. We might see Jesus' message and program as quaintly eccentric or charmingly iconoclastic (at least at a safe distance), but for those who take their very identity from the eyes of their peers, the idea of eating together and living together without any distinctions, differences, discriminations, or hierarchies is close to the irrational and the absurd. And the one who advocates or does it is close to the deviant and the perverted. He has no honor. He has no shame.

Radical Egalitarianism

Open commensality is the symbol and embodiment of radical egalitarianism, of an absolute equality of people that denies the validity of any discrimination between them and negates the necessity of any hierarchy among them. To all of this there is an obvious objection: you are just speaking of contemporary democracy and anachronistically retrojecting that back into the time and onto the lips of Jesus. I look, in reply and defense, both to general anthropology and to specific history during the first century.

Those who, like peasants, live with a boot on their neck can easily envision two different dreams. One is quick revenge—a world in which they might get in turn to put their boots on those other necks. Another is reciprocal justice—a world in which there would never again be any boots on any necks. Thus, for example, the anthropologist James C. Scott, moving from Europe to Southeast Asia, notes the popular tradition's common reaction to such disparate elite traditions as Christianity, Buddhism, and Islam, and argues very persuasively that peasant culture and religion are actually an anticulture, criticizing alike both the religious and political elites that oppress it. It is, in fact, a reactive inversion of the pattern of exploitation common to the peasantry *as such*:

> The radical vision to which I refer is strikingly uniform despite the enormous variations in peasant cultures and the different great traditions of which they partake. . . . At the risk of over generalizing, it is possible to describe some common

features of this reflexive symbolism. It nearly always implies
a society of brotherhood in which there will be no rich and
poor, in which no distinctions of rank and status (save
those between believers and non-believers) will exist.
Where religious institutions are experienced as justifying
inequities, the abolition of rank and status may well
include the elimination of religious hierarchy in favor of
communities of equal believers. Property is typically,
though not always, to be held in common and shared. All
unjust claims to taxes, rents, and tribute are to be nullified.
The envisioned utopia may also include a self-yielding and
abundant nature as well as a radically transformed human
nature in which greed, envy, and hatred will disappear.
While the earthly utopia is thus an anticipation of the
future, it often harks back to a mythic Eden from which
mankind has fallen away.*

That is the ancient peasant dream of radical egalitarianism. It does not
deny the other dream, that of brutal revenge, but neither does that latter
negate the former's eternal thirst for reciprocity, equality, and justice.

One instance from the first century shows both those dreams coming
together in the last days of the doomed Temple during the First Roman-
Jewish War. As Vespasian's forces moved steadily southward and tightened the noose around Jerusalem in the fall of 67 and winter of 68 C.E.,
groups of peasant rebels under bandit leaders were forced repeatedly
into the capital for refuge. They became known, collectively or in coali-
tion, as the Zealots, and one of their first actions was to install a new
High Priest. According to ancient tradition, the High Priest was chosen
from the family of Zadok, as had been true since at least the time of
Solomon. But when, in the second century B.C.E., the Jewish dynasty of
the Hasmoneans wrested control of their country from the Syrians, they
had simply appointed themselves High Priests. And thereafter, from

---

* James C. Scott, "Protest and Profanation: Agrarian Revolt and the Little Tradition," *Theory and Society* 4 (1977): 225–226.

Herod the Great to the outbreak of the revolt against Rome, the High Priests were selected from four families, likewise not of legitimate Zadokite origins. What the Zealots did was return to the legitimate high-priestly line, but within it they elected by lot rather than by choice. Josephus, telling the story in *Antiquities* 4.147–207, as an aristocratic priest is almost inarticulate with anger at what he considers an impious mockery. Here is the key section, in 155–156:

> They accordingly summoned one of the high-priestly clans, called Eniachin, and cast lots for a high priest. By chance the lot fell to one who proved a signal illustration of their depravity; he was an individual named Phanni, son of Samuel, of the village of Aphthia, a man who not only was not descended from high priests, but was such a clown that he scarcely knew what the high priesthood meant. At any rate they dragged their reluctant victim out of the country and, dressing him up for his assumed part, as on the stage, put the sacred vestments upon him and instructed him how to act in keeping with the occasion.

Lottery is what egalitarianism looks like in practice. If all members of some group are eligible for office, then the only fair human way to decide is by lot, leaving the choice up to God. That was how Saul, the first Jewish king, was elected from "all the tribes of Israel," according to 1 Samuel 10:21. And that was how the early Christians chose a replacement for the traitor apostle Judas from among "the men who have accompanied us" since the beginning, according to Acts of the Apostles 1:21–26. Obviously, of course, as in the implicit and presumed male exclusivity of the former case and the explicit and very deliberate male exclusivity of the latter one, discriminations can be present even in a lottery. They are there, too, in electing a High Priest only from a certain family. But granting that, a lottery attempts to deal equally among all candidates accepted as appropriate within a given context. Despite all of Josephus's tendentious rhetoric, what the Zealots did is quite clear and consistent. They restored the ancient Zadokite line according to selection by lot, and one presumes, of course, that such was to be the future mode of selection as well. Furthermore, this was probably more than just a new or legitimate High Priest. It was also, at least as far as the Zealots were concerned, a new and legitimate government of the city and the country. For those peasants, then, the idea of egalitarianism, even if not in its most radical form, was quite understandable and practicable.

Radical egalitarianism is not contemporary democracy. In the United States, for example, every appropriate person has a vote *in electing* the president, but although every appropriate person has also a legitimate right *to be* president, we are not yet ready for a national lottery instead of a presidential campaign. The open commensality and radical egalitarianism of Jesus' Kingdom of God are more terrifying than anything we have ever imagined, and even if we can never accept it, we should not explain it away as something else. I conclude, then, by putting Jesus' vision and program back into the matrix from which it sprang, the ancient and universal peasant dream of a just and equal world. These are the words of an unnamed peasant woman from Piana dei Greci, in the province of Palermo, Sicily, speaking to a northern Italian journalist during an 1893 peasant uprising:

> We want everybody to work, as we work. There should no longer be either rich or poor. All should have bread for themselves and for their children. We should all be equal. To have five small children and only one little room, where we have to eat and sleep and do everything, while so many lords have ten or twelve rooms, entire palaces. . . . It will be enough to put all in common and to share with justice what is produced.*

---

* Cited in Eric J. Hobsbawm, *Primitive Rebels: Studies in Archaic Forms of Social Movement in the 19th and 20th Centuries* (New York: Norton, 1965), page 183.

from One Jesus, Many Christs
by Gregory J. Riley

Christian tradition offers Jesus' story as the ful-fillment of Judaic prophecy. Gregory J. Riley (born 1947) sees Jesus as a successor to myth-ical Greek heroes.

THE EDUCATIONAL SYSTEM OF ANTIQUITY

The Gospels are books written in Greek. Viewed from a scholar's perspective, they are literary products of a certain merit, though not of the first rank. St. Jerome was embarrassed by some of the poor writing found in various parts of the New Testament. The professional scribes of the church who copied these manuscripts generation after generation regularly corrected infelicities of grammar and syntax, eventually producing a nearly flawless Greek text. Nevertheless, the grammar and modes of expression of the New Testament Gospel writers are in the main acceptable according to the literary standards of the common language, the *koinê* Greek, as it is called, of their day. The point of these observations is that the authors are educated people, not experts or professional writers, but educated, and that fact has rather profound implications.

Very few people in antiquity could read or write. Writing as we know it was first used in the ancient Near East about 3000 B.C., and people had been living without it in Egypt and Mesopotamia for hundreds of thousands of years. All of the basic structures and duties of civilization, even empires, were wholly in place and had been functioning completely without writing from time immemorial. Writing began, presumably, as an aid to trade and business, and then was later applied to government and taxation and religious establishments. If one were not in some complex business that required it, or a professional scribe, there was no reason to learn to write. An analogy might be something like being a professional electrician today. Most people need to know very little about installing or repairing electrical equipment or services, because they rely on professional electricians to perform this specialized function in society. The vast majority of people in the Mediterranean area and Europe functioned perfectly normally as farmers or bakers or homemakers without the ability to read or write right up to the modern era.

Writing was expensive. The list of surviving materials upon which people wrote is not long: papyrus sheets, animal skins, wooden tablets covered with wax, copper and lead sheets, stone slabs, and ostraca (pieces of broken pottery). Only the ostraca were free, but one could write only a few words on them. All the others were expensive and beyond the reach of most people. Papyrus was the paper of the ancient world—we even get our modern word "paper" from the name. The papyrus plant was grown and sheets manufactured from its pith in Egypt; from there it was exported to other areas. In Egypt, at the time the apostle Paul was writing (A.D. 50s), a single sheet of papyrus cost about two-thirds the daily wage of an unskilled laborer and about one-third that of a skilled workman. Only the relatively wealthy could afford it.

Education was also expensive, especially at levels beyond the basic skills of reading and writing. There was no system of state-supported education for basic literacy; parents had to pay for their own children's schooling. The theory of universal education had been voiced only a handful of times by a few philosophers and never put into practice.

Schools themselves were not to be found everywhere: cities had them, but most villages did not. The majority of people lived in villages, and *rusticus* meant "uneducated" as well as "villager." A popular saying for such people was "can't read, can't swim" (Plato *Laws* 3.689d). In villages, people often lived by barter, without money, and at a subsistence level. If they did send their sons to school for some perceived economic advantage, it would often be only to the *litterator,* the teacher of "letters," that is, an instructor of basic reading and writing. Very few but the wealthy and those who served the rich could afford to send their children to the *grammaticus* and then the *rhetor,* the instructors of the next levels of schooling, who taught literature and composition, and then declamation worthy of the courts, public speaking, and high office.

The texts for all three levels, however, were the great epics and poets, almost always Homer and the tragedians in Greek; in Latin, similar heroic tales were used, especially Virgil's epic of the founding of Rome, the *Aeneid.* There were no children's primers of easy stories, no books of the "See Spot run!" variety. Children were taught the alphabet, how to say and sound the letters and then how to write them. Then they were sent directly to the texts, to learn by reciting, memorizing, and copying the works of Homer, Hesiod, and the great tragic poets (Aeschylus, Sophocles, Euripides). So Protagoras, arguing with Socrates that virtue may be taught, tells us:

> Whenever [children] have learned their letters and are ready
> to understand the written word . . . [their teachers] set the
> works of good poets before them on their desks to read and
> make them learn them by heart. (Plato *Protagoras* 325e)

A third-century B.C. collection of school texts in Egypt shows that students were taught the individual letters, then the writing of single words, and then Homer; there were no intermediate "easy" texts, in fact no other texts at all. And Cicero, writing the *Tusculan Disputations* about 45 B.C. in Italy, in a discussion of the works of the poets, tells us that "We indeed, taught obviously by Greece, both read and learn by heart these (poets) from boyhood, and consider this to be liberal education and doctrine" (2.41, GJR). On the walls of Pompeii, buried and therefore preserved by the volcanic eruption of Mount Vesuvius in A.D. 79, one finds a large collection of graffiti, some scurrilous, some announcing this or that event of sale. But among them are many examples of *Arma virumque cano* ("Of arms and men I sing") and *Conticuere* ("They were silent"), the first line of Book I and the first word of Book II, respectively, of the *Aeneid*. This is clearly evidence of schoolchildren scrawling what they were learning to write. Education in the Greco-Roman world was based in the classics of Greek heroic literature and their offspring in Latin. If one was educated at all, no matter what the level of competence, one was educated on Homer and the heroes.

This educational philosophy was deeply embedded in the ancient mentality, that such literature formed one's character according to the revered models of the past. The quotation of Protagoras above continues by describing the moral purpose of such "poems, in which are many admonitions, and many tales, praises, and panegyrics of ancient good men, so that the child may imitate them eagerly and desire to be such a person" (Plato *Protagorus* 326a, GJR). Again, at a symposium, Socrates and others are asked to declare what useful knowledge each possesses. Niceratus, one of the banqueters, replies when it is his turn, "My father was anxious to see me develop into a good man, and as a means to this end he compelled me to memorize all of Homer" (Xenophon *Symposium* 3.6). The purpose of such an education was that one should "develop into a good man." Lucian in the second century A.D. tells us that schoolmasters gave a student "books that openly or by allegory teach him who was a great hero, who was a lover of justice and purity" (Lucian *Amores* 45). Schools enforced the worldview, the morals, and ethical ideals admired and imitated by the ancients essentially by requiring every student to learn from the same narrow selection of revered heroic texts.

There was no "popular" literature—no cheap novels, no magazines, no newspapers, no gothic romances. No works were written specifically for the mass audience—there was no publishing industry and most people were illiterate. Texts were hand copied, usually by slaves, and while sold occasionally for profit in the marketplace, the normal means of dissemination was by gift to friends. The world of necessary information was kept running by heralds, town criers who announced to all who could hear the dictates of magistrates. For judges, government officials, and political officeholders, the number of heralds employed far exceeded the number of scribes: most business was conducted and messages sent orally. Most towns had a nucleus of literate men who served as intermediaries when it was necessary, but the norm was the herald and the culture at large was based on oral communication and oral literature.

Among the very rich, among those who could afford to use writing materials extensively, there was a culture of letter exchange, poetry, and speeches on philosophy and ethics. But even this literature draws its inspiration from Homer and the classics. Pliny, for example, Roman governor of northern Turkey about A.D. 110–12, although writing in Latin, seasons his formal letters with quotations in Greek from Homer as one might today use quotations from the Bible, to offer inspired comfort, base a piece of advice on higher authority, or illustrate a truth. He clearly assumes the recipient will understand and recognize their authority.

Readings and performances by professional reciters of epic, the rhapsodes, were common. The illiterate masses heard and learned the heroic epics by this means. Competitions for skill in such recitations were held in many cities, even at the major athletic games. In his conversation with such a rhapsode, Ion by name, Socrates demonstrates that this great skill is really a result of divine inspiration. He describes the typical scene of a rhapsode giving a public recitation:

> There he is, at a sacrifice or festival, got up in his holiday attire, adorned with golden chaplets, and he weeps, though he has lost nothing of his finery. Or he recoils with fear, standing in the presence of more than twenty thousand

friendly people, though nobody is stripping him or doing him damage. (Plato *Ion* 535d)

Here the audience is twenty thousand people. Theaters held from five to thirty thousand people depending on the wealth of the city; Socrates is using a typical number to describe a common situation. Strabo, a Greek geographer (d. ca. A.D. 21), compares philosophy and heroic poetry, stating that "Philosophy is for the few, but poetry is more useful for the common people and is able to fill the theaters, but indeed especially that of Homer" (I.2.8, GJR). Public recitation of such stories seems to have been immensely popular. Public reading was a sign of high culture and a common form of entertainment at the symposia of the rich. Cicero even mentions with approval an old custom according to which dinner guests themselves "used to compose songs of the praises of famous men" (*Brutus* 19.75).

Education in Greek was based on Homer and the tragic poets from before the time of Socrates (d. 399 B.C.) to long after the reign of Constantine (d. A.D. 337) and into the Christian era of the Roman Empire. Even near the end of this period, Christians still did not develop their own curriculum or texts, but continued to use the same methods and system that had been in place for nearly a thousand years. Highly educated bishops and churchmen defended Greek literature as valuable and necessary preparation for service to the church; Basil (St. Basil "the Great," ca. 330–379) calls all of Homer's poetry a "high tribute to virtue" (*To Young Men, or How They Might Profit from Greek Literature* 5.6). There is no question that those who wrote the Gospels of the New Testament received the same education as other learned men of their culture. If one could read or write at all in Greek or Latin, one had learned to do so by reading and memorizing and copying the heroic literature. Thus both the writers of the Gospels and their readers knew what proper literature was supposed to be, what its ideals were, what its main characters were supposed to teach, and how its story line was to run—they expected a work like the story of Jesus to be the story of a hero.

● ● ●

The Story of Jesus and the Story of the Hero

One of the more interesting aspects of the preaching and teaching of the gospel was that the story of the life of Jesus was compressed into a bare outline containing very few elements at some time quite soon after the founding of the Church. The earliest writer in the New Testament is the apostle Paul, and the story apparently was already in outline form before he became a Christian within a decade of the death of Jesus (ca. A.D. 30); at least he says that he himself was taught it in this form. In a Letter to the Corinthian Church he states:

> For I handed on to you as of first importance what I in turn
>> had received:
>> that Christ died for our sins in accordance with the
>> scriptures,
>> and that he was buried,
>> and that he was raised on the third day in accordance
>> with the scriptures,
>> and that he appeared to Cephas, then to the twelve.
>> (1 Cor. 15:3–5)

The passage goes on to relate the postresurrection appearances to many others and finally to Paul himself. The outline has a poetic structure and was probably developed as a catechism for new Christians, one of whom eventually was Paul. He in turn taught it to the Corinthians early in his ministry among them. The written Gospels are rather full statements, including accounts of Jesus' birth, baptism, the many miracles and teachings, and especially the events leading up to and including his crucifixion and resurrection. Yet in the confessional form of the outline, all of this material is absent, though much of it must have been known. In the formula in 1 Corinthians 15, only the bare statement of four events is present.

Later in the history of the Church we find a venerable baptismal creed of the church at Rome, known as the Old Roman Creed, that contains a similar type of outline. It was used at least as early as the second half of the second century and shows a similar but not identical listing of bare events, this time numbering six. It has a triadic structure declaring faith in Father, Son, and Holy Spirit, as do all such baptismal creeds, taking their form from the command of the risen Christ in Matthew 28:19, "baptizing them in the name of the Father and of the Son and of the Holy Spirit." Only the first two parts are given here:

> I believe in God the Father the almighty
> and in Christ Jesus his only son, our Lord,
>> who was born of the Holy Spirit and Mary the virgin,
>> who was crucified under Pontius Pilate and buried;
>> he rose on the third day from [among] the dead;
>> he ascended into the heavens;
>> he sits at the right hand of the Father,
>> from where he will come to judge the living and the dead.

Much later in the history of the Church, in the time of Constantine, we find a similar simple outline as a central part of the Creed of Nicaea, drafted in 325, and the Creed of Constantinople of 381, although in these later creeds the outline is expanded with material that arose in the controversies over the nature of Christ. The point to observe is that this simple outline, the earliest catechism that we know of and the core of the great creeds of the Church, is the outline of the career of a hero.

Justin Martyr, in the middle of the second century, as noted in an earlier chapter, states just that in his defense of the faith (his *First Apology,* or "Speech for the Defense") written to emperor Antoninus Pius and his adoptive sons Marcus Aurelius and Lucius Verus. Justin was born a pagan (ca. A.D. 100) in Samaria and had studied all the major philosophies of his day. He wore the distinctive mantle of the professional philosopher to the day he was martyred (ca. 165). He was highly educated and, like many educated Christians, knew thoroughly and valued the poets and philosophers of Greek literature. Look again at the passage and see the outline of the life of Jesus:

• • •

> In saying that the Word, who is the first offspring of God,
>> was born for us without sexual union as Jesus Christ our
>>> teacher,
>> and that he was crucified and died,
>> and after rising again
>> ascended into heaven,
> we introduce nothing new beyond those whom you call
>> sons of Zeus. (*1 Apologia* 21)

Here is the same basic type of outline, not identical with either of the others but clearly descriptive of the career of Jesus. Justin is writing to the pagan emperor and knows that the emperor will quite easily recognize it as the kind of story he had heard since childhood. That would also have been true if the emperor had read Paul's catechism from 1 Corinthians 15, although he might have wondered to what "according to the scriptures" referred. He would have had no difficulty at all with the Old Roman Creed except for the final reference to the return "to judge the living and the dead"; he may have wondered why Jesus was replacing the older Greek heroes who already held the position of judges of the dead. Justin knew quite well of the apocalyptic return of Christ, as he makes clear elsewhere in the treatise, and knows that it is here that the stories of the heroes and that of Jesus begin to part company, so he leaves it out. At this point he wants to show the similarity of the Christian story to those of the "sons of Zeus."

Justin goes on to list a series of gods, heroes, and humans with differing relationships to the outline and to Zeus, all similar in ways to Jesus:

> Hermes, the interpreting Word and teacher of all; Asclepius, who was also a healer and after being struck by lightning ascended into heaven, as did Dionysus, who was torn in pieces; Heracles, who to escape his torment threw himself into the fire; the Dioscuri, born of Leda, and Perseus of

Danaë, and Bellerophon, who, though of human origin, rode on the horse Pegasus. Need I mention Ariadne and those who like her are said to have been placed among the stars? And what of your deceased emperors, whom you regularly think worthy of being raised to immortality, introducing a witness who swears that he saw the cremated Caesar ascending into heaven from the funeral pyre?

(*1 Apologia* 21)

We learn from his list how people of the time heard the aspects of the life of Jesus as similar to and in accord with those of the heroes and gods of their culture. Justin calls Hermes the "interpreting Word" and later the "announcing Word from God" (*1 Apologia* 22), because Hermes as the messenger of Zeus was by allegorical interpretation the Word of the invisible and unknown God of the universe, who makes him known to humans. This accords with the Christian claim that Jesus is the Word of God who makes God known: "No one has ever seen God; the only begotten God [Jesus] . . . has explained him" (John 1:18, GJR). So Jesus stands in the same relationship to God as did Hermes for pagans.

Asclepius, actually a grandson of Zeus, was the hero who became the patron god of healing. A bit later in his discussion Justin writes, "When we say that [Jesus] healed the lame, the paralytic, and those born blind, and raised the dead, we seem to be talking about things like those said to have been done by Asclepius" (*1 Apologia* 22). Dionysus, son of Zeus by Semele, also ascended to heaven "after being torn in pieces" by the Titans in the Orphic version of his story; he was a hero elevated to the status of Olympian god, the god of inspiration. Heracles, son of Zeus by Alcmena, at the end of his life put on a poisoned robe and was burned with unendurable pain. He ordered a huge funeral pyre to be lit and "to escape his torments he threw himself into the fire." He was worshiped everywhere in the Mediterranean as both hero and god; the mortal part of him was burned away in the fire and he ascended to heaven. Asclepius, Dionysus, and Heracles, prior to their ascents to heaven, all died rather violently. Justin says later, "If someone objects that [Jesus] was crucified, this is in common with the sons of Zeus, as you call them, who suffered as previously listed" (*1 Apologia* 22).

The Dioscuri were the twin brothers Castor and Pollux, who were great adventurers and went on the voyage of the Argonauts; at death they were placed in heaven among the stars as the constellation Gemini. Justin lists Perseus because he, like many others, was born of a virgin mother, Danaë. Bellerophon makes Justin's list because he "rode on the horse Pegasus," which brought him (almost) to heaven. Bellerophon in his stories did prove himself a hero in exploits and suffering; in his final ride on Pegasus he attempted to fly into heaven, but was thrown off and fell back to earth for this act of *hubris*. Justin says that Ariadne was "placed among the stars," but in fact it was the wreath given to the bride Ariadne by Dionysus, her husband, that was placed among the stars as the constellation Corona. Others like her who actually made it themselves were the Seven Sisters, who are the constellation Pleiades, and Orion, their would-be lover.

The issue that Justin is arguing with the emperor is that Rome should stop persecuting the Christians because they are saying nothing essentially different about Jesus the "Son of God" from what the Greek and Roman poets had said about their "sons of the gods." He writes, "Though we say the same as do the Greeks, we only are hated because of the name of Christ" (*1 Apologia* 24). The outline of the career of Jesus was not the point of the controversy between Rome and the Christians; that, as Justin shows, was essentially the same for all heroes. It was the Christian refusal to worship the same gods as did the Romans or to acknowledge their legitimacy—both Paul and Justin call them demons. In fact Justin says that although he and most other Christians had once been pagans and worshiped those gods, they now despised them. The Romans for their part accused Christians of gross immoralities, incest, and cannibalism. The differences were not minor, nor were the stakes low. Roman officials at the trials of the Christians often set up statues of the gods and emperors and required those accused to make a symbolic sacrifice to the images or die; Justin and many others like him went to their deaths willingly.

The Genetics of the Hero and the Virgin Birth

Like many, but not all, of the heroes, Jesus was reputed to have been a son of God born of a virgin mother. The title "son of god" did not necessarily imply divine genealogy in either the Jewish or Greek worlds. In Psalm 2:7, Yahweh declares of the king of Israel, "You are my son; today I have begotten you," at the enthronement ceremony. Justin repeats, in his defense of Jesus, what had long been Greek tradition: "Now if God's Son, who is called Jesus, were only an ordinary man, he would be worthy because of his wisdom to be called Son of God, for all authors call God father of humans and gods" (*1 Apologia* 22). In effect, all people, especially those of remarkable achievement, were "sons (and daughters) of God." Jesus is reported to have said much the same thing to the Jewish authorities in the Gospel of John:

> Is it not written in your law, "I said, you are gods"? If those to whom the word of God came were called 'gods'—and the scripture cannot be annulled—can you say that the one whom the Father has sanctified and sent into the world is blaspheming because I said, "I am God's Son"?
> (10:34–36)

Among Jews there was debate as to the genealogy of the messiah. Those who followed Christ saw in the text of Isaiah a prophecy of the virgin birth of Jesus: "Behold, a virgin shall conceive and bear a son . . . " (Isa. 7:14, RSV). Yet the proper interpretation of the text in Isaiah was disputed by those who did not believe, and a virgin birth was denied. A messiah for Jews did not have to have been virgin born: Simon Bar Cochbah, leader of the second great rebellion against Rome in A.D.

132–35, was declared to be the messiah by the most influential rabbi of his day, Rabbi Akiba, but no claim for a virgin birth was made; everyone knew who his father and mother were. In the New Testament itself, two versions of the virgin birth are to be found, in the Gospels of Matthew and Luke, and have become central features of the Christian understanding of the human and divine nature of Jesus. The other two Gospels, Mark and John, have no such story, and John even includes the saying of a group of detractors, "Is not this Jesus, the son of Joseph, whose father and mother we know?" (John 6:42). We are told by several church writers who later wrote of heresies that certain Jewish-Christian groups thought that Jesus was a "mere man" whose father was Joseph and that he had been chosen to be the Messiah because of his piety. So the virgin birth of Jesus was a matter of some controversy.

But there was no denial of virgin birth in the wider culture: heroes of every description were born of virgin humans as the partners of divine fathers and mothers. But these stories were notorious for their (apparent) ascription of sexual passion and immoral behavior to the gods. Ethically minded philosophers had long banished such ideas as inventions of the poets not worthy of the divine nature: God was without passion, in fact without a body, resting in silence and joy for eternity. Christians sided with the philosophers: Justin, in rejecting the old gods of the poets that he had once worshiped, tells the emperor that he has dedicated himself to the "unbegotten and impassable God" (*1 Apologia* 25). But so had the emperor in his own way, as had his successor, Marcus Aurelius (r. 161–80), to whom Justin dedicated his *Second Apology.* Marcus became one of the most influential Stoic philosophers of his day; his book *Meditations* is still read with profit today. Both sides of the argument, in less heated moments, would have agreed that a true understanding of divinity required the conclusion that God did not have physical sex with anyone.

So what happens in the case of the virgin birth of Jesus? By the time the birth stories of the Gospels of Matthew and Luke were composed, the conception of the deity as a wholly spiritual being was well in place among the philosophically minded. The old ideas of gods with bodies who looked like large and beautiful humans, made of heavenly but nevertheless material "stuff," were no longer defended seriously, though such ideas lived on in festivals, pageantry, and dramatic performances. Now there was but one God, sometimes seen as including all other divine expressions and sometimes excluding them as enemies. Zeus and Hera and Apollo could be positive manifestations of the one God, as in the writings of the Greek philosophers, or they could be demons, as in Zoroastrian and later Christian polemic. But in either case, God did not have passion: God was righteous and at peace, spiritual, self-sufficient, and eternal. The astronomers had discovered that the universe was enormous—God must be larger still, even infinitely large. Some called God "the Place," a name that pointed to the fact that God contained everything; God was the place in which everything existed, but who was not contained by anything. And God lived in complete silence, unknown and unknowable by us in our dark ignorance, weighed down as we are by bodies and material desires. Without God reaching out to us to communicate, we would never know of its existence. "It" is the proper pronoun here, since the divine nature had no gender, but contained all within itself as the source of all things. The ancient philosophical problem was conceived of as "the many and the One," the multiplicity of things in the world arising from the one God as source.

These changes and progress in ideas about God had some rather interesting consequences for understanding the birth of Jesus. Mary was a virgin, but she could in no way engender the Messiah in the manner of the poetic tradition. The poets told of Zeus and other gods lusting after beautiful virgins and having sexual relations with them. The new ideas conceived of a God who had neither a body nor the passion to go with it. Either Joseph would father the child or the one God would send the Spirit, but the old poetic methods of engendering a child were out of the question. Matthew does not explain how Mary came to be pregnant, saying only that she "was found to be with child from the Holy Spirit" (Matt. 1:18). Luke relates that the angel Gabriel tells Mary: "The Holy Spirit will come upon you, and the power of the Most High will overshadow you" (Luke 1:35). This is clearly a spiritual, nonphysical occurrence, and the authors are quite circumspect in their treatment of it. In time, a great deal of energy was expended by Christian writers and scribes to safeguard the virginity of Mary even after the birth of Jesus. They produced a doctrine of the perpetual virginity of Mary even in the face of such New Testament passages as "he [Joseph] . . . had no marital relations with her [Mary] until she had borne a son" (Matt. 1:25), and "Is this not [Jesus] the carpenter, the son of Mary and brother of James and Joses and Judas and Simon, and are not his sisters here with us?" (Mark 6:3).

Not all Christians believed in the virgin birth or thought it a necessary element in the story of Jesus. Recall that the early catechism of Paul makes no mention of Jesus' birth, though the later creeds composed for Roman readers do. Christianity spread among many people of the East who did not have access to Greek heroic tradition to the same extent as did those around the Mediterranean. They did not speak Greek, but Syriac or Aramaic or some other Semitic language. In Greek, the word for "spirit" is *pneuma*, of neuter grammatical gender. The Holy Spirit is properly an "it," which works perfectly for Luke's purpose in showing the nonphysical nature of the conception of Jesus. In Latin, *spiritus* is grammatically masculine and less precise for Luke's purpose, more in concert with the poetic tradition. But in Semitic languages, the word for "spirit" is grammatically feminine, and for a female Spirit to engender a child seems logically impossible:

> Some say, "Mary conceived by the Holy Spirit." They are in error. They do not know what they are saying. When did a woman ever conceive by a woman? Mary is the virgin whom no power defiled. [. . .] The powers defile themselves. The Lord would not have said, "My Father who is in heaven" unless he had had another father. (*Gospel of Philip* 55.23–36)

• • •

The passage is from the *Gospel of Philip*, a Syrian Christian writing of the second century. It is not a Gospel like those in the New Testament and does not compete with them for a place in the Bible, though it happens to carry the title "Gospel." It is instead a series of wise sayings representative of one branch of Christian thought in the Eastern empire in the second century. Note the way this group of Semitic-speaking Christians understood Jesus: the passage as a whole is arguing against the virgin birth, but the author knows full well that other Christians affirm it. Two proofs are brought up as countermeasures. First, the word "spirit" is feminine, and therefore the Holy Spirit is feminine and could not have caused a woman (Mary) to conceive a child. A large number of texts from Semitic areas of the Eastern empire speak of the Holy Spirit as the mother of Jesus and present a holy family of Father, Spirit/Mother, and Son in contrast to the holy family so common in Western Christian art and Christmas displays of Joseph, Mary, and baby Jesus. In these Semitic areas, as in our passage, the natural father of the physical body of Jesus is Joseph, while the "mother" of the divine nature in him is the Spirit. So Jesus has a "heavenly Father" (God) of his divine nature and "another father" (Joseph) of his physical body.

It is the second issue in the passage, however, that concerns us much more: the author is at pains to conserve the virgin purity of Mary against the defilement of the "powers." In Eastern tradition derived from Persia, the gods of the pagans were the demonic "powers" who ruled the world of darkness. Recall that many Christians had demonized the Greco-Roman gods who mated with humans; for them the gods of the pagans were servants of the Devil and the only possibility for sexual relations between gods and humans was demonic. So here the author declares that there was no virgin birth because the "powers," the demonic rulers of the world, did not "defile" Mary. There is a break in the papyrus that leaves us in doubt as to the remainder of one of the sentences (symbolized by the "[. . .]" in the translation above), but the general tenor of the passage is clear: a virgin birth by a "god" must mean physical sexual union between a demonic power and Mary and therefore is impossible—she cannot have been defiled. This author is willing to deny the virgin birth before allowing a deity, that is, for him is a demon, to impregnate Mary. Here, and emphatically, the old stories of the poets about the lusts of the gods meet their match.

But for most Christians, the circumspect spiritual accounts of Matthew and Luke sufficed. Gabriel told Mary that because the Spirit of God would engender the child, he would "be called Son of God" (Luke 1:35). There was another consequence of divine genealogy: Jesus called God *Abba*, "Daddy." He seems to have had a relationship with God as personal Father quite unlike what was customary in his own Jewish tradition, a much closer relationship than was common among the teachers and rabbis of his day. Later Jewish tradition had certainly taught that God was the "father" of Israel and that therefore God was the father of the individual Jew. And from much earlier, Greeks, as we saw in the text of Justin, often spoke of God as "father of gods and humans." This was, in fact, one of the most common epithets of Zeus in Homer. But Jesus seems to have had an especially close relationship with God, and this fact brought him into conflict with Jewish tradition and the Jewish authorities. For example, he contravenes the Law of Moses that permitted divorce by appealing to the (real and) original will of God: "from the beginning it was not so" (Matt. 19:8). And he contradicts the Mosaic Law "eye for eye" (Exod. 21:24) by commanding followers not to resist an evildoer (Matt. 5:39). Of the tradition to "hate your enemy," he says "Love your enemies . . . that you may be children of your Father in heaven" (Matt. 5:44–45), implying clearly that to do otherwise is to be something else.

Consider the controversy over the point in the Gospel of John. Jesus has just healed a paralyzed man at the pool of Bethesda on the Sabbath by commanding him, "Stand up, take up your mat and walk" (John 5:8). Certain Jewish authorities see the man carrying his bed and accost him for breaking the Sabbath. He replies that the one who had healed him told him to do so and eventually reports Jesus to them. They therefore go to Jesus and accuse him for "working" his miracles on the Sabbath. Jesus replies to the effect that his Father is in the business of doing good, Sabbath or no Sabbath, and therefore so is he; he is not going to stop because of some tradition. John the Gospel writer adds:

> For this reason the Jews were seeking all the more to kill him, because he was not only breaking the Sabbath, but was also calling God his own Father, thereby making himself equal to God. (John 5:18)

The Jewish authorities also believe that God is their Father, as is made clear later in the same Gospel (8:41). But here the level of intimacy and degree of relationship is different. They persecute Jesus because he is saying that God is his "own private Father"—the Greek text is quite clear that this is the point—setting him apart from the tradition and "making himself equal to God": he is God's son in a way no regular Jew could ever claim.

But this radical new sense of the close bond between God and Son of God does not stop with Jesus. It is basic to Jesus' religious mission to give to all his followers what he himself is and has, in effect to democratize his special status. This is the argument of this book and the basis of the appeal of the message about Jesus—everyone who followed him would become children of God in the special way that he was, not merely in the traditional way in which they already were considered so or that everybody was considered so. So Jesus taught his followers to pray "Our Father," and Paul taught that God had sent his Spirit into them to adopt them as children, that they too could call out to God, *Abba*—"Daddy."

REMARKABLE TALENTS

Such a lineage had consequences—children of the gods had talents beyond their mere mortal contemporaries. Jesus, according to our sources, was a healer and miracle worker and teacher. People hearing and seeing him were amazed and said, "Where did this man get all this? What is this wisdom that has been given to him? What deeds of power are being done by his hands!" (Mark 6:2). He stilled the storm, walked on water, multiplied the loaves and the fish, turned water into wine, healed the sick, and even raised the dead. These were amazing deeds, but the same or similar deeds had been claimed for others of divine lineage before. Tablets giving accounts of the healings of Asclepius could be found within his main sanctuary at Epidauros.

In the late fourth and third centuries B.C. there arose a type of literature known as "aretalogy," an account (*logos*) of the wonderful earthly deeds (*aretai*) of a god or hero. Scholars have long suspected that there existed such an account of the miracles of Jesus, written before the composition of the canonical Gospels and used by the authors of Mark and John. In John there is a series of miracles, the first of which are numbered. Changing water to wine is called "the first of his [Jesus'] signs" (John 2:11), and the healing of the nobleman's son is called "the second sign" (John 4:54). There may have been a numbered list of signs from which John worked, not all of which were used in the composition of the Gospel, for he concludes: "Jesus did many other signs . . . which are not written in this book" (John 20:30).

Jesus could have done anything, apparently: "Who then is this, that even the wind and sea obey him?" (Mark 4:41). If the early Christians had thought it necessary, he would have been able to fly or, if he had wished, to turn the Pharisees into green frogs. This last is not just humor—like so many heroes before, he was a kind of soldier or military captain locked in a deadly battle. He "frees the captives," those enslaved by dark forces, by casting out demons and healing diseases; he "binds the enemy" and sacks his belongings. But his kingdom and weapons are spiritual ones, and he does not choose to fight by other means. John tells us that just before the crucifixion, when asked by Pilate what he had done wrong, he replies (as so often, without answering the question):

My kingdom is not from this world. If my kingdom were

from this world, my followers would be fighting to keep me
from being handed over to the Jews. But as it is, my
kingdom is not from here. (John 18:36)

All the power there is is in his hands, yet he chooses not to defend himself. And perhaps most significantly for later Christian history and the
rise of the Church, he commands his followers not to defend themselves either: "Turn the other cheek." Follow the leader. Take up your
cross also. Fight with spiritual weapons only. And if necessary, go to
your death as well.

INTERWOVEN DESTINIES

Recall that the *Iliad* is part of an epic story that involved the whole of
the Greek world; essentially everyone was included. The gods and fate
had designed the plan and had placed at its center Achilles. He was
not only "the best of the Achaians," the best soldier, but in one
version of his possible lineage he had been destined to became the
heir to the throne of Zeus himself. He is the central pivotal point
around which the progress of the war and the plan of the gods revolve,
yet the plan is larger than he is and involves all lands and peoples
important to Greeks.

Jesus too is part of a story that involves the whole of the Greco-
Roman world, but his is on an even larger scale because it eventually
includes the cosmos itself and all of history. The difference in scale
stems from the deep influence of Persian apocalyptic conception in
postexilic Judaism that had expanded the scene to involve the whole
universe and expanded the enemies to include cosmic forces of evil.
We saw a related phenomenon in the story of the Four Ages in Hesiod,
where the cycle of ages comprised all of humanity and history. The Persians had added to this the coming of a captain of the forces of righteousness who would defeat the Devil and his dark powers. When

melded together as they were in Palestine, the two story lines result in what we find in the stories of Jesus, a hero from among the Jews with cosmic destiny. Nevertheless, the role played by the central human figure remains that of the classic hero.

The destinies of the world are woven together in the story of Jesus. Luke tells us that when the week-old child is dedicated at the temple, the aged Simeon recognizes the promised Messiah, whom he had been waiting to see before he died; he takes the child into his arms and proclaims, "This child is destined for the falling and the rising of many in Israel" (Luke 2:34). But not for Israel alone. Luke slowly develops his story into one that expands beyond the small nation of Israel to encompass the whole world; the risen Jesus instructs his disciples, "you will be my witnesses in Jerusalem, in all Judea and Samaria, and to the ends of the earth" (Acts 1:8). So in Paul's speech at Athens, "God . . . now . . . commands all people everywhere to repent, because he has fixed a day on which he will have the world judged in righteousness by a man whom he has appointed." (Acts 17:30–31).

The Trap of Fate and Free Will

One of the most endearing aspects of Greek heroic literature is that the individual heroes are often forced by an aspect of personal character into the tragedy that defines their lives. Achilles is a man of passionate anger when wronged, and while in a sense justified, it is his anger that eventually brings his fate upon him. For Helen of Troy, her very beauty is her qualification for tragic circumstance. For Antigone, it is her piety in insisting on the burial of her brother against the command of the king that brings her death. A similar connection between character and fate may be found in the stories of Hippolytus, Oedipus, and many others. Much the same could be said for Jesus. It is his very character, it seems, that caused him to be caught in his own web of fate—he can do no other than declare what is true, and that truth brings his fate upon him.

For each of the Gospel writers, but especially in Luke's story, Jesus' life is seen as having been predestined by God's plan. Although he had been crucified by Romans, he was "handed over to you according to the definite plan and foreknowledge of God" (Acts 2:23). Later the apostles give God praise that the authorities in executing Jesus did "whatever your hand and your plan had predestined to take place" (Acts 4:28). In fact, Jesus in the book of Revelation is called "the Lamb that was slaughtered from the foundation of the world" (Rev. 13:8). But he is not trapped or taken against his will. He knows, as did Achilles, that if he continues on the course set for him, he will be killed. The Gospel of Mark turns on this very point. Jesus' miracles and teaching bring him fame and a large following, but also offense and anger on the part of the authorities. In the midst of the story he tells his disciples that he will be killed, and Peter rebukes him, which elicits the angry retort, "Get behind me, Satan!" (Mark 8:33). From here on he sets his course toward Jerusalem and the cross.

He is at last forced, or directed by the will of God, into a situation intriguingly like that of Achilles, choosing death with honor over life. Jesus faces his fate and prays in Gethsemane that "the hour might pass from him" (Mark 14:35), but it does not. Like Achilles and many others, he chooses to go to his death. We never learn what the alternative might have been, if it existed at all. It is the defining moment in his life, the most important decision he ever makes, and he makes it entirely alone.

Consider this last issue from the point of view of the story as opposed to some theory of the historical memory of the events of Jesus' life. According to Mark, Jesus is alone in Gethsemane at the critical moment. He leaves most of the disciples at some place in the garden and goes farther on, taking with him only Peter, James, and John. He then leaves even these three and goes somewhat farther to pray concerning his choice: "Father, for you all things are possible; remove this cup from me; yet, not what I want, but what you want"

(Mark 14:36). He returns to find the three asleep. He awakens them to tell them to lend him some support; he retreats to pray and returns two times more to find them again asleep. He has been left to make the choice entirely alone. From the point of view of history, who would have known what he was praying about or that he was making the choice at all? But from the point of view of story, Mark knows that Jesus must face his fate and choose: he is a hero.

DIVINE ENEMIES

Heroes had divine enemies. Without such enemies they would never have faced the tragic circumstances that showed forth their character, for heroes were superior to mere mortals and would have overcome and won in any contest with lesser foes. It is the fact of divine power set against them that intrigues us as readers. We all live in an ambiguous world, perhaps a random world, but one that at times seems to be set against us. With it we must struggle by our best efforts, yet we know that one day it will overwhelm us also. Homer tells us that Zeus has two urns from which he dispenses the fate of each individual, "an urn of evils, an urn of blessings" (*Iliad* 24.528). He mixes evil and good for the (semi)fortunate, and only trouble for the unfortunate. No one, apparently, receives only blessing, for "such is the way the gods spun life for unfortunate mortals, that we live in unhappiness, but the gods themselves have no sorrows" (24.525–26).

The heroes fight against the gods most like themselves or against those with whom they compete most directly, which is at times the same deity. Jesus fights throughout his public life with the divine enemy most (un)like him and against whom he competes directly, the Devil, the other claimant to the title Lord. In Mark, the battle is engaged immediately after his commissioning as Son of God at the baptism administered by John the Baptist. The Spirit impels him into the desert to begin his fight with the Devil. He then casts out demonic powers from many oppressed and ill people. In Luke's story, this activity brings to Jesus a vision, and he stands watching "Satan fall from heaven like a flash of lightning" (Luke 10:18). The point is that he is the captain of the forces of the kingdom of God that have invaded the realm of the enemy; the preaching of the gospel is designed to cause people to "turn from darkness to light and from the power of Satan to God" (Acts 26:18). For the Greeks the divine enemies were inimical fate and the ambiguous jealousies of the gods, who as often fought against worshipers as heard their prayers. For the Persians, these forces were personified as the Devil and his minions, who sought to control the fortunes of all of creation. This is the form of the story as it was inherited by segments of Judaism after the exile, and this is the form of the enemy that stands behind the Gospels. Again, the scale is greater and the divine enemies are different from the ones in the stories of Homer, but the role is the same.

RULERS AS HUMAN ENEMIES

Both God and the inimical gods, understood to be the Devil and his demons, use the agency first of the Jerusalem authorities and then the Roman government to persecute and finally crucify Jesus. His life is seen to be lived out on two levels, in two dimensions, the earthly and human, on the one hand, and the invisible and divine, on the other. In the book of Acts, we find that the Jerusalemites were part of this life in two dimensions. They are told by Peter about Jesus, that "this man, handed over to you according to the definite plan and foreknowledge of God, you crucified and killed by the hands of those outside the law" (Acts 2:23). And later, in a prayer to God, Peter again claims that "both Herod and Pontius Pilate, with the Gentiles and the peoples of Israel, gathered together against your holy servant Jesus, whom you anointed, to do whatever your hand and your plan had predestined to take place" (Acts 4:27–28). Jesus' life and career are determined by higher powers, but played out on the human level among the various authorities and rulers who unconsciously follow dictates they do not understand.

Between the unknowable counsel of the highest God and the unwitting human rulers are the spiritual enemies, the inimical gods, who motivate the evil human agents into the persecution and destruction of the righteous ones. This produces a cosmic drama of four elements: God and the Devil unseen, their agents on earth, the human rulers who persecute the righteous, and the righteous themselves. The basic idea is old in the culture, stemming from Zoroastrianism but finding its own type of expression in Greece. The persecutors of the righteous are unwitting agents of the inimical gods, who themselves are unwitting agents in the plan of God. Only God knows the whole story, yet to some small extent the righteous on earth are allowed to see into the mystery. Paul expresses this well in his discussion of the mystery of the wisdom of God, that "None of the rulers of this age understood this; for if they had, they would not have crucified" Jesus (1 Cor. 2:8). They were unwitting agents of the divine plan.

The old idea that the human agents of evil would suffer the consequences for their acts, even though they are, without knowing it themselves, fulfilling a divine plan, is found in the Christian understanding of the fall of Jerusalem in A.D. 70 to the Roman legions. The Gospels predict the destruction as a consequence of the murder of Jesus. In the parable of the vineyard (Mark 12:1–9), when the tenants (Israel) refuse to pay the owner (God) his proper share of the crops, the owner sends first several servants (prophets) and then his son (Jesus) to collect. When the son of the owner is killed, Jesus asks: "What then will the owner of the vineyard do? He will come and destroy the tenants and give the vineyard to others" (Mark 12:9). In Luke, Jesus weeps over the city of Jerusalem, and predicts that it will be destroyed, "because you did not recognize the time of your visitation from God" (Luke 19:44). In Matthew, in the parable of the marriage feast, when the invited guests refuse to come to the feast and then kill the servants sent to them, "The king was enraged. He sent his troops, destroyed those murderers, and burned their city" (Matt. 22:7). This is the basis for the

Christian understanding of the eventual murder of thousands of Christians as martyrs. Eventually the Roman government was seen, especially in the book of Revelation, as the agent of the Devil in its persecution of Christians. They, like Jesus, were part of a cosmic drama far beyond their individual lives, playing a real part in a real, but unseen, divine plan.

THE TEST OF CHARACTER

Jesus experienced several tests of character and resolve in his story that often go unnoticed as tests, given our inheritance of the doctrine of Jesus as the Second Person of the Trinity. How could a test of character be a real one, if Jesus is God—"God cannot be tempted by evil" things (James 1:13). The point is not a small one, for during the theological controversies of later centuries it was discovered that if Christ were not fully human, then he could not stand in human stead for the salvation of the world; he could not die in the place of what he was not. But we at this point are not at the time of the Christological controversies of the fourth and fifth centuries, but much earlier, when not only the leader but all of the followers were required to show the quality of their souls through testing and suffering.

Recall that the first thing Jesus is required to do by God is to go out into the desert alone and be tempted by the Devil. More than once the offended "scribes and the Pharisees . . . cross-examine[d] him about many things, lying in wait for him, to catch him in something he might say" (Luke 11:53–54). His own closest disciple rebukes him for announcing that he is to go to his death, for the Messiah could not possibly be one to die; Jesus must stand against Peter as a representative of Satan. And later the chief priests send emissaries "to trap him in what he said" (Mark 12:13). He faces his most critical moment in the garden of Gethsemane where he "offered up prayers and supplications, with loud cries and tears, to the one who was able to save him from death, and he was heard because of his reverent submission" (Heb. 5:7). His prayers were heard, we assume, and he submitted, but he was not saved from death. Finally he goes literally to trial, caught for something that he probably did say about the temple, but that was garbled and turned into an accusation by false witnesses. Mark has the witness testify, "We heard him say, 'I will destroy this temple that is made with hands, and in three days I will build another, not made with hands' " (14:58). He is condemned and after that repeatedly beaten and finally crucified.

His trials teach him and test his character. In a passage clearly drawing on the heroic model and one seldom used in the later Christian world, the writer of the Letter to the Hebrews tells us that Jesus "learned obedience through what he suffered" (Heb. 5:8). What could this mean in the world of creeds? The text continues that God "perfected" him through sufferings (Heb. 2:10; 5:9). The idea of a messiah who is killed was found in the Scriptures in Isaiah 53, the famous passage about the suffering servant. But that was not the general expectation in the culture for the messiah; he should have been a victorious military leader like David (recall the title "son of David"). We see the same expectation in Peter's rebuke of Jesus: he cannot be allowed to be killed. That he should learn through and be perfected through suffering and then be killed is the heroic model. For the hero, *pathei mathos*, "learning comes through suffering."

BAIT IN A TRAP

Jesus was very definitely seen to be a test of the character of others, as a kind of bait in a trap that went unrecognized. Simeon in Luke's Gospel declares that that the child Jesus "is destined for the falling and the rising of many" (Luke 2:34), but that fact was hidden even from his own disciples. The Gospel writers tell us that not until after his resurrection did the disciples understand who he was. For example, when Jesus taught of the gate of the fold of sheep, the gatekeeper, and the good shepherd, the disciples "did not understand what he was saying to them" (John 10:6). And after Jesus entered Jerusalem riding on a donkey, thus fulfilling an Old Testament prophecy, the disciples were uncomprehending. Something was going on that they did not get: "His disciples did not understand these things at first; but when Jesus was glorified, then they remembered . . ." (John 12:16). Mark makes their stupidity a central feature of his Gospel. In a classic passage, Jesus is warning them:

> "Beware of the yeast of the Pharisees and the yeast of Herod." They said to one another, "It is because we have no bread." And becoming aware of it, Jesus said to them, "Why are you talking about having no bread? Do you still not perceive or understand? Are your hearts hardened? Do you have eyes, and fail to see? Do you have ears, and fail to hear?" (Mark 8:15–18)

Mark paints the disciples as the twelve stooges. The motif is known among scholars as the "incomprehension of the disciples" and is part of the "messianic secret." This is a literary device of Mark the author and a central feature of his Gospel. Jesus is unknown to all, even to his disciples, who should know him. All the demons, of course, recognize him immediately—he is like a light on a dark night to them—but Jesus commands them to be silent. Occasionally an enlightened human does recognize him, and even Peter finally declares, "You are the Christ," but Jesus each time "ordered them not to tell anyone about him" (Mark 8:30).

The motif may be found to some extent in each of the Gospels, reflecting both literary design and historical reality. Most people, in fact, especially those in authority, didn't recognize Jesus as Christ during his lifetime. He did not seem to fit the mold of a classic prophet or a messiah or a new king of Israel—he did not fit their expectations. When Jesus begins teaching in the temple in John, the authorities are amazed: "How has this man become learned, never having been educated?" (John 7:15, GJR). The crowd is divided: some side with him because of the miracles he performs; others including the authorities turn against him because he arose in Galilee. When Nicodemus attempts to defend him, he is rebuked: "Search [the Scriptures] and you will see that no prophet is to arise from Galilee" (John 7.52).

One of the most difficult issues raised by Jesus was his willfulness in breaking traditional rules connected with observance of Mosaic Law—he is perceived as a breaker of the Sabbath and other traditions. He associates not with rulers and the upper classes, but with prostitutes, tax collectors, and society's rejects. He does not seem to care about what he should—he recommends paying taxes to Caesar and seems not to want an independent political kingdom. In John, he predicts his death on a cross, and the crowd disbelieves again over the issue of a Christ who can be killed: "We have heard from the law that the Messiah remains forever. How can you say that the Son of Man must be lifted up [i.e., crucified]?" (John 12:34).

This was the final proof that he was not the fulfillment of Jewish expectation—he was not the messiah because the messiah could never be crucified, and he was not a prophet or the king of the Jews. The law had pronounced a curse on the crucified; therefore, or so it seemed, this man was not the promised one. So in the accounts of the trial he is beaten, humiliated, and mocked. He had told them to live righteously and exposed their hypocrisies; he seemed to be claiming some status, and that offended them. So they blindfold him and hit him and say "Prophesy!" He is made to wear a royal robe and crown of thorns, and they bow before him saying, "Hail, king of the Jews!" They crucify him and say, "Let the Messiah, the King of Israel, come down from the cross now, so that we may see and believe!" (Mark 15:32).

These were bad ideas. The bait in the trap comes in deceiving forms. It is meant to trick. It is designed in such a way that one is not supposed to be able to recognize it for what it really is, only to react to it according to one's own inner character and be exposed. In words from John's Gospel: "This is the judgment, that the light has come into the world, and people loved darkness rather than light because their deeds were evil" (John 3:19). The proof that these were bad ideas, that Jesus was something not to be mocked or left unrecognized, comes immediately—darkness at noon for three hours during the crucifixion and the rending of the curtain of the temple from top to bottom at the point of death (Mark 15:33, 38); Matthew adds an earthquake (27:51).

Recall that Odysseus returned home as a wrinkled and dirty beggar. How he was received determined life or death for those he met in his house. He did not look like the real Odysseus, the real lord of the island, but he was. He did not appear to have the power of the gods in his hands for retribution, but he did.

Herodotus tells us the story of Onesilus, who began a Cypriot revolt against the Persian Empire but was killed by traitors. The people of Amathus, at whose town the war had begun, severed his head and hung it up above the gates. Eventually it became hollow and bees used it for a hive, filling it with honeycomb. The people understood the threat: their act of *hubris* had made them liable to suffer the wrath of the dead but righteous man, and the skull filled with honey was the enigma. They were instructed by an oracle to take the head down and bury it and thereafter to honor Onesilus as a hero with an annual sacrifice (*Histories* 5.114).

In another story Herodotus tells of a wicked Persian governor who stole the treasures out of the shrine of the dead hero Protesilaus. Eventually he was besieged and captured, and when one of the guards began roasting a salt fish, it began to jump on the coals as though alive. The governor said, "This prodigy . . . applies to me: Protesilaus is telling me that though he is as dead as a dried fish, he yet has power from the gods to punish the one who wrongs him" (9.120). The governor and his son were both killed. That signs and portents should accompany the dead hero who has been mocked and unjustly treated was an old motif; they were signals from God that the hero had been wronged and that injustice would have its consequences.

• • •

EARLY DEATH IN THE MIDST OF LIFE

Jesus was killed in his thirties, as far as we can determine. Luke tells us that he was about thirty years old when he began his ministry (Luke 3:23), and an investigation of the Greek phrasing tells us that "thirty" does not mean exactly thirty. So Jesus was either twenty-eight or twenty-nine, or thirty-one or thirty-two, approximately, if Luke is correct. The length of his ministry is in question. Mark seems to have Jesus complete everything in one year, though this is not so stated; nor is it an issue in Mark—he never addresses the problem directly. John's account requires at least three years because of the number of major festivals mentioned and the large amount of travel he relates. Luke includes a unique parable of the barren fig tree that did not bear fruit for three years (Luke 13:6–9). The owner instructs the keeper to cut it down, but the keeper asks that it be left one more year that he might fertilize it and tend it; if it should not bear fruit after that, then let it be cut down. There is no interpretation of this parable in the text, and we do not know with certainty to what it refers, but it seems that Jesus himself is the keeper and God is the owner. If so, Luke may be telling us that the ministry of Jesus lasted four years, after which the ministry to Israel was "cut down" with the crucifixion of Jesus and the gospel was sent to the Gentiles, as we learn from the book of Acts. Jesus, by this reckoning, was between thirty-three and thirty-five years old when he was killed.

Jesus died a death that defined his life. If one returns for a moment to the outlines of his life, the catechisms and baptismal creeds cited earlier in this chapter, it is his death that is the central point of focus around which the story turns. He was killed because of what he was—his lineage, his abilities, his character. The way the world was conceived, he had to be killed—he was light shining in darkness, and the darkness would try if it could to kill him. Paul understands that the real enemies Jesus faced were the spiritual demonic "rulers of this age" (1 Cor. 2:8). God had predestined it, but the demonic forces did not understand the plan; in attacking him they destroyed themselves. The

hero is the bait in the trap, and his death seals the fate of the unrighteous. This is not as common a way of constructing reality any longer,
but it was the way of those in the first century. Jesus' kind of life
required his early and tragic death. If he had not been killed like one
of the heroes, it would only have meant that he was not worthy of that
status, that he was not a son of God, that he was not valuable enough
to draw down on himself the jealousies of the gods or fate or the wrath
of the powers and their religious authorities. The fact of his unjust
death not only proved the real value of his life, it authenticated his
right to complete the creedal journey, to ascend into heaven and
someday stand as judge.

THE PRIZE OF IMMORTALITY

The heroes gained immortality for themselves because of their divine
ancestry and their suffering. But among lesser souls, among mere mortals, there was little optimism concerning the possibilities for life after
death. Mystery religions offered initiations and promises, a subject for
a later chapter, but to judge from the vast majority of tomb inscrip-
tions, few were persuaded. To paraphrase an ancient saying, many
joined in the festival processions, but few actually believed. Even
among the philosophers, whose profession led them to meditate on
such questions, there was no settled opinion. Socrates, at the end of
Plato's *Apology*, in his speech in his own defense at his final trial, tells
the minority of the jury who voted for his acquittal:

> Death is one of two things. Either it is annihilation, and the
> dead leave no consciousness of anything, or, as we are told,
> it is really a change—a migration of the soul from this place
> to another. (40c)

Socrates is ambivalent, even agnostic, although he clearly prefers the second possibility. Plato believed strongly in the immortality of the soul, as did members of most other sophisticated schools of thought, each in its own way. Epicurus (341–270 B.C.), however, claimed that the soul was material and perished with the body. He taught his followers that "The most terrifying of evils, death, is nothing to us, since when we exist, death is not present. But when death is present, then we do not exist" (Diogenes Laertius 10.125). So the Epicureans repeated as a kind of gospel, "Death is nothing to us." Most people, apparently, agreed at least with the general conclusion that after death we do not survive in any substantial form.

But Jesus rose from the dead. It is difficult in the extreme for us to understand how this claim might have sounded in the world in which it was preached. Many uninformed Christian teachers today have claimed that the resurrection of Jesus was the one most unique feature of the gospel, that of all the other gods and heroes of antiquity Jesus alone rose from the dead. That, as Justin so clearly taught us above, is not even close to true. All the heroes, or nearly all, rose from the dead and ascended to heaven. But this was an impossibility for a mere human and a shocking claim for any real and historical man who lived in recent times. It meant that in our times one like the heroes of old had appeared among us and taught and suffered and died; because he rose from the dead, this was certain, and he had to be taken seriously. His resurrection was authentication of his status. In Paul's speech to the Athenians in the book of Acts, the listeners are to understand that Jesus is God's appointed one because God has "given assurance to all by raising him from the dead" (Acts 17:31).

In a fascinating passage that shows the interweaving of Jewish and Greco-Roman ideas, Paul wrote to the Romans, living in the very heart of the empire, that Jesus was "from the seed of David according to the flesh, designated as Son of God . . . by resurrection from the dead" (Rom. 1:3–4, GJR). The Greek text would allow the translation "son of God," or "a son of God," or even "a son of a god," though the last is clearly not the intention of Paul. The language itself, however, points to the fact that resurrection is proof that Jesus has God as father; it was proof of his divine genealogy. Paul sets up a parallelism here of two opposites: son of David and Son of God. Jesus is son of David according to the flesh, that is, a direct descendant of King David according to his human genealogy. That genealogy was, one assumes, at least claimed for him if not actually kept intact; the genealogies for Jesus found in Matthew and Luke do not agree with each other. But how do we know that he is Son of God? Recall that one does not need to be raised from the dead or have a virgin birth to be called "son of God" among Jews. And those who were so called, the kings, did not need to contrast the designation to their fleshly genealogy; it was in fact because of it that they were kings and adopted sons of God. Jesus is shown to be "son of God" because of the proof provided by the resurrection, something that no Jewish king needed or could possibly attain for the title. We are so used to thinking that there is only one Son of God and one culture informing our texts (that so many try to construct from the Old Testament alone), we forget that Paul could write in all seriousness, "in fact there are many gods and many lords" (1 Cor. 8:5). He doesn't believe in the worth of these gods and lords—he is no pluralist—but he does not deny their existence. And he knows the stories and so do his Roman readers. They all know that Jesus was son of God because he rose from the dead. That is what the stories had taught: if you rise from the dead, you had a divinity as one of your parents. Eventually Paul himself and some of his readers would be killed by order of one of these "lords," these so-called sons of god in the person of the Roman emperor.

But here Jesus and the Christians made a radical claim. Jesus had risen from the dead and so could anyone—now eternal life was available for all who dared to follow him to the end of their lives. The claim that a normal individual could gain immortality was not entirely new, not without precedent, as we shall see. But it had been reserved for the few, the initiates in secret mysteries or the expert practitioners of philosophy. The teachings of Jesus, on the other hand, were for everyone, but especially for those who could not afford initiations and were uneducated in philosophy. They were for the vast majority of the people in the lowest classes: "Blessed are you poor, for yours is the kingdom of God."

THE DEAD HERO AS PROTECTOR AND JUDGE

And finally, the dead Jesus becomes, in early Christian preaching, perhaps the most dangerous being ever to have been born, on the one hand, a protector of those who are his own and, on the other, one who will someday return from heaven to judge the living and the dead.

We have seen that the dead hero was a protector of the living, of those who turned to him or her for help, and an avenger of wrong, both against those who had wronged the hero, alive or dead, and against those who wronged the worshipers. A classic case of this is found in the *Libation Bearers* of Aeschylus. The wife of Agamemnon and her lover Aegisthus, had murdered him on the day of his triumphant return from Troy. Agamemnon's son was exiled and his daughter held in virtual slavery. In a chilling opening scene, the two now grown children and a chorus of assistants gather at Agamemnon's grave and call his spirit out of the ground to avenge himself and them. As they pray, the chorus observes that "powers gather under ground to give aid" (376–77), and Orestes prays, "Zeus, Zeus, force up from below ground the delayed destruction" on his mother and her lover (382–83). Subsequently, the dead hero brings destruction on those who wronged him in one of the most famous plays written in antiquity.

Socrates, at the end of Plato's *Apology,* tells those who voted for his acquittal not to grieve that he has been condemned unjustly and is about to die, for

> If on arrival in the other world, beyond the reach of our so-called justice, one will find there the true judges who are said to preside in those courts, Minos and Rhadamanthus and Aeacus and Triptolemus and all those other half-divinities

who were upright in their earthly life, would that be an unre-
warding journey? (41a)

These upright among the "half-divinities," heroes with one divine and
one human parent, had traditionally been appointed the judges of the
dead in the underworld, granting rewards and punishments after death
to individuals for deeds done while alive. Minos and Rhadamanthus
were brothers, sons of Zeus and the virgin Europa, and Aeacus was the
son of Zeus by Aegina; all three were famous as lawgivers and for personal integrity. According to another passage in Plato, the three are
appointed judges of the dead at the crossroads from which one path
leads to the Isles of the Blessed and the other to Tartarus, the place of
torture of the wicked (*Gorgias* 524a). Triptolemus was son of the king
of Attica, born at Eleusis, where he established the cult of Demeter
known as the Eleusinian mysteries. According to the myth of the cult,
he taught farming and the mysteries of Demeter to humanity as a kind
of culture hero and after death was made a god.

Earlier I observed that emperor Antoninus Pius, if he had ever had
the chance to read the Old Roman Creed (which he did not), may have
wondered why Jesus in Christian understanding replaced the older
Greek heroes who already held the position of judges of the dead. It is
here that the stories of the heroes and that of Jesus part company. Jesus
and the Gospel writers were heirs to more than one major culture;
through the other branch of Indo-European influence, specifically Persian Zoroastrianism, they had inherited apocalyptic eschatology as it
was mediated by Jewish writers in the period from the Exile to the first
century. Eschatology was not unknown among the Greeks, as we saw
in the poem of Hesiod on the Four Ages, but it was never as developed
in Greece as it was in Persia and then among some sects of the Jews.
There, one major role of the quintessential hero had been projected
into the future—he was the captain of the forces of righteousness that
would destroy the forces of the Devil and his minions in a cataclysmic
last battle, to be followed by a new and clean heaven and earth. Among
the Jews this role was assimilated to old ideals of the Israelite kingdom

of David and Canaanite mythology, and the coming one became the future "son of David," the anointed one ("messiah") of God. Yet neither the Zoroastrian captain nor the Jewish messiah was supposed to suffer horribly and die on a cross. These were never thought to have to endure death, resurrection, and ascension, but instead were supposed to march on to a divinely directed military victory on a cosmic scale and remain forever. This was not yet the career of Jesus. Christians used these apocalyptic ideas to understand how Jesus would someday return from heaven a second time to fulfill this role. As for his first appearance, Justin was right—the story of Jesus, so far, was the story of a hero.

from The Anti-Christ

by Friedrich Nietzsche

German philosopher Friedrich Nietzsche (1844–1900) was a brilliantly provocative critic of Christianity, but an admirer of Jesus. This translation is by H. L. Mencken.

What concerns *me* is the psychological type of the Savior. This type might be depicted in the Gospels, in however mutilated a form and however much overladen with extraneous characters—that is, *in spite* of the Gospels; just as the figure of Francis of Assisi shows itself in his legends in spite of his legends. It is *not* a question of mere truthful evidence as to what he did, what he said and how he actually died; the question is, whether his type is still conceivable, whether it has been handed down to us.— All the attempts that I know of to read the *history* of a "soul" in the Gospels seem to me to reveal only a lamentable psychological levity. Mssr. Renan, that mountebank *in psychologicus*, has contributed the two most unseemly notions to this business of explaining the type of Jesus: the notion of the *genius* and that of the *hero* ("*heros*"). But if there is anything essentially unevangelical, it is surely the concept of the hero. What the Gospels make instinctive is precisely the reverse of all heroic struggle, of all taste for conflict: the very incapacity for resistance is here converted into something moral: ("resist not evil!"—the most profound sentence in the Gospels, perhaps the true key to them), to wit, the blessedness of peace, of gentleness, the inability to be an enemy. What is the meaning of "glad tidings"?—The true life, the life eternal has been found—it is not merely promised, it is here, it is in *you*; it is the life that lies in love free from all retreats and exclusions, from all keeping of distances. Every one is the child of God—Jesus claims nothing for himself alone—as the child of God each man is the equal of every other man. . . . Imagine making Jesus a *hero*!—And what a tremendous misunderstanding appears in the word "genius"! Our whole conception of the "Spiritual," the whole conception of our civilization, could have had no meaning in the world that Jesus lived in. In the strict sense of the physiologist, a quite different word ought to be used here. . . . We all know that there is a morbid sensibility of the tactile nerves which causes those suffering from it to recoil from every touch, and from every effort to grasp a solid object. Brought to its logical conclusion, such a physiological *habitus* becomes an instinctive hatred of all reality, a flight into the "intangible," into the "incomprehensible"; a distaste for all formulae, for all conceptions of time and space, for everything established—customs, institutions, the church; a feeling of being at home in a world in which no sort of reality survives, a merely "inner" world, a "true" world, an "eternal" world . . . "The Kingdom of God is within *you*". . . .

The instinctive hatred of reality: the consequence of an extreme susceptibility to pain and irritation—so great that merely to be "touched" becomes unendurable, for every sensation is too profound. *The instinctive exclusion of all aversion, all hostility, all bounds and distances in feeling*: the consequence of an extreme susceptibility to pain and irritation—so great that it senses all resistance, all compulsion to resistance, as unbearable *anguish* (—that is to say, as *harmful*, as *prohibited* by the instinct of self-preservation), and regards blessedness (joy) as possible only when it is no longer necessary to offer resistance to anybody or anything, however evil or dangerous—love, as the only, as the *ultimate* possibility of life.

These are the two *physiological realities* upon and out of which the doctrine of salvation has sprung. I call them a sublime superdevelopment of hedonism upon a thoroughly unsalubrious soil. What stands most closely related to them, though with a large admixture of Greek vitality and nerve-force, is epicureanism, the theory of salvation of paganism. Epicurus was a *typical decadent*: I was the first to recognize him.—The fear of pain, even of infinitely slight pain—the end of this *can* be nothing save a *religion of love*.

I have already given my answer to the problem. The prerequisite to it is the assumption that the type of the Savior has reached us only in a greatly distorted form. This distortion is very probable: there are many reasons why a type of that sort should not be handed down in a pure form, complete and free of additions. The milieu in which this strange figure moved must have left marks upon him, and more must have been imprinted by the history, the *destiny*, of the early Christian communities; the latter indeed, must have embellished the type retrospectively with characters which can be understood only as serving the purposes of war and of propaganda. That strange and sickly world into which the Gospels lead us—a world apparently out of a Russian novel, in which the scum of society, nervous maladies and "childish" idiocy keep a tryst—must, in any case, have *coarsened* the type: the first disciples, in particular, must have been forced to translate an existence visible only in symbols and incomprehensibilities into their own crudity, in order to understand it at all—in their sight the type could take on reality only after it had been recast in a familiar mold. . . . The prophet, the messiah, the future judge, the teacher of morals, the worker of wonders, John the Baptist—all these merely presented chances to misunderstand it. . . . Finally, let us not underrate the [nature] of all great, and especially all sectarian veneration: it tends to erase from the venerated objects all its original traits and idiosyncrasies, often so painfully strange—*it does not even see them*. It is greatly to be regretted that no Dostoyevsky lived in the neighborhood of this most interesting *decadent*—I mean someone who would have felt the poignant charm of such a compound of the sublime, the morbid and the childish. In the last analysis, the type, as a type of the decadence, may actually have been peculiarly complex and contradictory: such a possibility is not to be lost sight of. Nevertheless, the probabilities seem to be against it, for in that case tradition would have been particularly accurate and objective, whereas we have reasons for assuming the contrary. Meanwhile, there is a contradiction between the peaceful preacher of the mount, the seashore and the fields, who appears like a new Buddha on a soil very unlike India's, and the aggressive fanatic, the mortal enemy of theologians and ecclesiastics, who stands glorified by Renan's malice as "the grand master of irony." I myself haven't any doubt that the greater part of this venom (and no less of spirit) got itself into the concept of the Master only as a result of the excited nature of Christian propaganda: we all know the unscrupulousness of sectarians when they set out to turn their leader into an *apologia* for themselves. When the early Christians had need of an adroit, contentious, pugnacious and maliciously subtle theologian to tackle other theologians, they *created* a "god" that met that need, just as they put into his mouth without hesitation certain ideas that were necessary to them but that were utterly at odds with the Gospels—"the second coming," "the last judgment," all sorts of expectations and promises, current at the time.—

I can only repeat that I set myself against all efforts to intrude the fanatic into the figure of the Savior: the very word *imperieux* [imperious], used by Renan, is alone enough to *annul* the type. What the "glad tidings" tell us is simply that there are no more contradictions; the kingdom of heaven belongs to *children*; the faith that is voiced here is no more an embattled faith—it is at hand, it has been from the beginning, it is a sort of recrudescent childishness of the spirit. The physiologists, at all events, are familiar with such a delayed and incomplete puberty in the living organism, the result of degeneration. A faith of this sort is not furious, it does not denounce, it does not defend itself: it does not come with "the sword"—it does not realize how it will one day set man against man. It does not manifest itself either by miracles, or by rewards and promises, or by "scriptures": it is itself, first and last, its own miracle, its own reward, its own promise, its own "kingdom of God." This faith does not formulate itself—it simply *lives*, and so guards itself against formulae. To be sure, the accident of environment, of educational background gives prominence to concepts of a certain sort: in primitive Christianity one finds *only* concepts of a Judeo-Semitic character (—that of eating and drinking at the last supper belongs to this category—an idea which, like everything else Jewish, has been badly mauled by the church). But let us be careful not to see in all this anything more than symbolical language, semantics,[1] an opportunity to speak in parables. It is only on the theory that no work is to be taken literally that this anti-realist is able to speak at all. Set down among Hindus, he would have made use of the concepts of Sankhya,[2] and among Chinese he would have employed those of Lao-tse[3]—and in neither case would it have made any difference to him.—With a little freedom in the use of words, one might actually call Jesus a "free spirit"[4]—he cares nothing for what is established: the word *killeth*,[5] whatever is established *killeth*. The idea of "life" as an *experience*, as he alone conceives it, stands opposed to his mind to every sort of word, formula, law, belief and dogma. He speaks only of inner things: "life" or "truth" or "light" is his word for the innermost—in his sight everything else, the whole of reality, all nature, even language, has significance only as sign, as allegory.—Here it is of paramount importance to be led into no error by the temptations lying in Christian, or rather *ecclesiastical* prejudices: such a symbolism *par excellence* stands outside all religion, all notions of worship, all history, all natural science, all worldly experience, all knowledge, all politics, all psychology, all books, all art—his "wisdom" is precisely a *pure ignorance*[6] of all such things. He

---

1. The word "Semiotik" is in the text, but it is probable that "Semantik" is what Nietzsche had in mind.
2. One of the six great systems of Hindu philosophy.
3. The reputed founder of Taoism.
4. Nietzsche's name for one accepting his [Nietzsche's] philosophy.
5. That is, the strict letter of the law—the chief target of Jesus' early preaching ["killeth"].
6. A reference to the "pure ignorance" ("reine Thorheit") of Parsifal.

has never heard of *culture*; he doesn't have to make war on it—he doesn't even deny it . . . . The same thing may be said of the *state*, of the whole bourgeois social order, of labor, of war—he has no ground for denying "the world," for he knows nothing of the ecclesiastical concept of "the world". . . . *Denial* is precisely the thing that is impossible to him.—In the same way he lacks argumentative capacity, and has no belief that an article of faith, a "truth," may be established by proofs (—*his* proofs are inner "lights," subjective sensations of happiness and self-approval, simple "proofs of power"—). Such a doctrine *cannot* contradict: it doesn't know that other doctrines exist, or *can* exist, and is wholly incapable of imagining anything opposed to it. . . . If anything of the sort is ever encountered, it laments the "blindness" with sincere sympathy—for it alone has "light"—but it does not offer objections. . . .

In the whole psychology of the "Gospels," the concepts of guilt and punishment are lacking, and so is that of reward. "Sin," which means anything that puts a distance between God and man, is abolished— *this is precisely the "glad tidings."* Eternal bliss is not merely promised, nor is it bound up with conditions: it is conceived as the *only* reality— what remains consists merely of signs useful in speaking of it.

The *results* of such a point of view project themselves into a new way of life, the special evangelical *way of life.* It is not a "belief" that marks off the Christian; he is distinguished by a different mode of action; he acts *differently.* He offers no resistance, either by word or in his heart, to those who stand against him. He draws no distinction between strangers and countrymen, Jews and Gentiles ("neighbor," of course, means fellow-believer, Jew). He is angry with no one, and he despises no one. He neither appeals to the courts of justice nor heeds their mandates ("Swear not at all" [Matthew V:34]). He never under any circumstances divorces his wife, even when he has proofs of her infidelity.—And under all of this is one principle; all of it arises from one instinct.—

The life of the Savior was simply a carrying out of this way of life— and so was his death. . . . He no longer needed any formula or ritual in his relations with God—not even prayer. He had rejected the whole of the Jewish doctrine of repentance and atonement; he *knew* that it was only by a *way* of life that one could feel one's self "divine," "blessed," "evangelical," a "child of God." *Not* by "repentance," *not* by "prayer and forgiveness" is the way to God: *only the Gospel way* leads to God—it is itself "God!" What the Gospels *abolished* was the Judaism in the concepts of "sin," "forgiveness of sin," "faith," "salvation through faith"— the whole *ecclesiastical* dogma of the Jews was denied by the "glad tidings."

The deep instinct which prompts the Christian how to *live* so that he will feel that he is "in heaven" and is "immortal," despite many reasons for feeling that he is not "in heaven": this is the only psychological reality in "salvation."—A new way of life, *not* a new faith. . . .

If I understand anything at all about this great symbolist, it is this: that he regarded only *subjective* realities as realities, as "truths"—that he saw everything else, everything natural, temporal, spatial and historical, merely as signs, as materials for parables. The concept of "the Son of God" does not connote a concrete person in history, an isolated and definite individual, but an "eternal" fact, a psychological symbol set free from the concept of time. The same thing is true, and in the highest sense, of the God of this typical symbolist, of the "kingdom of God," and of the "sonship of God." Nothing could be more un-Christian than the *crude ecclesiastical* notions of God as a *person*, of a "kingdom of God" that is to come, of a "kingdom of heaven" beyond, and of a "son of God" as the *second person* of the Trinity. All this—if I may be forgiven the phrase—is like thrusting one's fist into the eye (and what an eye!) of the Gospels: a disrespect for symbols amounting to *world-historical cynicism*. . . . But it is nevertheless obvious enough what is meant by the symbols "Father" and "Son"—not, of course, to every one—: the word "Son" expresses *entrance* into the feeling that there is a general transformation of all things (beatitude), and "Father" expresses *that feeling itself*—the sensation of eternity and of perfection.—I am ashamed to remind you of what the church has made of this symbolism: has it not set an

Amphitryon[7] story at the threshold of the Christian "faith"? And a dogma of "immaculate conception" for good measure? . . . *And thereby it has robbed conception of its immaculateness—*

The "kingdom of heaven" is a state of the heart—not something to come "beyond the world" or "after death." The whole idea of natural death is *absent* from the Gospels: death is not a bridge, not a passing; it is absent because it belongs to a quite different, a merely apparent world, useful only as a symbol. The "hour of death" is *not* a Christian idea—"hours," time, the physical life and its crises have no existence for the bearer of "glad tidings." The "kingdom of God" is not something that men wait for: it had no yesterday and no day after tomorrow, it is not going to come at a "millennium"—it is an experience of the heart, it is everywhere and it is nowhere. . . .

This "bearer of glad tidings" died as he lived and *taught—not* to "save mankind," but to show mankind how to live. It was a *way* of life that he bequeathed to man: his demeanor before the judges, before the officers, before his accusers—his demeanor on the *cross.* He does not resist; he does not defend his rights; he makes no effort to ward off the most extreme penalty—more, he *invites it.* . . . And he prays, suffers and loves *with* those, *in* those, who do him evil. . . . *Not* to defend one's self, *not* to show anger, *not* to lay blames. . . . On the contrary, to submit even to the Evil One—to *love* him. . . .

—We free spirits—we are the first to have the necessary prerequisite to understanding what nineteen centuries have misunderstood—that instinct and passion for integrity which makes war upon the "holy lie" even more than upon all other lies. . . . Mankind was unspeakably far from our benevolent and cautious neutrality, from that discipline of the spirit which alone makes possible the solution of such strange and subtle things: what men always sought, with shameless egoism, was

7. Amphytrion was the son of Alcaeus, King of Tiryns. His wife was Alcmene. During his absence she was visited by Zeus, and bore Heracles.

their *own* advantage therein; they created the *church* out of denial of the Gospels. . . .

Whoever sought for signs of an ironical divinity's hand in the great drama of existence would find no small indication thereof in the *stupendous question-mark* that is called Christianity. That mankind should be on its knees before the very antithesis of what was the origin, the meaning and the *law* of the Gospels—that in the concept of the "church" the very things should be pronounced holy that the "bearer of glad tidings" regards as *beneath* him and *behind* him—it would be impossible to surpass this as a grand example of *world-historical irony.*

—Our age is proud of its historical sense: how, then, could it delude itself into believing that the *crude fable of the wonder-worker and Savior* constituted the beginnings of Christianity—and that everything spiritual and symbolical in it only came later? Quite to the contrary, the whole history of Christianity—from the death on the cross onward—is the history of a progressively clumsier misunderstanding of an *original* symbolism. With every extension of Christianity among larger and ruder masses, even less capable of grasping the principles that gave birth to it, the need arose to make it more and more *vulgar* and *barbarous*—it absorbed the teachings and rites of all the *subterranean cults* of the *imperium Romanum,* and the absurdities engendered by all sorts of sickly reasoning. It was the fate of Christianity that its faith had to become as sickly, as low and as vulgar, as the needs were sickly, low and vulgar to which it had to administer. A *sickly barbarism* finally lifts itself to power as the church—the church, that incarnation of deadly hostility to all honesty, to all loftiness of soul, to all discipline of the spirit, to all spontaneous and kindly humanity.—*Christian* values—*noble* values: it is only we, we free spirits, who have reestablished this greatest of all antitheses in values! . . .

I cannot, at this place, avoid a sigh. There are days when I am visited by a feeling blacker than the blackest melancholy—*contempt of man.* Let me leave no doubt as to *what* I despise, *whom* I despise: it is the man of today, the man with whom I am unhappily contemporaneous. The man of today—I am suffocated by his foul breath! . . . Toward the past, like all who understand, I am full of tolerance, which is to say, *generous* self-control: with gloomy caution I pass through whole millennia of this madhouse of a world, call it "Christianity," "Christian faith" or the "Christian church," as you will—I take care not to hold mankind responsible for its lunacies. But my feeling changes and breaks out irresistibly the moment I enter modern times, *our* times. Our age *knows better*. . . . What was formerly merely sickly now becomes indecent—it is indecent to be a Christian today. *And here my disgust begins.* I look about me: not a word survives of what was once called "truth"; we can no longer bear to hear a priest pronounce the word. Even a man who makes the most modest pretensions to integrity *must* know that a theologian, a priest, a pope of today not only errs when he speaks, but actually *lies*—and that he no longer escapes blame for his lie through "innocence" or "ignorance." The priest knows as every one knows, that there is no longer any "God," or any "sinner," or any "Savior"—that "free will" and the "moral order of the world" are lies—: serious reflection, the profound self-conquest of the spirit, *allow* no man to pretend that he does *not* know it. . . . *All* the ideas of the church are now recognized for what they are—as the worst counterfeits in existence, invented to debase nature and all natural values; the priest himself is seen as he actually is—as the most dangerous form of parasite, as the venomous spider of creation. . . . We know, our *conscience* now knows—just *what* the real value of all those sinister inventions of priest and church has been and *what ends they have served*, with their debasement of humanity to a state of self-pollution, the very sight of which excites loathing—the concepts "the other world," "the last judgment," "the immortality of the soul," the "soul" itself: they are all merely so many instruments of torture, systems of cruelty, whereby the priest becomes master and remains master. . . . Everyone knows this, *but nevertheless things remain as before*. What has become of the last trace of decent feeling, of self-respect, when our statesmen, otherwise an unconventional class of men and thoroughly anti-Christian in their acts, now call themselves Christians and go to the communion table? . . . A prince at the head of his armies, magnificent as the expression of the egoism and arrogance of his people—and yet acknowledging, without any shame, that he is a Christian! . . . Whom, then, does Christianity deny? *What* does it call "the world"? To be a *soldier*, to be a judge, to be a patriot; to defend one's self; to be careful of one's honor; to desire one's own advantage; to be *proud* . . . every act of every day, every instinct, every valuation that shows itself in a *deed*, is now anti-Christian: what a *monster of falsehood* the modem man must be to call himself nevertheless, and *without* shame, a Christian!

—I shall go back a bit, and tell you the authentic history of Christianity.—The very word "Christianity" is a misunderstanding—at bottom there was only one Christian, and he died on the cross. The "Gospels" died on the cross. What, from that moment onward, was called the "Gospels" was the very reverse of what he had lived: "bad tidings," a *Dysangelium*.[8] It is an error amounting to nonsensicality to see in "faith," and particularly in faith in salvation through Christ, the distinguishing mark of the Christian: only the Christian *way of life*, the life *lived* by him who died on the cross, is Christian. . . . To this day *such* a life is still possible, and for certain men even necessary: genuine, primitive Christianity will remain possible in all ages. . . . *Not* faith, but acts; above all, an *avoidance* of acts, a different *state of being*. . . . States of consciousness, faith of a sort, the acceptance, for example, of anything as true—as every psychologist knows, the value of these things is perfectly indifferent and fifth-rate compared to that of the instincts: strictly speaking, the whole concept of intellectual causality is false. To reduce being a Christian, the state of Christianity, to an acceptance of truth, to a mere phenomenon of consciousness, is to formulate the negation of Christianity. *In fact, there are no Christians.* The "Christian"—he who for two thousand years has passed as a Christian—is simply a psychological

8. So in the text. One of Nietzsche's numerous coinages, obviously suggested by "Evangelium," the German for "gospel."

self-delusion. Closely examined, it appears that, *despite* all his "faith," he has been ruled *only* by his instincts—and what instincts!—In all ages—for example, in the case of Luther—"faith" has been no more than a cloak, a pretense, a *curtain* behind which the instincts have played their game—a shrewd *blindness* to the domination of *certain* of the instincts. . . . I have already called "faith" the specially Christian form of *shrewdness*—people always *talk* of their "faith" and act according to their instincts. . . . In the world of ideas of the Christian there is nothing that so much as touches reality: on the contrary, one recognizes an instinctive *hatred* of reality as the motive power, the only motive power at the bottom of Christianity. What follows therefrom? That even here, [psychologically], there is a radical error, which is to say one conditioning fundamentals, which is to say, one in *substance*. Take away one idea and put a genuine reality in its place—and the whole of Christianity crumbles to nothingness!—Viewed calmly, this strangest of all phenomena, a religion not only depending on errors, but inventive and ingenious *only* in devising injurious errors, poisonous to life and to the heart—this remains a *spectacle for the gods*—for those gods who are also philosophers, and whom I have encountered, for example, in the celebrated dialogues at Naxos. At the moment when their disgust leaves them (—and us!) they will be thankful for the spectacle afforded by the Christians: perhaps because of *this* curious exhibition alone the wretched little planet called the Earth deserves a glance from omnipotence, a show of divine interest. . . . Therefore, let us not underestimate the Christians: the Christian, false *to the point of innocence*, is far above the ape—in its application to the Christians a well-known theory of descent becomes a mere piece of politeness. . . .

—The fate of the Gospels was decided by death—it hung on the "cross." . . . It was only death, that unexpected and shameful death; it was only the cross, which was usually reserved for the canaille only— it was only this appalling paradox which brought the disciples face to face with the real riddle: *"Who was it? what was it?"*—The feeling of dismay, of profound affront and injury; the suspicion that such a death might involve a *refutation* of their cause; the terrible question, "Why just in this way?"—this state of mind is only too easy to understand. Here everything *must* be accounted for as necessary; everything must have a meaning, a reason, the highest sort of reason; the love of a disciple excludes all chance. Only then did the chasm of doubt yawn: "*Who* put him to death? Who was his natural enemy?"—this question flashed like a lightning-stroke. Answer: dominant Judaism, its ruling class. From that moment, one found one's self in revolt *against* the established order, and began to understand Jesus as *in revolt against the established order*. Until then this militant, this nay-saying, nay-doing element in his character had been lacking; what is more, he had appeared to present its opposite. Obviously, the little community had *not* understood what was precisely the most important thing of all: the example offered by this way of dying, the freedom from and superiority to every feeling of *[resentment]*—a plain indication of how little he was understood at all! All that Jesus could hope to accomplish by his death, in itself, was to offer the strongest possible proof, or *example*, of his teachings in the most public manner . . . . . But his disciples were very far from forgiving his death—though to have done so would have accorded with the Gospels in the highest degree; and neither were they prepared to *offer* themselves, with gentle and serene calmness of heart, for a similar death. . . . On the contrary, it was precisely the most unevangelical of feelings, *revenge*, that now possessed them. It seemed impossible that the cause should perish with his death: "recompense" and "judgment" became necessary (—yet what could be less evangelical than "recompense," "punishment," and "sitting in judgment"!). Once more the popular belief in the coming of a messiah appeared in the foreground; attention was riveted upon an historical moment: the "kingdom of God" is to come, with judgment upon his enemies. . . . But in all this there was a wholesale misunderstanding: imagine the "kingdom of God" as a last act, as a mere promise! The Gospels had been, in fact, the incarnation, the fulfillment, the *realization* of this "kingdom of God." It was only now that all the familiar contempt for and bitterness against Pharisees and theologians began to appear in the character of the Master—he was thereby *turned* into a Pharisee and theologian himself! On the other hand, the savage veneration of these completely unbalanced souls could no longer endure the Gospel doctrine, taught by Jesus, of the equal right of all men to be children of God: their revenge took the form of *elevating* Jesus in an extravagant fashion, and thus separating him from themselves: just as, in earlier times, the Jews, to revenge themselves upon their enemies, separated themselves from their God, and placed him on a great height. The One God and the Only Son of God: both were products of *[resentment]*.

—And from that time onward an absurd problem offered itself: "how could God allow it!" To which the deranged reason of the little community formulated an answer that was terrifying in its absurdity: God gave his son as a *sacrifice* for the forgiveness of sins. At once there was an end of the gospels! Sacrifice for sin, and in its most obnoxious and barbarous form: sacrifice of the *innocent* for the sins of the guilty! What appalling paganism!—Jesus himself had done away with the very concept of "guilt," he denied that there was any gulf fixed between God and man; he *lived* this unity between God and man, and that was precisely his "glad tidings." . . . And *not* as a mere privilege!—From this time forward the type of the Savior was corrupted, bit by bit, by the doctrine of judgment and of the second coming, the doctrine of death as a sacrifice, the doctrine of the *resurrection*, by means of which the entire concept of "blessedness," the whole and only reality of the gospels, is juggled away—in favor of a state of existence *after* death! . . . St. Paul, with that rabbinical impudence which shows itself in all his doings, gave a logical quality to that conception, that *indecent* conception, in this way: "*If* Christ did not rise from the dead, then all our faith is in vain!"—And at once there sprang from the Gospels the most contemptible of all unfulfillable promises, the *shameless* doctrine of personal immortality. . . . Paul even preached it as a reward. . . .

One now begins to see just *what* it was that came to an end with the death on the cross: a new and thoroughly original effort to found a

Buddhistic peace movement, and so establish *happiness on earth*—real, *not* merely promised. For this remains—as I have already pointed out—the essential difference between the two religions of decadence: Buddhism promises nothing, but actually fulfils; Christianity promises everything, but *fulfils nothing.*—Hard upon the heels of the "glad tidings" came the worst imaginable: those of Paul. In Paul is incarnated the very opposite of the "bearer of glad tidings"; he represents the genius for hatred, the vision of hatred, the relentless logic of hatred. *What,* indeed, has not this dysangelist sacrificed to hatred! Above all, the Savior: he nailed him to *his own* cross. The life, the example, the teaching, the death of Christ, the meaning and the law of the whole gospels—nothing was left of all this after that counterfeiter in hatred had reduced it to his uses. Surely *not* reality; surely *not* historical truth! . . . Once more the priestly instinct of a Jew perpetrated the same old master crime against history—he simply struck out the yesterday and the day before yesterday of Christianity, and *invented his own history of Christian beginnings.* Going further, he treated the history of Israel to another falsification, so that it became a mere prologue to *his* achievement: all the prophets, it now appeared, had referred to his "Savior." Later on the church even falsified the history of man in order to make it a prologue to Christianity. . . . The figure of the Savior, his teaching, his way of life, his death, the meaning of his death, even the consequences of his death—nothing remained untouched, nothing remained in even remote contact with reality. Paul simply shifted the center of gravity of that whole life to a place *behind* this existence in the *lie* of the "risen" Jesus. At bottom, he had no use for the life of the Savior—what he needed was the death on the cross, *and* something more. To see anything honest in such a man as Paul, whose home was at the center of the Stoical enlightenment, when he converts an hallucination into a *proof* of the resurrection of the Savior, or even to believe his tale that he suffered from this hallucination himself—this would be a genuine [folly] in a psychologist. Paul willed the end; *therefore* he also willed the means. . . . What he himself didn't believe was swallowed readily enough by the idiots among whom he spread his teaching.—What *he* wanted, was power; in Paul the priest once more reached out for power—he had use only for such concepts, teachings and symbols as served the purpose of tyrannizing over the masses and organizing mobs. *What* was the only part of Christianity that Mohammed borrowed later on? Paul's invention, his device for establishing priestly tyranny and organizing the mob: the belief in the immortality of the soul—*that is to say, the doctrine of "judgment".* . . .

When the center of gravity of life is placed, *not* in life itself, but in "the beyond"—in *nothingness*—then one has taken away its center of gravity altogether. The vast lie of personal immortality destroys all reason, all natural instinct—henceforth, everything in the instincts that is beneficial, that fosters life and that safeguards the future is a cause of suspicion. So to live that life no longer has any meaning: *this* is now the "meaning" of life. . . . Why be public-spirited? Why take any pride in descent and forefathers? Why labor together, trust one another, or concern one's self about the common welfare, and try to serve it? . . . Merely so many "temptations," so many strayings from the "straight path." "*One* thing only is necessary." . . . That every man, because he has an "immortal soul," is as good as every other man; that in an infinite universe of things the "salvation" of *every* individual may lay claim to eternal importance; that insignificant bigots and the three-fourths insane may assume that the laws of nature are constantly *suspended* in their behalf—it is impossible to lavish too much contempt upon such a magnification of every sort of selfishness to infinity, to *insolence*. And yet Christianity has to thank precisely *this* miserable flattery of personal vanity for its *triumph*—it was thus that it lured all the botched, the dissatisfied, the fallen upon evil days, the whole refuse and off-scouring of humanity to its side. The "salvation of the soul"—in plain words: "the world revolves around *me*." . . . The poisonous doctrine, "*equal rights for all*," has been propagated as a Christian principle: out of the secret nooks and crannies of bad instinct Christianity has waged a deadly war upon all feelings of reverence and distance between man and man, which is to say, upon the first *prerequisite* to every step upward, to every development of civilization—out of the [resentment] of the masses it has forged its chief weapons against *us*, against everything noble, joyous and high-spirited on earth, against our happiness on earth. . . . To allow "immortality" to every Peter and Paul was the greatest, the most vicious outrage upon *noble* humanity ever perpetrated.—*And* let us not underestimate the fatal influence that Christianity has had, even upon politics! Nowadays no one has courage any more for special rights, for the right of dominion, for feelings of honorable pride in himself and his equals—for the *pathos of distance*. . . . Our politics is sick with this lack of courage! The aristocratic attitude of mind has been undermined by the lie of the equality of souls; and if belief in the "privileges of the majority" makes and *will continue to make* revolutions—it is Christianity, let us not doubt, and *Christian* valuations, which convert every revolution into a carnival of blood and crime! Christianity is a revolt of all creatures that creep on the ground against everything that is *lofty*: the gospel of the "lowly" *lowers*. . . .

from Christ: A Crisis in
the Life of God

by Jack Miles

Jack Miles (born 1942) suggests that God shared the ancient Jews' suffering by manifesting himself as a victimized Jewish peasant, thereby redefining Jewish conceptions of victory and defeat.

W hy did God become a Jew and subject himself to public execution by the enemy of his chosen people? He did so in order to confess that, by choice or of necessity, he was a god disarmed. He knew that genocide against his chosen people was imminent and that he would do nothing to prevent it. The one thing he could choose to do, as the Jew he became, was to break his silence about his own scandalous inaction.

God revealed to the seer Daniel at the court of the king of Babylon that when Babylon fell, the kingdom of God would not come immediately. Instead, there would come—in a succession symbolized in Daniel's vision (Dan. 7) by a series of beasts—the kingdoms of the Babylonians, the Medes, the Persians, and the Greeks of Alexander the Great. Only then would God's kingdom come, symbolized in the vision by "one like a son of man." But as the Gospel opens, instead of God's kingdom, there has come the kingdom of the Romans, and the iron fist of this new Babylon is tightening around Judea in the last decades before a catastrophic rebellion. If, as the Book of Daniel makes clear, God foresees the historical future in detail, then he knows that he will not rescue his people from the defeat that lies ahead. Rome, enraged by Jewish rebelliousness, will perpetrate genocide, and God will do nothing. The one thing he can do—and does do as Jesus of Nazareth, God the Son—is break his silence about his own inaction.

The word *genocide* above refers to the ferocious escalation of violence that took place in the generation immediately after the execution of Jesus and came to its first climax with a Jewish revolt against Rome in 66–70 C.E. The Jews were a formidable opponent for imperial Rome. They were, more than is sometimes remembered, populous, well organized, well financed, and passionately motivated. Rome did not finally defeat them and suppress their rebellion until after it peaked for a second time, in 132–135 C.E. After this final Jewish revolt, an uprising led by the messiah Simon Bar Kokhba, Rome changed the name of Jerusalem to Aelia Capitolina and made it a capital offense for any Jew to set foot in the erstwhile City of David. Jewish sovereignty in the Land of Israel then came to an end for fully eighteen centuries.

Rome's imperial agenda did not extend to the extermination of all the Jews of the empire. In that one regard, the Roman suppression of world Jewry's bid for freedom differed from the Nazi "Final Solution" of 1941–45. In two other regards, however, Rome's victory in its sixty years' war with the Jews may plausibly bear the grim designation *genocide*. First, the Roman intent in destroying the Jewish Temple was to end the distinctive national life that the Jewish people had led as a nation within the empire. Second, the portion of the world Jewish population that perished in the first of the Jewish Wars alone is comparable to the portion that perished in the Nazi *shoah*.[*]

Contemporary estimates of the world Jewish population in the first

---

[*] I use this Hebrew noun, which means simply "catastrophe," in preference to the more usual *holocaust*, a word that some find offensive because its original setting is in the Jewish religion itself. *Shoah* is the noun most commonly used in Israel to refer to the slaughter of the Jews of Europe during World War II.

century range from a low of 5.5 million to a high of more than 8 million. Of these, 1 million to 2.5 million lived in Palestine; 4.5 million to 6 million lived in the diaspora. In the years before the doomed uprisings, the Jews of the Roman empire, notwithstanding worsening oppression within their homeland, were more numerous, more powerful, and better organized within the greater multinational social order of their day than were the Jews of Europe before the outbreak of World War II. Their remarkable unity—all Jews looking to Jerusalem as their spiritual capital and all supporting the Temple by the payment of a Temple tax—mimicked the organization of the Roman empire itself. This political coherence was admired by the other, less autonomous peoples of the empire, but it was understandably suspect in the eyes of the imperial authorities themselves.

Perhaps because of latent Roman resentment of Jewish success within the empire, not to mention various officially conceded Jewish legal exemptions and privileges, the Jewish revolts were put down with exceptional violence. The first-century historian Josephus, a Romanized Jew, reports that 1.1 million died in Titus's siege of Jerusalem in 70 C.E. The Roman historian Tacitus estimates six hundred thousand dead. Though many modern historians have regarded these numbers as exaggerations, Josephus in reporting his figure recognizes that it will seem incredible and explains that Passover pilgrims from the diaspora had swollen the resident population of Jerusalem to a degree that, though not out of the ordinary for this pilgrimage city, might well seem unbelievable to outsiders. He then engages in a surprisingly modern back-calculation from the number of animals slain for the feast—256,500—to a Passover population of 2,700,200 at the time the siege began.

Jerusalem in that era, it must be remembered, was like Mecca in our own: the site of an astounding annual concentration of pilgrims, overwhelmingly male, for whose ritual purposes an equally astounding number of animals were slaughtered. When the Roman siege began, the temporary population of Jerusalem was further swollen by refugees from parts of Palestine where Roman forces had already, and with great force, been putting down the Jewish rebellion for three full years. In view of all this, the large casualty figures quoted by Josephus and Tacitus are not as implausible as they might otherwise seem.

Even adjusting those figures downward, however, it seems clear that the first-century slaughter of the Jews of Palestine was large enough to be comparable in its impact to the twentieth-century slaughter of the Jews of Europe. The destruction of the Temple in and of itself would have had a major psychological impact, but this loss came coupled with staggering casualties; mass enslavements and ensuing depopulation in the promised land; and, not least, the memory of hideous atrocities. Generally faulted for obsequiousness toward Rome, Josephus does not flinch from reporting terror-crucifixions outside the walls of Jerusalem—mass crucifixions aimed at driving the defenders of the city to despair and panic—or from reporting that when some of the defenders did flee, Roman mercenaries took to disemboweling them in search of swallowed gold coins until stopped by the Roman commander himself.

Tales like these bear comparison with the grisliest from the Nazi concentration camps. The memory of them, combined with so devastating a loss of life in the Promised Land and with major pogroms against Jews in a number of cities within the Roman empire, can scarcely fail to have raised many of the radical or desperate questions about God that, to some, seem to have arisen for the first time in the twentieth century. As for radical or desperate answers to those questions, one seems to have been the Christian vision of the divine warrior self-disarmed.

Historically, there is little doubt that the Jews who rose against Rome expected that their God would come to their assistance, as he had in the historic victories whose celebration remains central to Judaism. There can be equally little doubt that these rebels, as they imagined the God who would assist them, imagined him as knowing the future in detail. This is the image of God expressed so vividly in the Book of Daniel. Literary criticism attending to the character of God within the Old Testament and the New is free to accept this understanding of God (as well as the time and place of the Book of Daniel as given in the text) and then to stipulate about God, as we have done earlier in this book, that, from the Babylonian exile onward, his character is such that he knows the future in the detailed way that human beings know the past.

Yet to imagine a first-century Jew imagining God in this way, even before the disastrous Jewish Wars, is to imagine a Jew in distress. Instead of the predicted kingdom of God, there has come the kingdom of the Romans, and its oppressiveness dwarfs that of all previous oppressors. What was a devout first-century Jew reading the Book of Daniel in a trusting, straightforward, precritical way to think as he or she noted its disconfirmation by events? Had God been mistaken? Had he failed to foresee the rise of Rome? What the radical reversal in the divine identity implied by the pacifist preaching of Jesus suggests is that a Jewish writer of powerful imagination projected this crisis of faith into the mind of God, transforming it into a crisis of conscience. God had broken his own covenant, and the fact that he had broken it had to matter to him. He knew he should have stopped Rome. He knew he had not done so. From that simple notion, a composition of enormous complexity could be derived.

A good many historical critics, it should be noted, have based their reading of the Gospels on speculation about the historical consciousness of Jesus. Beginning with Albert Schweitzer in 1901, many have believed that Jesus—living under Roman rule, intensely aware of Jewish tradition, and experiencing what we would call cognitive dissonance between the two—inserted himself into the apocalyptic mythology of his day by personifying the "son of man" image of Daniel 7 and then identifying himself as the personage in question. Jesus believed, Schweitzer concluded, that by his own agency and, finally, his own death, Rome would fall, history would end, and God's Kingdom would be established for all time.

More recent scholarship tends to believe that this and related, more or less learned scriptural identifications were made not by Jesus during his lifetime but only about Jesus after his death. So it may well have been, yet the protagonist of the Gospels as we encounter him on the page acts *as if* he has made these identifications himself, and on this literary datum may be grounded an interpretation in which historical speculation about the remembered mind of Jesus yields to literary speculation about the imagined mind of God at that historical juncture. For literary purposes, in other words, it does not matter whether the historical Jesus referred to himself as "Son of Man" or not, so long as the literary character Jesus Christ does so on the page. Nor need it matter that the effect this character produces on the page, as the page is read by some contemporary interpreter, may not have been intended by all or even by any of the writers who produced the Gospels. It is proper to a literary classic that it touch readers generation after generation, century after century, in ways that transcend the intentions of the originating author.

But having gone thus far in claiming space for a literary reading of the Gospels, let me immediately concede that nonhistorical readings vary in the degree to which they are informed by history. A fantastical or mystical or morally didactic reading, for example, might prescind almost entirely from historical information. The reading offered in this book, by contrast, admits history roughly to the extent that it is admitted in the interpretation of a historical novel. Moreover, though one does not read a historical novel in order to extract history from it, a general awareness of historical time and geographic place colors and contributes to the aesthetic effect, which, as interpreted, may be historically suggestive without entailing any outright historical claim.

Against the usual Christian spiritualization of the Old Testament, the interpretation offered here is, then, a relative materialization of the New Testament, in which God's real-world, land-and-wealth-and-offspring promises to the Jews are expected to remain on his mind—which is to say, on Jesus' mind—and in which they are allowed, without shame, to remain on his hearers' minds as well. What such an interpretation of the Gospels suggests about the historical situation behind them is that a theodicy—a moral justification of the behavior of God—whose plausibility had survived several centuries of fluctuating foreign oppression finally came into crisis under the steadily worsening Roman oppression of the first century.

According to the received theodicy, first formulated after Israel was conquered by Assyria and Babylonia, that double defeat did not mean what it seemed to mean. The Lord's victory over Egypt had been a real victory, but his apparent defeat by Assyria and Babylonia was not a real defeat. No, Assyria and Babylonia were actually tools in the hands of the Lord, who, far from defeated, was in perfect control of events and merely punishing Israel for its sins. Painful as it might seem to accept the claim that a national god who had once been so favorable had now turned hostile, the alternative was the loss of that god as a potential future support and protection. Since Israel's sense of itself as a people had become inseparable from its sense of covenant with the Lord, life with him even in an angry and punitive mood was preferable to life altogether without him.

By the expedient of attributing its enemies' victories to the action of its own god, Israel saved that god from suffering the same kind of defeat that Israel itself had suffered. But the price of this expedient was high. It required a massive inculpation of the people of Israel—a blaming of the victim, if you will—and an uncomfortable emphasis on anger and vindictiveness in the characterization of the god. Even at the start, these features of the theodicy were felt to be so costly that it was necessary to add, when presenting it, that God would not always conduct himself thus. Israel's national good fortune would be restored before long, and with it a much happier relationship between the god and his people.

But for how many centuries of continuing oppression, especially as different oppressors succeeded one another, could this revision of the covenant remain adequate? The historical suggestion implied by the literary reading of the Gospels offered here is that for a significant segment of the Jewish population, a further revision came to seem necessary. It became necessary to concede the obvious and to redefine the Lord as a god whose return to action as a warrior was not just delayed but altogether canceled, and then to adjust his warlike character accordingly. Not the least part of this adjustment was a revision of his relationship to the other nations of the world; for if the Lord could no longer function effectively as anybody's enemy, then he was necessarily everybody's friend. And if his covenant love was now indiscriminate and universal, then so also must be the love of his covenant partner.

Israel, as God's partner in the original covenant, was expected to demonstrate its status as such by its exclusive devotion *to the Lord*. As the new covenant is proclaimed, Israel's sin, its infidelity and failure to be exclusive in its devotion, is more forgotten than forgiven. The God who will no longer reward or punish his covenant partners as he once did can no longer require of them what he once required. Henceforth, it is not their devotion to him but their devotion to one another and, even more remarkably, to strangers that will signal their status as his. To the extent that they keep this one commandment, to that extent the divine warrior will be excused from ever again taking up arms. Israel will have no enemy because no one will have an enemy other than Satan, the enemy of all.

God Incarnate does indeed understand himself to be, as to his human identity, the "Son of Man" of Daniel 7. But in this capacity, rather than establish the Kingdom of God by military force, he preaches military renunciation: He urges his followers to turn the other cheek. Going dramatically beyond even that, he reveals what he will *not* do—what no one any longer must expect him to do—by going without protest to his own execution on the gallows of the oppressor. The covenant revision is communicated, in sum, not only by prophetic preaching but also by a traumatic, cathartic, climactic, and, not least, ironic sacred drama in which the central role is played by God himself.

Did the historical Jesus actually foresee the worst for his nation, despair of anything like divine rescue, and then—by a bold but conceivable modification of Israelite prophecy—infer that, rather than the prophet of God, he was God himself become incarnate to turn the bad news into an ironic kind of good news? As noted, the all-but-universal assumption on the part of contemporary historical critics is that others turned Jesus into Christ and then into God after his death.

I myself, rather than suppose that Jesus was a simple preacher drafted, as it were, against his will into a larger role, find it historically more plausible to suppose that he was complicitous in his own mythologization, a messenger who intended somehow to become the message, a provocateur who stimulated others to further provocation. Israel Knohl[*] and Michael O. Wise[**] claim, on evidence from the Dead Sea Scrolls, to have identified historical figures who, before Jesus, believed themselves or were believed by their followers to be divine, suffering messiahs. One need not accept the exact identifications they propose to recognize that, on the evidence they adduce, the idea of combining these elements—divinity, suffering, and messianism—had grown religiously plausible in Palestinian Jewry well before its Christian enactment.

The new research has attracted as much attention as it has because a chasm separates the claim that the Messiah must suffer from the far bolder claim that the suffering messiah is God Incarnate. And, to be sure, even though Jesus makes this claim in the Gospel of John, it remains possible that the idea behind the claim may not in fact have emerged until decades after his death—that is, until closer to the time when the Gospel of John was written. A careful and conservative scholar, the late Raymond E. Brown, asked forty years ago in his great commentary on John

> whether there is any likelihood that Jesus made such a public claim to divinity as that represented in [John 8:58, "Before Abraham was, I AM"], or are we dealing here exclusively with the profession of faith of the later Church? As a general principle it is certainly true that through their faith the evangelists were able to clarify a picture of Jesus that was obscure during [his] ministry. However, it is difficult to avoid the impression

---

[*] *The Messiah Before Jesus: The Suffering Servant of the Dead Sea Scrolls* (Berkeley: University of California Press, 2000).

[**] *The First Messiah: Investigating the Savior Before Christ* (San Francisco: Harper-SanFrancisco, 1999).

created by all the Gospels that the Jewish authorities saw something blasphemous in Jesus' understanding of himself and his role. There is no convincing proof that the only real reason why Jesus was put to death was because he was a social, or ethical, reformer, or because he was politically dangerous. But how can we determine scientifically what the blasphemous element was in Jesus' stated or implied claims about himself? In the clarity with which John presents the divine "I AM" statement of Jesus, is he making explicit what was in some way implicit? No definitive answer seems possible on purely scientific grounds.

There, as it seems to me, the matter still rests. I am content, however, to leave further discussion of this point to the historians, for the explosion of religious and literary creativity that turned material defeat into spiritual victory is no less remarkable as the achievement of Jesus' Jewish contemporaries after his death than as his own creation. The spectacle of the Lord of Hosts put to death by the enemy ought, in principle, to have ended forever a covenant predicated on the Lord's ability to protect his friends and defeat their foes. In practice, for those who made the commemoration of that awful spectacle a covenant ritual, its meaning was that a new covenant between God and mankind had taken effect that was immune to defeat, a covenant that could withstand the worst that Satan, standing (as in the Book of Revelation) for all historical enemies past or future, could inflict. Whatever provoked this brilliant adjustment of the idea of covenant (and scholars, significantly, are unanimous that the Gospels were all written after the destruction of Jerusalem in 70 C.E.), it is conceptually analogous to the adjustment made when the victories of Assyria and Babylonia were defined as the punitive actions of God. The far-reaching implications of this revision are a matter to which we shall return at the start of Part Four. What the revision creates, in the end, is a new theodicy, a new way of maintaining that there is still a god and that he still matters in the face of historical experience to the contrary.

While I was at work on this book, Rabbi Ovadia Yosef, the spiritual leader of Israel's right-wing Shas party, created a scandal by suggesting in a sermon that the Jews who suffered and died in the Nazi Shoah may have died because of Jewish sin. When this statement came up in conversation in Los Angeles, a friend of mine recalled with anger and sadness that, as a boy in the 1940s, he had heard the rabbi in his Orthodox *shul* preach this interpretation of the Shoah not just once but repeatedly. Reactions *against* such statements—including both my friend's anger and the scandal that erupted in Israel over Ovadia Yosef—are, of course, as much a part of contemporary Jewish thought as are the statements themselves, but the sadness and the scandal are instructive for anyone attempting to make sense of Jesus.

How did the divine warrior end up preaching pacifism? Christian theology has tended to speak of this change as spiritual growth in God, though rarely using a phrase like "spiritual growth." The answer suggested here is that God made a new human virtue of his divine necessity. He found a way to turn his defeat into a victory, but the defeat came first. For some, to be sure, no divine defeat is so devastating as to extinguish forever the hope of victory. But for others, considering the number and magnitude of the defeats, a different conclusion has seemed inevitable: If God must be defined as a historical-time, physical-world warrior whose victory has simply been postponed indefinitely, then there might as well be no such god. Indefinite postponement is tantamount to cancellation. Effectively, after such a conclusion, the only choices left are atheism or some otherwise unthinkably radical revision in the understanding of God.

This is a question that is called with devastating starkness in Elie Wiesel's *Night* (1958):

> The SS hanged two Jewish men and a youth in front of the whole camp. The men died quickly, but the death throes of the youth lasted for half an hour. "Where is God? Where is he?" someone asked behind me. As the youth still hung in

torment in the noose after a long time, I heard the man call again, "Where is God now?" And I heard a voice in myself answer: "Where is he? He is here. He is hanging there on the gallows."

If God will not rescue us, then is there a god? If there is and he still will not rescue us, then is he a weakling or a fiend? It should go without saying that Wiesel did not write this scene as an apology for Christianity. But the scene cannot fail to evoke the Crucifixion for Christian readers, and Wiesel cannot have failed to notice and intend this.

In sum, the disarmament of the divine warrior in the first century mirrors, though with different consequences, his disarmament in the twentieth century. The dedication to *The Prophets*, the most widely read of the books of the late Abraham Joshua Heschel, the most influential Jewish theologian of the twentieth century, reads:

> TO THE MARTYRS OF 1940–45
> *All this has come upon us*
> *Though we have not forgotten Thee,*
> *Or been false to Thy covenant.*
> *Our heart has not turned back,*
> *Nor have our steps departed from Thy way*
> *. . . for Thy sake we are slain. . . .*
> *Why dost Thou hide Thy face?*
> —*from Psalm 44*

Heschel had every reason to think of these lines—from Psalm 44, quoted in full above—when thinking of the martyrs of 1940–45, but other Jews nineteen centuries before him, thinking of other martyrs, had no less reason to turn to the same Psalm. And one of them, whether or not the one in question was Jesus himself, may have gone on—like the Jew witnessing the hanging in *Night*—to imagine that the Jew on the gallows, this time, was truly God himself.

from Constantine's Sword
by James Carroll

James Carroll (born 1943) worked as a priest and a writer, before giving up the priesthood. He has written nine novels, as well as a memoir, An American Requiem, *which won the National Book Award.* Constantine's Sword *examines the Catholic Church's teachings about Judaism as it pertains to Jesus' story.*

W hat religion was Jesus?

A college professor I know routinely includes this question on a comprehensive quiz he gives to incoming freshmen each year. The pattern of responses is constant. Some students answer "Catholic," most answer "Christian." A distinct minority answers "Jewish." It is easy to condescend to students who do not know that Jesus was a Jew, but in fact there are good reasons to be confused about his religious identity. Some of those reasons have to do with the difficulty of imagining what this extraordinary person's inner life consisted of, and some with whether our compartmentalized idea of religion is relevant to the question. Part of the difficulty has to do with the rampant ambiguities of "Judaism" itself at the time Jesus lived, and part has to do with Christianity's long attempt to purge itself of Semitic content.

The famous "quest for the historical Jesus" that so gripped Protestant scholars in the nineteenth century led both to a new appreciation of Jesus' ties to his native Jewish milieu and to a new emphasis on what separated Jesus from his Jewishness. Jewish scholars at first welcomed Christian explorations into the Jewishness of Jesus, thinking that, as Susannah Heschel puts it, "the more Jewish Jesus could be shown to have been, the more Christians would respect Judaism." But that is not what happened. "Christians had a different agenda," Heschel writes. "For them, the more Jewish Jesus was shown to be, the less original and unique he was. If Jesus had simply preached the ordinary Judaism of his day, the foundation of Christianity as a distinctive and unparalleled religion was shattered . . . As strongly as nineteenth-century Jews tried to show an identity between Jesus and Judaism, Christians tried to demonstrate a difference."

That theological debate was skewed by political developments, especially in Germany, where, ludicrous as it may now seem, the image of the Aryan Christ emerged as something to be taken seriously. Under Otto von Bismarck (1815–1898), pan-German nationalism jelled, spawning a unifying racial theory, which led to a purified notion of a German *volk*. Similar efforts had marked Christian dogma and practice, going back to the early times of the Church, but nineteenth-century nationalism brought a new edge to such discussions. Ideas of racial purity as a component of social identity influenced religious identity, leading to a notion of Christianity stripped of all Semitic influence. As important a figure as the philosopher Johann Fichte (1762–1814), for example, had posited a Jesus who was not Jewish at all, and throughout the century theologians followed suit. This would be one of the ways that German Protestant scholars tilled the soil for Nazi antisemitism, promulgating an idolatry of Aryan racial identity by defining Jesus over against Jewishness, not only religiously but racially. Eventually German Protestant hymnals would be "de-Judaized" by the removal of words like "amen," "hallelujah," and "hosanna."

In the Christian world, the influence of nineteenth-century German Protestant theology was so dominant that it was felt even within Roman Catholicism, especially in the matter of a historical quest for Jesus that led to his removal from the Jewish milieu. As critics of that "quest" remind me now, the illustrated books used in Catholic schools that I attended as a child had been subtly shaped by visual cues. Jesus, Mary, Joseph, and all their intimates, save one, were portrayed with the racial and sartorial characteristics—blue eyes, light brown flowing hair, graceful robes—of northern Europe, in stark distinction to the pictured Pharisees, Sadducees, and high priests, with their odd headdresses, phylacteries, tasseled prayer shawls, oversized noses, and dark skin. It was as if the residents of the towns of Galilee were of a different racial strain than those of Judea—indeed, in the nineteenth century Jesus commonly came to be referred to as "the Galilean," or "the Nazarene," an implicit distancing from "Judea," the region of the Jews. The only obvious Semite in Jesus' inner circle, of course, was the one named for that region, Judas. The betrayer functioned in this filtered narrative as the one Jew, and the story forever emphasized his motive as greed.

The occupations of the fishermen friends of Jesus, like Jesus' own trade of carpenter—think of these pastel scenes of the boy and his dad in that airy, neatly swept workshop, making cabinets—were emphasized to contrast with the Judas-like moneygrubbers whom Jesus would go to Judea to attack. The nineteenth-century quest for the historical Jesus, in other words, in its effort to get behind the façade of an overly divinized Lord, led to the application of nineteenth-century racial categories and cultural stereotypes to first-century Palestine, a way of making Jesus human without making him Jewish. I have been saying "nineteenth-century," emphasizing the German Protestant origins of this mindset, but this was all still thoroughly in place in the crucifix and stained glass of St. Mary's Roman Catholic Church in Alexandria, Virginia, and in the textbooks and bulletin-board posters of my parochial school, by which, despite myself, I continue to measure God. One would think that six years of Scripture study and theology in a rigorous seminary at the time of the revolutionary Vatican II would have remedied this shallow notion of who Jesus was, but German Protestant theology and scholarship, still largely uncriticized for its implicit anti-Judaism, was in the early 1960s more influential in Catholic circles than ever.

True, the most patently childish notions—that cabinetmaker's work-shop, Jesus hand-carving birds, then bringing them to life—had dropped away. But an idea that distanced Jesus even further from Jew-ishness had taken over my understanding. I learned to think of Jesus as a mystical genius whose direct experience of God the Father, whom he called Abba ("Daddy"), was such that he had no need of any mediating culture. Religion is by definition such a culture. Here is how one of the theologians I learned this from, Bernard Cooke, explains it: "What was distinctive about Jesus' experience [of God] was its intimacy and imme-diacy. All the textual evidence points to the fact that Jesus' knowledge of his Abba was immediate personal acquaintance."

The word "religion" shares a root with "ligament," meaning "tie." Religion exists to overcome the gulf between creatures and Creator. It is a system of beliefs and rituals that ties the human to God. But Jesus was presented, in this understanding, as the one man who had no need of such a tie. "Believe me that I am in the Father and the Father is in me," the Gospel of John reports him as saying. The theology that develops from that mystical union makes Jesus himself the ligament. So the question of the religious identity of Jesus never arises—not Jewish religion, not Christian religion—because his knowledge of God is immediate. He has no need of the ligament of religion. If he at first participated in Jewish ritual, he did so for the sake of form, not because he needed it. And the Gospels show him distancing himself from Jewish religious observances. As Paula Fredriksen points out, for example, the Gospel of Mark shows Jesus dismissing central religious traditions of Judaism like "Shabbat, food, tithing, Temple offerings, purity—as the 'traditions of men.' To these he opposes what Jesus ostensibly propounds as 'the commandment of God' (7:8). The strong rhetoric masks the fact that these laws are biblical and, as such, the common concern of all religious Jews: It is God in the Torah, not the Pharisees in their interpretations of it, who com-manded these observances."

When the disciples of Jesus asked him how to pray—this story became the core of my belief in him—he replied with the Our Father.

Christians recite this prayer in rote fashion, as if it were the farthest thing from religiously revolutionary, when in fact it is nothing less than an invitation to call God "Daddy"—that is, to think of the Almighty One, the Ineffable, in the most intimate way. Ironically, this aspect of Jesus' spirituality, which for most Christians has had the effect of distancing him from Judaism, actually shows him participating in its vital and at that time multifaceted manifestation. As the Catholic scholar John Pawlikowski has written, "In particular, Jesus' stress on his intimate link with the Father picks up an a central feature of Pharisaic thought." Indeed, there is evidence that, by the time of Jesus, Jews were regularly praying to God as Father. But that was never explained to us. The intimacy Jesus claimed to have with God the Father was made to seem unique, entirely his. More than anything else, to us, it set him apart from Jews.

Based on what was presented to us, we could only have concluded that, if anything, Jesus' Abba experience put him at odds with Jewish religion, for, as Cooke puts it, "There were fundamental incongruities between the Abba he experienced and the God known and explained by those around him." This spirituality had the simple effect of deleting any reference to Jewish cult in the life of Jesus. It was impossible to picture him in that tasseled prayer shawl, wearing phylacteries, entering the Temple not to protest but to pray. Having learned in parochial school that Jesus was racially not Jewish, I learned in graduate theological school that he was religiously not Jewish either. Susannah Heschel characterizes the Aryanizing of Jesus as an effort "to create a *judenrein* Christianity for a *judenrein* Germany," but this spiritualizing of Jesus was a *judenrein* of such subtlety that I did not know, until reflecting on Heschel's recent work, that it had completely dominated my religious imagination. What religion was Jesus? I'd have surely answered Jewish, unlike those ill-informed college freshmen— but their answers were more honest than mine.

What is a Jew anyway? At the end of the second millennium, Jews themselves carry on the argument, with the ultra-Orthodox of Mea

Shearim, their enclave in Jerusalem, aiming anathemas at the secular children of David Ben Gurion, modern Israel's first prime minister. Hitler said that a Jew was anyone who had at least one Jewish grandparent, and, as if to spite him, many Jews adopted that definition. The rabbis, holding to matrilineal descent, define a Jew as someone having a Jewish mother. In the state of Israel, a Jew can be an atheist, although not a baptized Christian. Part racial, part religious, the meaning of Jewishness today is ambiguous. In his memoir, the drama critic Richard Gilman described a life's journey that had taken him from the Jewish faith into which he was born, into unbelief, then into Roman Catholicism, from which he subsequently "lapsed." And where did that leave him? As "a lapsed Jewish-atheist-Catholic. Fallen from all three, a triple deserter!" But not quite. In the end, he had, without choosing it, resumed his original identity. "The difference is that you stay Jewish in your bones and pores, there's no lapsing from that; changed names or nose bobs won't do."

The contemporary argument among ultra-Orthodox Jews, Reform Jews, and secular Jews over the question Who is a Jew? points to a piece of the social and political context that is mainly missing from the Christian memory of foundational events. To imagine that first Jesus and then his followers were in conflict with "the Jews," a conflict with the sequential climaxes that occurred when "the Jews" killed Jesus and then certain of his followers, is, of course, to ignore the fact that Jesus and his first followers were themselves Jews. But on a more basic level, it is to assume that there was a social-religious entity called "the Jews." Obviously, a period of time had to pass before something called "Christianity" came into being as a distinct community, but emphasis on that evolution ignores the fact that, in the same period, there was not clearly defined "Judaism" either. Indeed, the suffix "ism," suggesting a set of coherent ideological boundaries, a membership definition, a precisely notated theology and cult, is anachronistic. If my great-uncle's story was misremembered by my family, it was because the post-1916 Irish imagination could no longer contain the ambiguous experience of a dual loyalty to London and Dublin. If the story of Jesus is misremembered, with devastating effect on the Jews, however defined, it is first because a later Christianity presumed a univocal—and, not incidentally, flawed—Judaism against which to define its uniqueness and value. But there was no such Judaism.

"When Jesus was born," the Columbia University scholar Alan Segal writes, "the Jewish religion was beginning a new transformation, the rabbinic movement, which would permit the Jewish people to survive the next two millennia. The complex of historical and social forces that molded rabbinic Judaism also affected the teachings of Jesus, helping to form Christianity into a new and separate religion." Segal entitled his book *Rebecca's Children*, reflecting a theme already noted, that it is useful to think of the two religions as siblings, which, like Jacob and Esau, struggled against each other even in their mother's womb. The history of the origins of Jewish-Christian conflict suggests that the metaphor of rivalrous fraternity is more than a metaphor; it actually defines the way these two religions came into being. In Jesus' lifetime and shortly after it, Segal writes, "Dislocation, war, and foreign rule forced every variety of Jewish community to rebuild its ancient national culture into something almost unprecedented, a religion of personal and communal piety. Many avenues were available to Jews for achieving this new sense of personal piety, one of which was Jesus' movement."

When a Christian asks Who is a Jew? he risks falling into the trap of a mythic projection of perennial Christian anxiety, defining Jewishness in a way that serves a Christian purpose. Obviously, Judaism defines itself in its own terms. In trying to understand the origins of Jewish-Christian conflict, perhaps it would be more useful to put the question as those first rivals within the broad Jewish community might have, which would be to ask, in effect, Who is the "true Israel"?

Competing answers were offered by the groups characterized in the New Testament. There were the Pharisees, whose movement evolved into rabbinic Judaism, referred to earlier. Some Pharisees were priests, although most were laymen, and their religious impulse, competing with Temple sacrifice, emphasized the study of Torah in their synagogues and the rigorous keeping of the Law. Josephus says that six thousand Jews were Pharisees. There were Sadducees, whom we might recognize as aristocrats, and some of them were high priests whose religious focus was the sacrificial cult of the Jerusalem Temple. They were inclined to cooperate with the Roman occupiers. It is not clear how large this party was, but according to the distinguished scholar E. P. Sanders, there were many thousands of priests. Josephus argues that the majority of Jews would have inclined toward such cooperation with Rome. The Sadducees, in effect, formed a core of the establishment. There were Essenes, famous now for their caves in Qumran, but in the first century they were a countersect that rejected the corruptions of the cities, and in particular of Herod's Temple, which to them was a Hellenized blasphemy. Herod the Great (c. 73–4 B.C.E.), the half-Jewish Roman puppet, had ruled as king of Israel, including Judea and Galilee, since 37 B.C.E. He is remembered by Christians for the story of his slaughter of the innocent at the time of Jesus' birth, but his greatest undertaking was the restoration of the Temple in Jerusalem, which for him fulfilled a political purpose as much as a religious one. The Temple was designed to impress his Roman overlords as much as his Jewish subjects. But because of that duality, the Temple was a flashpoint to the Essenes, who wanted to replace the Romans as rulers of Israel with their own leaders. Josephus put their number at more than four thousand.

The numbers offered by Josephus, while not to be taken as precise, indicate that relatively few Jews belonged to the identifiable parties. But the broader population would have had clear sympathies one way or another. At one extreme—in our terms, perhaps, the "liberals"— would have been the Hellenizers, those open to the customs of the Gentiles. By and large, these Jews would have been of the Diaspora— Greek speakers, men and women who had learned to live within and take for granted the pagan culture of Greek and Roman cities. Most famous of these would have been Philo of Alexandria (c. 30 B.C.E.–45 C.E.), who wrote favorably, for example, of the emperor Augustus. But many Palestinian Jews would probably have rejected Hellenization, and that is especially true of the rural people, whose experience of the wider world would have been limited.

At the other extreme from "liberals" would have been "zealots," whether pacifists or violent revolutionaries—pietists or apocalyptic believers who looked for divine intervention as a means of restoring Israel. An example of such a movement, perhaps, would have been that of John the Baptist. He was a radical spiritualist, yet his direct challenge to Herod, for which he was beheaded, demonstrates the impossibility of separating religion from politics in this milieu. In addition to the main parties and the sects, there were powerful regional divisions among those who identified themselves as the "true Israel." Judeans were dominant because the cultic center was in Jerusalem, yet there were Samaritans who, worshiping at their own Mount Gerizim instead of on Mount Zion, were disdained by Judeans. And there were the villagers of Galilee, whom city-dwelling Judeans would have looked down upon as peasants. In turn, Galileans would have regarded the Jewish oligarchs of Jerusalem both as near traitors for accommodating Rome and as idolaters for allowing images of Caesar to be venerated, if only on coins. (Jesus' question about the coin, "Whose likeness and inscription is this?," is a sly jibe at his challengers' idolatry.)

The true Israel. Centered in the Temple. The Torah. The oneness of God. The idea of election. The covenant. Each of these metaphors had adherents who gave it priority. But it is important to recall the rather obvious fact that such debate, in Fredriksen's phrase, "coexisted with consensus." Indeed, agreement on those elements as essential, however much one or the other was emphasized, would have been the precondition of diversity within the community. Still, it is impossible to detect in the vibrant religious expressions of first-century Palestine an all-encompassing Jewish orthodoxy. The very sectarianism of Israel in the time of Jesus appears to be its defining note. Segal argues that sectarian multiplicity amounted to an efficient channeling of conflict among classes and across ideologies, achieving a remarkable social balance in an era of massive cultural mutation. That is why Jesus was acting exactly like a Jew of his time when, apparently influenced by John the Baptist, he initiated yet another sectarian movement, and like a Jew of his place—Galilee—when he targeted the Herod-compromised Temple in Jerusalem as the site of his defining spiritual-political act.

So the college students who didn't label Jesus as a Jew inadvertently score a point, because Jesus, while taking his membership in the covenant people Israel for granted, would likely have thought of himself not as a Judean (from which our word "Jew" derives, but which to him would have implied geography) but as a Galilean. "The Nazarene" after all. What was it to be a first-century Galilean? In trying to imagine Jesus' experience—and in trying to understand how his became a story told against Judaism instead of within Judaism—there is a key element yet to be considered. It is the most important element, yet it is also one often left aside. To tell the story of Christian origins (or the origins, for that matter, of rabbinic Judaism) without reference to it is equivalent to telling the story of the 1916 Irish Rising without reference to the Great War. And war—war every bit as savage, in relative terms, as World War I—is the missing element.

War was not in any way missing from Palestine when Jesus was born. Nor was war missing from the direct experience of his followers, his followers' children, of their children, and of their great-nephews. The origins of the Jesus movement, and ultimately of Christianity, cannot be understood apart from the century-long Roman war against the Jews, albeit a war punctuated by repeated acts of Jewish rebellion. That is the social and political context that is all too often missing from the memory: Jesus and his movement were born in the shadow of what would stand as the most grievous violence against the Jewish people until Hitler's attempt at a Final Solution. (I would add here that it is equally misguided to consider the late-twentieth-century ferment in Christian theology, symbolized by the Second Vatican Council, apart front the trauma of the Holocaust, including the failure of the Christian churches to resist it.)

Between half a million and a million Jews lived in Palestine at the time of Jesus' birth. Some scholars put the Jewish population there as high as two and a half million, with a few hundred thousand Gentiles.

Sanders accepts a figure of "less than a million, possibly only about half that." Later we will see that Josephus posits Jewish casualty figures in the war with Rome that Sanders finds too high. Whatever the totals, the ratio of Jewish dead in Palestine at the hands of Rome may well approximate the twentieth-century record of one in three. Already, when Jesus was born, the inhabitants of his region were a defeated, violated people. The brutally effective Roman general Pompey (106–48 B.C.E.), undertaking a major clampdown on the Asian provinces of the empire, had set his legions loose throughout the area little more than half a century before (63 B.C.E.). He conquered Jerusalem. Thus began a period of oppressive colonial occupation that would climax twice: when Roman garrisons leveled Jerusalem in 70 C.E., and again—once and for all—in 135 C.E.

Largely because we are heirs to a Roman imperial culture that controlled the writing of history, we are inclined to read Rome's story through rose-colored lenses. We tend to see the march of the Roman Empire as a civilizing work of human progress. Every schoolchild knows that the darkness of barbarianism was penetrated by Julius Caesar, who brought order to its chaos. "All Gaul," we learned, "is divided into three parts." But we never asked who was doing the dividing, or how the dividees felt about it. We accepted the idea of a system according to which only citizens had rights, and roles in the story. Saint Paul's story, for example, takes a dramatic turn when, as Acts tells it, he announces his citizenship. Only then are the Romans who arrested him bound by what we call due process. In the story of Rome, all others, especially that invisible mass of slaves, are the forever unnamed—and forever unentitled to any semblance of due process. We mark Rome's progression from a republic to a dictatorship, and while we take note of the madness of a Caligula (12–41 C.E.), who had himself worshiped as a god, or a Nero (37–68 C.E.), who killed himself saying, "What an artist I perish," reports of their brutality serve mainly to emphasize the relative worthiness of most rulers. We are conditioned to think of the decline and fall of Rome sentimentally, as tragedy pure and simple. The gradual dissipation of imperial power, leading to vulnerability before the northern hordes, is the condition only of a new darkness.

But what if Roman imperial power itself, not in decline but at the peak, was the real darkness? A British critic and author of several important works on early Christianity, A. N. Wilson, says that Rome "was the first totalitarian state in history," the first to extend absolute control over the lives of a vast population. When compared to other empires of antiquity, Rome comes off well in some ways. The Greeks under Alexander, for example, imposed their language on those they conquered, while the Romans allowed local languages and cultures to remain intact. That is why Greek was the lingua franca of the Hellenized world. In addition, the breadth of religious diversity in Rome itself shows that the caesars tolerated, and even admitted to the pantheon, local gods. But the Roman war machine, once set running, was ruthless beyond what the world had seen. And though local gods were left alone, Rome was perhaps the first empire to require of its subjects an at least outward show of assent to the proposition that the emperor, too, was God.

It is the glories of Roman dominance that are emphasized in the cultural memory of Western civilization—those arrow-straight roads, elegant aqueducts, timeless laws, conjugated language—to the exclusion of what the imposition of these glories cost those on whom they were imposed. What if, when we thought of Caesar, we thought less of Cleopatra's lover or Virgil's patron or Marcus Aurelius's delicate conscience than, say, of a Joseph Stalin or a Pol Pot whose program worked? How would history tell the story of the twentieth century if it were the first century of the thousand-year Reich? It all depends on where you stand. It may be anachronistic to judge the policies of a great empire of antiquity by the standards of the U.N. Declaration of Human Rights, but if being human means anything, it is that a minimal level of decent treatment is required in every culture and era. It is clear that from the point of view of those on the bottom of the Roman pyramid—indeed, under it—that such minimal standard was not met.

To the peasant peoples of the Roman-dominated world, to the

millions of slaves and petty laborers (in Rome itself, fully one million of the population of two million were slaves), to the lepers and beggars, to the troublemakers whose lives could be snuffed out with little notice taken, no characterization of Caesar's evil would have been too extreme. We have looked back at Rome from above—from the point of view, that is, of those who benefited from its systems, traveled its roads, beheld its architectural wonders, learned to think in its language—but what of that vast majority who drew no such benefit? There is no understanding either the Jesus movement itself or the foundational memory of its violent conflict with the Jews if we cannot look back from below, from the vantage of these for whom the Roman systems were an endless, ever-present horror. It was to them, above all, that the message of Jesus came to seem addressed.

Most of the subjugated peoples in the Mediterranean world yielded to the Romans in what Romans regarded as essential, and those who refused to do this found themselves required to yield in everything, surrendering whatever was distinctive in their cultural identities to the dominant occupier. That is why we know so little of the Phoenicians, say, or the Nabataeans. The people in Palestine proved to be especially stubborn, clinging doggedly, and despite efforts at coercion and co-optation, to a self-understanding that permanently set them apart. But Jewish resistance arose from something far deeper than some pseudo-genetic stiff-necked stubbornness that would one day inspire an anti-semitic stereotype. For the Jews of Palestine, the indignity of an emperor-worshiping colonizer's foot on the throat was compounded by the religious convictions that no such emperor was divine and, more pointedly, that their freedom in this new violated land was a gift from the one true God—their God. Despite everything that set them apart, the rivalrous groups of Jews agreed that the land was a sacred symbol of that God's enduring promise. So for Palestinian Jews of all stripes, the Roman occupation as such was a religious affront as well as a political one. Furthermore, and equally across the board, a Jew's belief in the covenant included the belief that, one way or another, sooner or later, God would fulfill the promise again, as God had done repeatedly in history. God would do this once the purpose of this humiliating defeat—some, like John the Baptist, said its purpose was to bring the people to repentance—was fulfilled. God would do it by vanquishing the foreign invader and restoring to Israel its holy freedom. In other words, Jews *as Jews* had a reason to resist Rome, and a reason to believe, despite Rome's overwhelming military superiority, that the resistance would be effective.

What Jews did not have was anything approaching agreement on the form this resistance should take. And it is here that the other, negative meaning of Jewish sectarianism surfaces. Typically, imperial powers depend on the inability of oppressed local populations to muster a unified resistance, and the most successful occupiers are skilled at exploiting the differences among the occupied. Certainly that was the start of the British Empire's success, and its legacy of nurtured local hatreds can be seen wherever the Union Jack flew, from Muslim-Hindu hatred in Pakistan and India, to Catholic-Protestant hatred in Ireland, to, yes, Jew-Arab hatred in modern Israel. Rome was as good at encouraging internecine resentments among the occupied as Britain ever was. At one level, it is a matter only of exploiting the temperamental differences that perennially divide conservatives, moderates, and radicals from one another. E. P. Sanders says that for Jews confronted with "the great empires of the Mediterranean," the various parties had to decide "when to fight, when to yield; when to be content with partial independence, when to seek more. In terms of internal affairs, the primary issue was who would control the national institution: the temple, the sacrifices, the tithes and other offerings, and the administration of the law."

Sectarian conflict amounted to more than mere squabbling. There were grave tensions involving the life and death of the nation of Israel, and every aspect of its existence could be disputed because Israel's God had become involved at every level. Today, even believers take for granted the "wall of separation," in Jefferson's phrase, between areas of God's concern and those of government's, but it was not so at the time of Jesus. "There was no simple distinction," Sanders says, "between 'church' and 'state' or 'religion' and 'politics.' God, in the eyes of Jews, cared about all aspects of life; no part of it was outside 'religion.' Thus, in any case in which there was a choice—whether between would-be rulers, competing architectural plans for the temple, or various prohibitions on the sabbath—Jews would attempt to discern and follow *God's* will. Not infrequently they disagreed." In every case, their disagreement served the purposes of Rome.

To the radical revolutionaries who wanted to mount an immediate, violent assault on the occupier, the impulse of aristocrats to cut the best deal with the enemy looked like collaboration or treason; equally, from inside the Temple precincts, the radicals' fanaticism looked like suicide. So the establishment party of Sadducees, associated with the priestly class, participated from their place at the Temple in the administration of Roman power in Jerusalem; the separatist Zealots, like the monastics at Qumran, pursued a rejectionist path; the Pharisees advocated an adherence to Mosaic law as a way of ushering in God's liberating intervention; and the Sicarii launched knife-wielding terrorist attacks against agents of the occupiers. What the Romans could depend on—a classic exercise of divide-and-keep-conquered—was each group's readiness to identify a competing group as the primary enemy, often leaving Rome above the fray. For our purposes, the point is that even in the way events of this era are remembered, the unleashed sectarian impulse continued to keep the Roman overlords at the margin of the story.

Take two examples, one from the beginning and one from the end of the story of Jesus, as his followers told it to each other and the world. First, in the year 4 B.C.E., which also happened to be the year of Jesus' birth, Herod the Great died. His death left a temporary power vacuum, which caused violent outbreaks among forces loyal to various pretenders to succeed Herod as Rome's client king and among the followers of messianic movements who sought to seize an opening against Rome. The Romans smashed every rebellion and, with those legions pouncing from Syria, restored direct imperial rule. As summed up by the scholars Richard Horsley and Neil Asher Silberman: "The

Roman armies had swept through many of the towns and villages of the country, raping, killing, and destroying nearly everything in sight. In Galilee, all centers of rebellion were brutally suppressed; the rebel-held town of Sepphoris was burned to the ground, and all its surviving inhabitants were sold into slavery." Thousands of Jews were killed. Villages in Galilee were laid waste. In Jerusalem, where rebels had briefly taken charge, the Romans showed the lengths to which they were prepared to go to maintain control by swiftly executing anyone even suspected of collusion in the rebellion—Josephus puts the number at two thousand. The Roman means of execution, of course, was crucifixion, and Josephus makes the point that indeed the victims were crucified. This means that just outside the wall of the Jewish capital, crosses were erected—not three lonely crosses on a hill, as in the tidy Christian imagination, but perhaps two thousand in close proximity. On each was hung a Jew, and each Jew was left to die over several days the slow death of suffocation, as muscles gave out so that the victim could no longer hold himself erect enough to catch a breath. And once squeezed free of life, the corpses were left on their crosses to be eaten by buzzards. This grotesquery was its own justification. Its power was magnified because for Jews, coming into contact with a corpse made one ritually impure—a priest, for example, could not bury a parent. Such impurity could even be acquired by "overshadowing" a corpse, or being "overshadowed" by one. The shadows of those crucifixes, in other words, were also the point. The Jews who'd been left alive were being reminded whom they were dealing with in Rome, reminded for weeks by the sight and stench of the bodies. The image of those scores of crosses would stamp Jewish consciousness for a generation.

The opening chapters of the Gospel of Matthew evoke the political and social stresses of the world into which Jesus was born, but doesn't it seem odd that the ruthlessness displayed in Matthew's account of the slaughter of the innocents—the murder of every male child under two in the town of Bethlehem, a very few miles from those crosses—belonged not to the Romans but to the Jewish king Herod? This is not to dismiss that crime, if it occurred, nor to deny Herod's brutality, especially in the madness of his last years, but only to note that in the Christian memory—the Gospel of Matthew, usually dated to the decade of the 80s C.E., was written long after these events took place— the Roman crime is forgotten while the Jewish one is highlighted. Similarly with the Gospel of Luke, which was composed about the same time as Matthew. Luke's nativity-narrative reference to Caesar Augustus (63 B.C.E.–14 C.E.) as issuing a decree "that all the world should be enrolled," which moved the action of the Mary and Joseph story to Bethlehem in the first place, cries out for elaboration. It was the same Caesar Augustus who declared himself "Savior of the world," making him anathema to Jews. When he came to power with the Senate's authority in 27 B.C.E., it was as the head of a republic, but when he died in 14 C.E., it was as the emperor of a dictatorship, one tool of which was that world census. The perfect symbol of Caesar's regime was the gibbet on which those who refused to be part of his all-encompassing blasphemy were hung to die.

Now the second example, from the end of Jesus' life. When that Roman gibbet finally enters his story, by an extraordinary set of narrative machinations it is hardly Roman at all. Certainly the Gospel accounts are explicit in describing the Romans as the executioners of Jesus, but if they are coconspirators with the Jewish high priests and leaders of the Jewish ruling body, the Sanhedrin, they are decidedly *unindicted* coconspirators, which in modern law is a distinction between parties to a crime and perpetrators of it. According to the Christian memory, as conjured again by Matthew, the hand of the hand-washing Pilate (whose term as procurator, or appointed governor, in Judea ran from 26 to 36 C.E.) is forced by the bloodthirstiness of the crowd. "I am innocent of this man's blood," Pilate says. This procurator is remembered somewhat differently by the Jewish philosopher Philo of Alexandria, who lived when Pilate did, and wrote sometime around 41 C.E. that the Roman used "bribes, insults, robberies, outrages, wanton injuries, constantly repeated executions without trial, ceaseless and supremely grievous cruelty." Crossan, having cited these words, nevertheless asserts that Pilate "was neither a saint nor a monster." Fredriksen, however, makes the point that Philo, Josephus, and the Roman historian Tacitus all single out Pilate "as one of the worst provocateurs." Even by the standards of brutal Rome, Pilate seems to have been savage. When, six or so years after the death of Jesus, he wantonly slaughtered Samaritans for gathering to venerate Moses on a sacred mountain they associated with him, Pilate was recalled to Rome.

Given the ways in which his occupying force routinely maintained control over a restless population, the Roman commander's self-exculpation, as recorded in Matthew, in the matter of one particular crucifixion is the moral equivalent of Adolf Eichmann's standing in his glass booth and declaring himself innocent. "And all the people," Matthew says, "answered, 'His blood be on us and on our children!' " Which, of course, it has been.

This start-to-finish pattern in the Gospels of deflecting blame away from Romans and onto Jews is commonly taken now as evidence of a primordial Christian anti-Judaism, or worse: an anti-Judaism at the service of a craven attempt to placate Roman authorities. But this perception fails to take the "Christian" impulse here as one of people who are in fact Jews. So this anti-Judaism is evidence not of Jew hatred but of the sectarian conflict *among* Jews. Yes, there may have been an element of attempted ingratiation with Romans, but Jewishness was not the point of distinction in that attempt. As early as 64 C.E., well before the Gospels were composed, the emperor Nero had singled out the Jewish sect that claimed Jesus as its *Christus*, blaming them for the fire that had just then ravaged Rome. Tacitus writes of the violence that Nero inflicted on them, which is the first recorded mention of the movement. The Christian Jews were labeled as arsonists. They were crucified, burned, and driven out. One of them would flee from Rome to the Aegean island of Patmos to compose the fire-ridden Apocalypse, which labels Rome the beast. The Christian Jews were punished not for what they believed or refused to believe, or for any political threat they posed, but because, as a readily identifiable and vulnerable group, consisting in all likelihood mainly of slaves and lower-class workers with whom other Jews seemed not to identify, they were useful to Nero in providing the angry citizens of Rome with another target for their hatred besides him.

A. N. Wilson makes the point that Nero's savage scapegoating of the Christian Jews was for them an organizational boon, giving the until then inconsequential movement a reputation in the empire and numerous martyrs around whom to rally. Two of these, apparently, were Peter and Paul. Long-run organizational boon or not, in the short run Nero's persecution traumatized the Christian Jews, why knew they had been falsely punished. They knew themselves not to be the violent threat to Roman order that Nero accused them of being. If the Gospels, just then starting to jell in their final forms, emphasized a relative friendliness to Rome, there was a reason for it. The followers of Jesus had just been slandered, defined not merely as Rome's mortal enemy but as violent insurrectionists. It was not true, and the Gospels were slanted, in effect, to emphasize that followers of Jesus fully intended to render unto Caesar what was Caesar's. Sectarian tensions between Christians and what Wilson calls the "generality" of Jews may have been exacerbated by the narrow scapegoating, but again, those tensions were multilayered, still decidedly intra-Jewish. But soon enough, after the Gospels had jelled, Rome's murderous assault on the Jews of Judea would make Nero's violence seem benign, and explode the boundaries against which Christian-Jewish stresses had begun to press. The trauma of bloodshed on an imperial scale, unprecedented for the Jews, is the necessary context for understanding what was happening in those years among the Jews. Christian anti-Judaism, in others words, is not the first cause here; the Roman war against Judaism is.

By the Irish analogy, think of the ultimate effect of British imperial power among the Irish themselves. The Irish war with England, begun in 1916, was extremely violent, including as it did the twentieth century's first indiscriminate shelling of an urban center, Dublin. Part of England's "draconian reaction" was the unleashing on an unarmed populace of the criminal-terrorist Black and Tans and the post-1918 deployment of trench-veteran tommies, who viewed the Irish war as an extension of the no-holds-barred war against the Hun and fought accordingly. And the first result of all this violence? The Irish population, which in 1916 had been overwhelmingly inclined to favor London—as my great-uncle probably would have—over the self-appointed, self-aggrandizing liberators of the Irish Republican Brotherhood, by 1920 thought of London as the devil's own. The fierce, universal Irish hatred of England, a twentieth-century cliché, was in fact born in the twentieth century—just then. Thus even a diehard like Winston Churchill came to recognize that an English victory over this despicable people, short of the outright elimination of the native population, was impossible. Empowered to do so by Eamon de Valera, Michael Collins negotiated the Anglo-Irish Treaty of 1921. There would not be another until 1986.

There was a second result of the violence of that war. In addition to a unifying Irish hatred of the English, there would be a terribly disunifying Irish hatred of the self. "I tell you this—early this morning I signed my death warrant," Collins wrote to a friend after agreeing to the treaty, instinctively grasping what awaited him at home. No sooner had the Anglo-Irish war ended than the even more dispiriting Irish civil war began. Forces loyal to de Valera would eventually murder Collins, proving him a prophet. De Valera rejected the central terms of the treaty—an oath of allegiance to the Crown, British hegemony over the six counties in the north—but would later accept them once the paroxysm of Irish self-hatred had run its course. The Irish civil war—unlike, say, the American one—accomplished nothing, except to enable one Irish faction to vent its rage on another. Irish sectarian hatred served the overlord's purpose well, resulting in an Irish impotence the English could depend on for most of a century. Indeed, Irish sectarian violence was efficiently, if slyly, stoked by London all that time, from Lloyd George's government to Margaret Thatcher's.

Intra-Jewish conflict served Rome's purposes in just such a way. There is perhaps something craven in the Gospels' emphasis on "Jews" as a threat to order in the empire, as opposed to "Christians," and it does not mitigate the Gospel writers' responsibility for driving this wedge to note that they were responding to Roman oppression. But the more fundamental point is that in doing this, the followers of the murdered Jesus were only demonstrating how effective the imperial overlord had been in infecting the dominated population with its own cynicism and contempt. This dynamic becomes even clearer in the context that has provided us our starting point: One measure of the diabolical efficacy of Nazi torment in Auschwitz, besides the way Jews were victims of SS guards, was the way Jews were victims of fellow Jews, the capos who served as SS surrogates. The collapse of the moral universe that led Jews to participate in their own destruction in the death camps, or to take upon themselves a feeling of guilty responsibility for the evil around them, only emphasizes the abject evil of an absolutely oppressive system. That evil lies in the system's capacity to destroy the innocence of everyone it touches. When Jewish factions turned Rome's venom against each other, Rome won yet another victory. There is no question here of "Christian innocence," because among human beings there is no innocence when the question becomes survival. Extreme violence and extreme measures to survive it form the ground on which this entire story stands.

It is nevertheless important to emphasize that, well after the life of Jesus, those who remembered the conflicts surrounding both its beginning and its end mainly as conflicts among Jews—Herod's villainy, not Caesar's; the high priest's, not Pilate's—were being true to the ways these events come to be understood in the period of heightened Jewish sectarianism that followed Jesus' death. Not "innocent," yet they were not liars either. The Gospel of Matthew was not composed by someone who had been there, not composed by someone who knew well that Pilate was a sadist who'd have thought nothing of dispatching an unknown Galilean troublemaker, and, knowing this, still consciously and falsely portrayed the Romans as innocent and "the Jews" as guilty. It would be a slander to say such a thing of Matthew (or the writers of that Gospel), just as it would slander my mother to say she lied to me when she led me to think her uncle was a hero of the Easter Rising.

Earlier, I cited John Dominic Crossan's 1995 characterization of the claim that the Jews murdered Jesus as "the longest lie," but in a subsequent work, in 1998, he amended that judgment. The authors of the foundational Christian documents, writing years after the event, "did not say this: I know that the Roman authorities crucified Jesus, but I will blame the Jewish authorities; I will play the Roman card; I will write propaganda that I know is inaccurate. If they *had* done that, the resulting text would have been a lie." Crossan does not attribute such venality to the Gospels, because to do so would impose a post-Enlightenment notion of history on a far more complex phenomenon. Rigid concern for "how it happened" is a contemporary preoccupation of ours, but no such emphasis informed the way the ancients wrote history. Reports of the words and deeds of the late Jesus evolved as his movement grew, and so did the understanding of who his friends and enemies were, depending on the experience through time of who the friends and enemies of the movement were. "As Christian Jewish communities are steadily more alienated from their fellow Jews, so the 'enemies' of Jesus expand to fit those new situations. By the time of 'John' in the 90s, those enemies are 'the Jews'—that is, all those other Jews except us few right ones. If we had understood (the literary genre) gospel, we would have understood that. If we had understood gospel, we would have expected that. It is, unfortunately, tragically late to be learning it."

from A Week on the Concord
and Merrimack Rivers

by Henry David Thoreau

Transcendentalist Henry David Thoreau's (1817–1862) A Week on the Concord and Merrimack Rivers *included ideas culled from ten years' worth of his notes and journals. This passage suggests that Christian forms may keep us from Christian meaning.*

trust that some may be as near and dear to Buddha, or Christ, or Swedenborg, who are without the pale of their churches. It is necessary not to be Christian to appreciate the beauty and significance of the life of Christ. I know that some will have hard thoughts of me, when they hear their Christ named beside my Buddha, yet I am sure that I am willing they should love their Christ more than my Buddha, for the love is the main thing, and I like him too. "God is the letter Ku, as well as Khu." Why need Christians be still intolerant and superstitious? The simple-minded sailors were unwilling to cast overboard Jonah at his own request.

Where is this love become in later age?
Alas! 't is gone in endless pilgrimage
From hence, and never to return, I doubt,
Till revolution wheel those times about.

• • •

One man says,—

> The worlde's a popular disease, that reigns
> Within the froward heart and frantic brains
> Of poor distempered mortals.

Another, that

> all the world's a stage,
> And all the men and women merely players.

The world is a strange place for a playhouse to stand within it. Old Drayton thought that a man that lived here, and would be a poet, for instance, should have in him certain "brave, translunary things," and a "fine madness" should possess his brain. Certainly it were as well, that he might be up to the occasion. That is a superfluous wonder, which Dr. Johnson expresses at the assertion of Sir Thomas Browne that "his life has been a miracle of thirty years, which to relate were not history but a piece of poetry, and would sound like a fable." The wonder is, rather, that all men do not assert as much. That would be a rare praise, if it were true, which was addressed to Francis Beaumont,—"Spectators sate part in your tragedies."

Think what a mean and wretched place this world is; that half the time we have to light a lamp that we may see to live in it. This is half our life. Who would undertake the enterprise if it were all? And, pray, what more has day to offer? A lamp that burns more clear, a purer oil, say winter-strained, that so we may pursue our idleness with less obstruction. Bribed with a little sunlight and a few prismatic tints, we bless our Maker, and stave off his wrath with hymns.

> I make ye an offer,
> Ye gods, hear the scoffer,
> The scheme will not hurt you,
> If ye will find goodness, I will find virtue.

Though I am your creature,
And child of your nature,
I have pride still unbended,
And blood undescended,
Some free independence,
And my own descendants.

I cannot toil blindly,
Though ye behave kindly,
And I swear by the rood,
I'll be slave to no God.
If ye will deal plainly,
I will strive mainly,
If ye will discover,
Great plans to your lover,
And give him a sphere
Somewhat larger than here.

"Verily, my angels! I was abashed on account of my servant, who had no Providence but me; therefore did I pardon him."[1]

Most people with whom I talk, men and women even of some originality and genius, have their scheme of the universe all cut and dried,—very *dry*, I assure you, to hear, dry enough to burn, dry-rotted and powder-post, methinks,—which they set up between you and them in the shortest intercourse; an ancient and tottering frame with all its boards blown off. They do not walk without their bed. Some, to me, seemingly very unimportant and unsubstantial things and relations are for them everlastingly settled,—as Father, Son, and Holy Ghost, and the like. These are like the everlasting hills to them. But in all my wanderings I never came across the least vestige of authority for these things. They have not left so distinct a trace as the delicate flower of a remote

1. *The Gulistan* of Sadi

geological period on the coal in my grate. The wisest man preaches no doctrines; he has no scheme; he sees no rafter, not even a cobweb, against the heavens. It is clear sky. If I ever see more clearly at one time than another, the medium through which I see is clearer. To see from earth to heaven, and see there standing, still a fixture, that old Jewish scheme! What right have you to hold up this obstacle to my under-standing you, to your understanding me! You did not invent it; it was imposed on you. Examine your authority. Even Christ, we fear, had his scheme, his conformity to tradition, which slightly vitiates his teaching. He had not swallowed all formulas. He preached some mere doctrines. As for me, Abraham, Isaac, and Jacob are now only the sub-tilest imaginable essences, which would not stain the morning sky. Your scheme must be the framework of the universe; all other schemes will soon be ruins. The perfect God in his revelations of himself has never got to the length of one such proposition as you, his prophets, state. Have you learned the alphabet of heaven and can count three? Do you know the number of God's family? Can you put mysteries into words? Do you presume to fable of the ineffable? Pray, what geogra-pher are you, that speak of heaven's topography? Whose friend are you, that speak of God's personality? Do you, Miles Howard, think that he has made you his confidant? Tell me of the height of the mountains of the moon, or of the diameter of space, and I may believe you, but of the secret history of the Almighty, and I shall pronounce thee mad. Yet we have a sort of family history of our God,—so have the Tahitians of theirs,—and some old poet's grand imagination is imposed on us as adamantine everlasting truth, and God's own word. Pythagoras says, truly enough, "A true assertion respecting God is an assertion of God;" but we may well doubt if there is any example of this in literature.

The New Testament is an invaluable book, though I confess to having been slightly prejudiced against it in my very early days by the church and the Sabbath-school, so that it seemed, before I read it, to be the yellowest book in the catalogue. Yet I early escaped from their meshes. It was hard to get the commentaries out of one's head and taste its true flavor. I think that Pilgrim's Progress is the best sermon which has been preached from this text; almost all other sermons that I have heard, or heard of, have been but poor imitations of this. It would be a poor story to be prejudiced against the Life of Christ because the book has been edited by Christians. In fact, I love this book rarely, though it is a sort of castle in the air to me, which I am permitted to dream. Having come to it so recently and freshly, it has the greater charm, so that I cannot find any to talk with about it. I never read a novel, they have so little real life and thought in them. The reading which I love best is the scriptures of the several nations, though it happens that I am better acquainted with those of the Hindoos, the Chinese, and the Persians, than of the Hebrews, which I have come to last. Give me one of these bibles, and you have silenced me for a while. When I recover the use of my tongue, I am wont to worry my neighbors with the new sentences; but commonly they cannot see that there is any wit in them. Such has been my experience with the New Testament. I have not yet got to the crucifixion, I have read it over so many times. I should love dearly to read it aloud to my friends, some of whom are seriously inclined; it is so good, and I am sure that they have never heard it, it fits their case exactly, and we should enjoy it so much together,—but I instinctively despair of getting their ears. They soon show, by signs not to be mistaken, that it is inexpressibly wearisome to them. I do not mean to imply that I am any better than my neighbors; for, alas! I know that I am only as good, though I love better books than they.

It is remarkable that, notwithstanding the universal favor with which the New Testament is outwardly received, and even the bigotry with which it is defended, there is no hospitality shown to, there is no appreciation of, the order of truth with which it deals. I know of no book that has so few readers. There is none so truly strange, and heretical, and unpopular. To Christians, no less than Greeks and Jews, it is foolishness and a stumbling-block. There are, indeed, severe things in it which no man should read aloud more than once. "Seek first the kingdom of heaven." "Lay not up for yourselves treasures on earth." "If thou wilt be perfect, go and sell that thou hast, and give to the poor, and thou shalt have treasure in heaven." "For what is a man profited, if he shall gain the whole world, and lose his own soul? Or what shall a man give in exchange for his soul?" Think of this, Yankees! "Verily, I say unto you, if ye have faith as a grain of mustard seed, ye shall say unto this mountain, Remove hence to yonder place, and it shall remove; and nothing shall be impossible unto you." Think of repeating these things to a New England audience! thirdly, fourthly, fifteenthly, till there are three barrels of sermons! who, without cant, can read them aloud? Who, without cant, can hear them, and not go out of the meeting-house? They never *were* read, they never *were* heard. Let but one of these sentences be rightly read, from any pulpit in the land, and there would not be left one stone of that meeting-house upon another.

Yet the New Testament treats of man and man's so-called spiritual affairs too exclusively, and is too constantly moral and personal, to alone content me, who am not interested solely in man's religious or moral nature, or in man even. I have not the most definite designs on the future. Absolutely speaking, Do unto others as you would that they should do unto you is by no means a golden rule, but the best of current silver. An honest man would have but little occasion for it. It is golden not to have any rule at all in such a case. The book has never been written which is to be accepted without any allowance. Christ was a sublime actor on the stage of the world. He knew what he was thinking of when he said, "Heaven and earth shall pass away, but my words shall not pass away." I draw near to him at such a time. Yet he taught mankind but imperfectly how to live; his thoughts were all directed toward another world. There is another kind of success than his. Even here we have a sort of living to get, and must buffet it somewhat longer. There are various tough problems yet to solve, and we must make shift to live, betwixt spirit and matter, such a human life as we can.

A healthy man, with steady employment, as woodchopping at fifty cents a cord, and a camp in the woods, will not be a good subject for Christianity. The New Testament may be a choice book to him on some, but not on all or most of his days. He will rather go a-fishing in his leisure hours. The Apostles, though they were fishers too, were of the solemn race of sea-fishers, and never trolled for pickerel on inland streams.

from The Gospel According to Jesus
by Stephen Mitchell

Here translator and critic Stephen Mitchell comments on Matthew's and Mark's respective versions of the Crucifixion.

The final scene, in which all we can know with certainty is the stark fact of the crucifixion. Yet we can be certain that Jesus didn't see his own suffering as tragic, since it happened according to God's will.

And they brought him to the place called Golgotha (which means "the place of the skull"). And some women offered him drugged wine, but he wouldn't take it.

And at about nine o'clock they crucified him.

And above his head the charge against him was written: THE KING OF THE JEWS. And with him they crucified two Zealots, one on his right and one on his left.

And at about three o'clock in the afternoon, Jesus uttered a loud cry, and died.

And some women offered him: Literally, "And they offered him."

The "wine" referred to must have been the concoction which was given to Jews who were about to suffer the penalty of death, in order that they might lose consciousness. The preparation of this drugged wine seems to have been left to the hands of the ladies of Jerusalem, who, doubtless, regarded making and giving it as a deed of piety.

(C. G. Montefiore, *The Synoptic Gospels*, vol. 1, Macmillan, 1927, p.381)

Matthew reads, "They gave him wine mixed with gall to drink, but when he tasted it, he wouldn't drink it." Luke and John make no reference to wine.

but he wouldn't take it: He wanted to die fully conscious.

the charge against him: Even if this is not historical, it is clear that the Romans executed Jesus as a dangerous revolutionary.

two Zealots: The Greek word literally means "bandit" or "robber." Josephus, who collaborated with the Romans, regularly used it in a derogatory sense for the Jewish freedom-fighters known as Zealots, in the same way that Dr. Johnson might have called (perhaps did call) George Washington "a damned rebel."

uttered a loud cry: According to Mark, followed by Matthew, Jesus' last words were a quotation from Psalm 22 ("My God, my God, why have you forsaken me?"); according to Luke, a quotation from Psalm 30 ("Father, into your hands I commend my spirit"). But since the disciples had scattered, it is unlikely that any of them witnessed the crucifixion. Even if they did, they would have been allowed to watch it only from a considerable distance, as Mark says of Mary Magdalene and certain other women (15:40), and they wouldn't have been able to distinguish Jesus' words.

• • •

Many scholars think that, like the other borrowings from Psalm 22, these words too were borrowed from the same source, not by Jesus, but by the Evangelist, or by tradition. Jesus died with a "loud cry." What did he say? What had he said? Pious fantasy soon found answers; hence what we now read in Mark and Luke. Jesus was the Messianic hero predicted and represented in the Psalm. Therefore, he is made to quote its opening words, not because those who put the words in his mouth thought that he was, or believed he was, forsaken of God, but because they are the opening words of the Psalm.

(Montefiore, *Synoptic Gospels*, vol. 1, p. 383)

The famous words of Luke 23:34 ("Father, forgive them, for they know not what they do") are missing from many of the most ancient manuscripts and are almost certainly a later addition. As touching as they are, we should realize that they come from a consciousness radically different from Jesus'. Jesus knew that God is our immediate mirror: what we give, we receive; as we judge, we are judged; when we forgive, we are forgiven. There is measure for measure, cause and effect, and no notion of an intercessor. The God whom "Jesus" is addressing in these words is a stern king who acts mercifully only with reluctance, and only after persuasion by the good prince.

and died: The Evangelists add an account of the burial: "And late in the afternoon, since it was Friday and the Sabbath was approaching, Joseph of Arimathea, a respected member of the Sanhedrin, who was himself looking for the kingdom of God, took courage and went to Pilate and asked him for the body of Jesus. And Pilate ordered that it be given to him. And Joseph bought a linen cloth, and took the body down, and wrapped it in the cloth. And he laid it in a tomb that had been cut in the rock. And he rolled a large stone against the door of the tomb, and departed" (Mark 15:41, Luke 23:54; Matthew 27:58; Mark 15:46; Matthew 27:60).

These verses may be historical, or they may be apologetic, to pre-pare for the myth of the empty tomb. Some scholars think it probable that Jesus' body was taken down from the cross by the soldiers and thrown into a mass grave.

I would like to append Nietzsche's deeply insightful account of the cru-cifixion and of how the apostles used it. (Christian readers may find it easier to forgive his passionate revulsion from the apostles if they can understand his passionate love for Jesus.)

The fate of the gospel was determined by the death—it hung on the "cross.". . . It was only the death, this unex-pected shameful death, only the cross, which was in general reserved for the rabble—it was only this most horrible paradox that brought the disciples face to face with the true riddle: "*Who was that? What was that?*"—The feeling of being bewildered and shocked to their very depths, the sus-picion that such a death might be the *refutation* of their cause, the terrifying question mark "Why did this happen?"—this condition is only too easy to understand. Here everything *had* to be necessary, had to have meaning, significance, the highest significance; a disciple's love doesn't recognize the accidental. Only now did the chasm open up: "*Who* killed him? *Who* was his natural enemy?"— this question leaped forth like a lightning bolt. Answer: *ruling* Judaism, its upper class. From this moment they felt themselves in rebellion *against* the social order, in retrospect they understood Jesus as having been *in rebellion against the social order*. Until then this warlike, nay-saying and -doing trait had been *lacking* in his image; even more, he was the contradiction of it. Obviously the little community did *not* understand the main point, the exemplary character of this way of dying, the freedom, the superiority *over* every feeling of resentment:—an indication of how little of him they really understood! Jesus himself couldn't have intended anything by his death except to publicly give the sternest test, the *proof* of his teaching. . . . But his disciples were far from *forgiving* this death—which would have been gospel-like in the highest sense; not to speak of *offering* themselves for a similar death in sweet and gentle peace of heart. . . . Precisely the most ungospel-like feeling, *revenge*, came uppermost again. The matter couldn't possibly be finished with this death: "retribution" was needed, "judgment" (—yet what can be more ungospel-like than "retribution," "punishment," "sitting in judgment"!). Once more the popular expectation of a Messiah came into the foreground; a historic moment appeared: the "kingdom of God" is coming as a judgment over his enemies. . . . But with this, everything is misunderstood: the "kingdom of God" as a closing act, as a promise! For the gospel had been precisely the presence, the fulfillment, the *reality* of this "kingdom." Just such a death *was* this very "kingdom of God.". . .

And now an absurd problem arose: "How *could* God have allowed that to happen?" To this, the disturbed reason of the little community found a terrifyingly absurd answer: God gave his Son for the forgiveness of sins, as a *sacrifice*. All at once the gospel was done for! The *guilt sacrifice*, and this in its most repulsive, most barbaric form, the sacrifice of the *guiltless* for the sins of the guilty! What ghastly paganism!— For Jesus had abolished the very concept of "guilt"—he had denied any separation between God and man, he *lived* this unity of God and man as *his* "good news". . . . And not as a special privilege!—From now on, step by step, there enters into the figure of the redeemer the doctrine of a judgment and a second coming, the doctrine of his death as a sacrificial death, the doctrine of the *resurrection*, with which the whole concept of "blessedness," the whole and only reality of the gospel, is conjured away—in favor of a state *after* death!

(Friedrich Nietzsche, *The Antichristian*)

But because Nietzsche's insight bristles with offense and antagonism, I want to end this commentary by making the same point in the sweet, serene tones of Lao-tzu:

The Master gives himself up
to whatever the moment brings.
He knows that he is going to die,
and he has nothing left to hold on to:
no illusions in his mind,
no resistances in his body.
He doesn't think about his actions;
they flow from the core of his being.
He holds nothing back from life;
therefore he is ready for death,
as a man is ready for sleep
after a good day's work.

(chapter 50)

sources: Mark 15:22; Mark 15:25; Matthew 27:37, Mark 15:26; Mark 15:27; Mark 15:34,37

from The Man Who Died

by D. H. Lawrence

David Herbert Lawrence (1885–1930) shocked many readers with his sexually suggestive novels. This piece originally appeared as a story called "The Escaped Cock." Lawrence later published it in tandem with a tale of Jesus' relationship with the pagan god Isis; he called the two-part work The Man Who Died.

Tthere was a peasant near Jerusalem who acquired a young game-cock which looked a shabby little thing, but which put on brave feathers as spring advanced and was resplendent with arched and orange neck by the time the fig trees were letting out leaves from their end tips.

This peasant was poor, he lived in a cottage of mud-brick, and had only a dirty little inner courtyard with a tough fig-tree for all his territory. He worked hard among the vines and olives and wheat of his master, then came home to sleep in the mud-brick cottage by the path. But he was proud of his young rooster. In the shut-in yard were three shabby hens which laid small eggs, shed the few feathers they had, and made a disproportionate amount of dirt. There was also, in a corner under a straw roof, a dull donkey that often went out with the peasant to work, but sometimes stayed at home. And there was the peasant's wife, a black-browed youngish woman who did not work too hard. She threw a little grain, or the remains of the porridge mess, to the fowls, and she cut green fodder with a sickle, for the ass.

The young cock grew to a certain splendour. By some freak of destiny, he was a dandy rooster, in that dirty little yard with three patchy hens. He learned to crane his neck and give shrill answers to the crowing of other cocks, beyond the walls, in a world he knew nothing of. But there was a special fiery colour to his crow, and the distant calling of the other cocks roused him to unexpected outbursts.

"How he sings," said the peasant, as he got up and pulled his day-shirt over his head.

"He is good for twenty hens," said the wife.

The peasant went out and looked with pride at his young rooster. A saucy, flamboyant bird that has already made the final acquaintance of the three tattered hens. But the cockerel was tipping his head, listening to the challenge of far-off unseen cocks, in the unknown world. Ghost voices, crowing at him mysteriously out of limbo. He answered with a ringing defiance, never to be daunted.

"He will surely fly away one of these days," said the peasant's wife.

So they lured him with grain, caught him, though he fought with all his wings and feet, and they tied a cord round his shank, fastening it against the spur; and they tied the other end of the cord to the post that held up the donkey's straw pent-roof.

The young cock, freed, marched with a prancing stride of indignation away from the humans, came to the end of his string, gave a tug and a hitch of his tied leg, fell over for a moment, scuffled frantically on the unclean earthen floor, to the horror of the shabby hens, then with a sickening lurch, regained has feet, and stood to think. The peasant and the peasant's wife laughed heartily, and the young cock heard them. And he knew, with a gloomy, foreboding kind of knowledge, that he was tied by the leg.

He no longer pranced and ruffled and forged his feathers. He walked within the limits of his tether somberly. Still he gobbled up the best bits of food. Still, sometimes, he saved an extra-best bit for his favourite hen of the moment. Still he pranced with quivering, rocking fierceness upon such of his harem as came nonchalantly within range, and gave off the invisible lure. And still he crowed defiance to the cock-crows that showered up out of limbo, in the dawn.

But there was now a grim voracity in the way he gobbled his food, and a pinched triumph in the way he seized upon the shabby hens. His voice, above all, had lost the full gold of its clangour. He was tied by the leg and he knew it. Body, soul and spirit were tied by that string.

Underneath, however, the life in him was grimly unbroken. It was the cord that should break. So one morning, just before the light of dawn, rousing from his slumbers with a sudden wave of strength, he leaped forward on his wings, and the string snapped. He gave a wild strange squawk, rose in one lift to the top of the wall, and there he crowed a loud and splitting crow. So loud, it woke the peasant.

At the same time, at the same hour before dawn, on the same morning, a man awoke from a long sleep in which he was tied up. He woke numb and cold, inside a carved hole in the rock. Through all the long sleep his body had been full of hurt, and it was still full of hurt. He did not open his eyes. Yet he knew that he was awake, and numb, and cold, and rigid, and full of hurt, and tied up. His face was banded with cold bands, his legs were bandaged together. Only his hands were loose.

He could move if he wanted: he knew that. But he had no want. Who would want to come back from the dead? A deep, deep nausea stirred in him, at the premonition of movement. He resented already the fact of the strange, incalculable moving that had already taken place in him: the moving back into consciousness. He had not wished it. He had wanted to stay outside, in the place where even memory is stone dead.

But now, something had returned to him, like a returned letter, and in that return he lay overcome with a sense of nausea. Yet suddenly his hands moved. They lifted up, cold, heavy and sore. Yet they lifted up, to drag away the cloth from his face, and to push at the shoulder bands. Then they fell again, cold, heavy, numb, and sick with having moved even so much, unspeakably unwilling to move further.

With his face cleared, and his shoulders free, he lapsed again, and lay dead, resting on the cold nullity of being dead. It was the most desirable. And almost, he had it complete: the utter cold nullity of being outside.

Yet when he was most nearly gone, suddenly, driven by an ache at the wrists, his hands rose and began pushing at the bandages of his knees, his feet began to stir, even while his breast lay cold and dead still.

And at last, the eyes opened. On to the dark. The same dark! yet perhaps there was a pale chink, of the all-disturbing light, prizing open the pure dark. He could not lift his head. The eyes closed. And again it was finished.

Then suddenly he leaned up, and the great world reeled. Bandages fell away. And narrow walls of rock closed upon him, and gave the new anguish of imprisonment. There were chinks of light. With a wave of strength that came from revulsion, he leaned forward, in that narrow well of rock, and leaned frail hands on the rock near the chinks of light.

Strength came from somewhere, from revulsion; there was a crash and a wave of light, and the dead man was crouching in his lair, facing the animal onrush of light, Yet it was hardly dawn. And the strange, piercing keenness of daybreak's sharp breath was on him. It meant full awakening.

Slowly, slowly he crept down from the cell of rock, with the caution of the bitterly wounded. Bandages and linen and perfume fell away, and he crouched on the ground against the wall of rock, to recover oblivion. But he saw his hurt feet touching the earth again, with unspeakable pain, the earth they had meant to touch no more, and he saw his thin legs that had died, and pain unknowable, pain like utter bodily disillusion, filled him so full that he stood up, with one torn hand on the ledge of the tomb.

To be back! To be back again, after all that! He saw the linen swathing-bands fallen round his dead feet, and stooping, he picked them up, folded them, and laid them back in the rocky cavity from which he had emerged. Then he took the perfumed linen sheet, wrapped it round him as a mantle, and turned away, to the wanness of the chill dawn.

He was alone; and having died, was even beyond loneliness.

Filled still with the sickness of unspeakable disillusion, the man stepped with wincing feet down the rocky slope, past the sleeping soldiers, who lay wrapped in their woollen mantles under the wild laurels. Silent, on naked scarred feet, wrapped in a white linen shroud, he glanced down for a moment on the inert, heap-like bodies of the soldiers. They were repulsive, a slow squalor of limbs, yet he felt a certain compassion. He passed on towards the road, lest they should wake.

Having nowhere to go, he turned from the city that stood on her hills. He slowly followed the road away from the town, past the olives, under which purple anemones were drooping in the chill of dawn, and rich-green herbage was pressing thick. The world, the same as ever, the natural world, thronging with greenness, a nightingale winsomely, wistfully, coaxingly calling from the bushes beside a runnel of water, in the world, the natural world of morning and evening, forever undying, from which he had died.

He went on, on scarred feet, neither of this world nor of the next. Neither here nor there, neither seeing nor yet sightless, he passed dimly on, away from the city and its precincts, wondering why he should be travelling, yet driven by a dim, deep nausea of disillusion, and a resolution of which he was not even aware.

Advancing in a kind of half-consciousness under the dry stone wall of the olive orchard, he was roused by the shrill wild crowing of a cock just near him, a sound which made him shiver as if electricity had touched him. He saw a black and orange cock on a bough above the road, then running through the olives of the upper level, a peasant in a grey woolen shirt-tunic. Leaping out of greenness, came the black and orange cock with the red comb, his tail-feathers streaming lustrous.

"O stop him, Master!" called the peasant. "My escaped cock!"

The man addressed, with a sudden flicker of smile, opened his great white wings of a shroud in front of the leaping bird. The cock fell back with a squawk and a flutter, the peasant jumped forward, there was a terrific beating of wings, and whirring of feathers, then the peasant had the escaped cock safely under his arm, its wings shut down, its face crazily craning forward, its round eyes goggling from its white chops.

"It's my escaped cock!" said the peasant, soothing the bird with his left hand, as he looked perspiringly up into the face of the man wrapped in white linen.

The peasant changed countenance, and stood transfixed, as he looked into the dead-white face of the man who had died. That dead-white face, so still, with the black beard growing on it as if in death; and those wide-open black sombre eyes, that had died! and those washed scars on the waxy forehead! The slow-blooded man of the field let his jaw drop, in childish inability to meet the situation.

"Don't be afraid," said the man in the shroud. "I am not dead. They took me down too soon. So I have risen up. Yet if they discover me, they will do it all over again. . . ."

He spoke in a voice of old disgust. Humanity! Especially humanity in authority! There was only one thing it could do. He looked with black, indifferent eyes into the quick shifty eyes of the peasant. The peasant quailed, and was powerless under the look of deathly indifference, and strange cold resoluteness. He could only say the one thing he was afraid to say:

"Will you hide in my house, Master?"

"I will rest there. But if you tell anyone, you know what will happen. You will have to go before a judge."

"Me! I shan't speak. Let us be quick!"

The peasant looked round in fear, wondering sulkily why he had let himself in for this doom. The man with scarred feet climbed painfully up to the level of the olive garden, and followed the sullen, hurrying peasant across the green wheat among the olive trees. He felt the cool silkiness of the young wheat under his feet that had been dead, and the roughishness of its separate life was apparent to him. At the edges of rocks, he saw the silky, silvery-haired buds of the scarlet anemone bending downwards. And they too were in another world. In his own world he was alone, utterly alone. These things around him were in a world that had never died. But he himself had died, or had been killed from out of it, and all that remained now was the great void nausea of utter disillusion.

They came to a clay cottage, and the peasant waited dejectedly for the other man to pass.

"Pass!" he said. "Pass! We have not been seen."

The man in white linen entered the earthen room, taking with him the aroma of strange perfumes. The peasant closed the door, and passed through the inner doorway into the yard, where the ass stood within the high walls, safe from being stolen. There the peasant, in great disquietude, tied up the cock. The man with the waxen face sat down on a mat near the hearth, for he was spent and barely conscious. Yet he heard outside the whispering of the peasant to his wife, for the woman had been watching from the roof.

Presently they came in, and the woman hid her face. She poured water, and put bread and dried figs on a wooden platter.

"Eat, Master!" said the peasant. "No one has seen."

But the stranger had no desire for food. Yet he moistened a little bread in the water, and ate it, since life must be. But desire was dead in him, even for food and drink. He had risen without desire, without even the desire to live, empty save for the all-overwhelming disillusion that lay like nausea where his life had been. Yet perhaps, deeper even than disillusion, was a desireless resoluteness, deeper even than consciousness.

The peasant and his wife stood near the door, watching. They saw with terror the livid wounds and the thin waxy hands and the thin feet of the stranger, and the small lacerations in the still dead forehead. They smelled with terror the scent of rich perfumes that came from him, from his body. And they looked at the fine, snowy, costly linen. Perhaps really he was a dead king, from the region of terrors. And he was still cold and remote in the region of death, with perfumes coming from his transparent body as if from some strange flower.

Having with difficulty swallowed some of the moistened bread, he lifted his eyes to them. He saw them as they were: limited, meagre in their life, without any splendour of gesture and of courage. But they were what they were, slow inevitable parts of the natural world. They had no nobility, but fear made them compassionate.

And the stranger had compassion on them again, for he knew that they would respond best to gentleness, giving back a clumsy gentleness again.

"Do not be afraid," he said to them gently. "Let me stay a little while with you. I shall not stay long. And then I shall go away forever. But do not be afraid. No harm will come to you through me."

They believed him at once, yet the fear did not leave them. And they said:

"Stay, Master, while ever you will. Rest! Rest quietly!"

But they were afraid.

So he let them be, and the peasant went away with the ass. The sun had risen bright, and in the dark house with the door shut, the man was again as if in the tomb. So he said to the woman, "I would lie in the yard."

And she swept the yard for him, and laid him a mat, and he lay down under the wall in the morning sun. There he saw the first green leaves spurting like flames from the ends of the enclosed fig-tree, out of the bareness to the sky of spring above. But the man who had died could not look, he only lay quite still in the sun, which was not yet too hot, and had no desire in him, not even to move. But he lay with his thin legs in the sun, his black perfumed hair falling into the hollows of his neck, and his thin colourless arms utterly inert. As he lay there, the hens clucked and scratched, and the escaped cock, caught and tied by the leg again, cowered in a corner.

The peasant woman was frightened. She came peeping, and, seeing him never move, feared to have a dead man in the yard. But the sun had grown stronger, he opened his eyes and looked at her. And now she was frightened of the man who was alive, but spoke nothing.

He opened his eyes, and saw the world again bright as glass. It was life, in which he had no share any more. But it shone outside him, blue sky, and a bare fig-tree with little jets of green leaf. Bright as glass, and he was not of it, for desire had failed.

Yet he was there, and not extinguished. The day passed in a kind of coma, and at evening he went into the house. The peasant man came home, but he was frightened, and had nothing to say. The stranger too ate of the mess of beans, a little. Then he washed his hands and turned to the wall, and was silent. The peasants were silent too. They watched their guest sleep. Sleep was so near death he could still sleep.

Yet when the sun came up, he went again to lie in the yard. The sun was the one thing that drew him and swayed him, and he still wanted to feel the cool air of morning in his nostrils, see the pale sky overhead. He still hated to be shut up.

As he came out, the young cock crowed. It was a diminished, pinched cry, but there was that in the voice of the bird stronger than chagrin. It was the necessity to live, and even to cry out the triumph of life. The man who had died stood and watched the cock who had escaped and been caught, ruffling himself up, rising forward on his toes, throwing up his head, and parting his beak in another challenge from life to death. The brave sounds rang out, and though they were diminished by the cord round the bird's leg, they were not cut off. The man who had died looked nakedly on life, and saw a vast resoluteness everywhere flinging itself up in stormy or subtle wave-crests, foam-tips emerging out of the blue invisible, a black and orange cock or the green flame-tongues out of the extremes of the fig-tree. They came forth, these things and creatures of spring, glowing with desire and with assertion. They came like crests of foam, out of the blue flood of the invisible desire, out of the vast invisible sea of strength, and they came coloured and tangible, evanescent, yet deathless in their coming. The man who had died looked on the great swing into existence of things that had not died, but he saw no longer their tremulous desire to exist and to be. He heard instead their ringing, ringing, defiant challenge to all other things existing.

The man lay still, with eyes that had died now wide open and darkly still, seeing the everlasting resoluteness of life. And the cock, with the flat, brilliant glance, glanced back at him with a bird's half-seeing look. And always the man who had died saw not the bird alone, but the short, sharp wave of life of which the bird was the crest. He watched the queer, beaky motion of the creature as it gobbled into itself the scraps of food; its glancing of the eye of life, ever alert and watchful, overweening and cautious, and the voice of its life, crowing triumph and assertion, yet strangled by a cord of circumstance. He seemed to hear the queer speech of very life, as the cock triumphantly imitated the clucking of the favourite hen, when she had laid an egg, a clucking which still had, in the male bird, the hollow chagrin of the cord round his leg. And when the man threw a bit of bread to the cock, it called with an extraordinary cooing tenderness, tousling and saving the morsel for the hens. The hens ran up greedily, and carried the morsel away beyond the reach of the string.

Then, walking complacently after them, suddenly the male bird's leg would hitch at the end of his tether, and he would yield with a kind of collapse. His flag fell, he seemed to diminish, he would huddle in the shade. And he was young, his tail-feathers, glossy as they were, were not fully grown. It was not till evening again that the tide of life in him made him forget. Then when his favourite hen came strolling uncon-cernedly near him, emitting the lure, he pounced on her with all his feathers vibrating. And the man who had died watched the unsteady, racking vibration of the bent bird, and it was not the bird he saw, but one wave-tip of life overlapping for a minute another, in the tide of the swaying ocean of life. And the destiny of life seemed more fierce and compulsive to him even than the destiny of death. The doom of death was a shadow compared to the raging destiny of life, the determined surge of life.

At twilight the peasant came home with the ass, and he said "Master! It is said that the body was stolen from the garden, and the tomb is empty, and the soldiers are taken away, accursed Romans! And the women are there to weep."

The man who had died looked at the man who had not died.

"It is well," he said. "Say nothing, and we are safe."

And the peasant was relieved. He looked rather dirty and stupid, and even as much flaminess as that of the young cock, which he had tied by the leg, would never glow in him. He was without fire. But the man who had died thought to himself: "Why, then, should he be lifted up? Clods of earth are turned over for refreshment, they are not to be lifted up. Let the earth remain earthy, and hold its own against the sky. I was wrong to seek to lift it up. I was wrong to try to interfere. The ploughshare of devastation will be set in the soil of Judæa, and the life of this peasant will be overturned like the sods of the field. No man can save the earth from tillage. It is tillage, not salvation. . . ."

So he saw the man, the peasant, with compassion; but the man who had died no longer wished to interfere in the soul of the man who had not died, and who could never die, save to return to earth. Let him return to earth in his own good hour, and let no one try to interfere when the earth claims her own.

So the man with scars let the peasant go from him, for the peasant had no re-birth in him. Yet the man who had died said to himself: "He is my host."

And at dawn, when he was better, the man who had died rose up, and on slow, sore feet retraced his way to the garden. For he had been betrayed in a garden, and buried in a garden. And as he turned round the screen of laurels, near the rock-face, he saw a woman hovering by the tomb, a woman in blue and yellow. She peeped again into the mouth of the hole, that was like a deep cupboard. But still there was nothing. And she wrung her hands and wept. And as she turned away, she saw the man in white, standing by the laurels, and she gave a cry, thinking it might be a spy, and she said:

"They have taken him away!"

So he said to her:

"Madeleine!"

Then she reeled as if she would fall, for she knew him. And he said to her:

"Madeleine! Do not be afraid. I am alive. They took me down too soon, so I came back to life. Then I was sheltered in a house."

She did not know what to say, but fell at his feet to kiss them.

"Don't touch me, Madeleine," he said. "Not yet! I am not yet healed and in touch with men."

So she wept because she did not know what to do. And he said:

"Let us go aside, among the bushes, where we can speak unseen."

So in her blue mantle and her yellow robe, she followed him among the trees, and he sat down under a myrtle bush. And he said:

"I am not yet quite come to. Madeleine, what is to be done next?"

"Master!" she said. "Oh, we have wept for you! And will you come back to us?"

"What is finished is finished, and for me the end is past," he said. "The stream will run till no more rains fill it, then it will dry up. For me, that life is over."

"And will you give up your triumph?" she said sadly.

"My triumph," he said, "is that I am not dead. I have outlived my mission, and know no more of it. It is my triumph. I have survived the day and the death of my interference, and am still a man. I am young still, Madeleine, not even come to middle age. I am glad all that is over. It had to be. But now I am glad it is over, and the day of my interference is done. The teacher and the saviour are dead in me; now I can go about my business, into my own single life."

She heard him, and did not fully understand. But what he said made her feel disappointed.

"But you will come back to us?" she said, insisting.

"I don't know what I shall do," he said. "When I am healed, I shall know better. But my mission is over, and my teaching is finished, and death has saved me from my own salvation. Oh, Madeleine, I want to take my single way in life, which is my portion. My public life is over, the life of my self-importance. Now I can wait on life, and say nothing, and have no one betray me. I wanted to be greater than the limits of my hands and feet, so I brought betrayal on myself. And I know I wronged Judas, my poor Judas. For I have died, and now I know my own limits. Now I can live without striving to sway others any more. For my reach ends in my finger-tips, and my stride is no longer than the ends of my toes. Yet I would embrace multitudes, I who have never truly embraced even one. But Judas and the high priests saved me from my own salvation, and soon I can turn to my destiny like a bather in the sea at dawn, who has just come down to the shore alone."

"Do you want to be alone henceforward?" she asked. "And was your mission nothing? Was it all untrue?"

"Nay!" he said. "Neither were your lovers in the past nothing. They were much to you, but you took more than you gave. Then you came to me for salvation from your own excess. And I, in my mission, I too ran to excess. I gave more than I took, and that also is woe and vanity. So Pilate and the high priests saved me from my own excessive salvation. Don't run to excess now in giving, Madeleine. It only means another death."

She pondered bitterly, for the need for excessive giving was in her, and she could not bear to be denied.

"And will you not come back to us?" she said. "Have you risen for yourself alone?"

He heard the sarcasm in her voice, and looked at her beautiful face which still was dense with excessive need for salvation from the woman she had been, the female who had caught men at her will. The cloud of necessity was on her, to be saved from the old, wilful Eve, who had embraced many men and taken more than she gave. Now the other doom was on her. She wanted to give without taking. And that, too, is hard, and cruel to the warm body.

"I have not risen from the dead in order to seek death again," he said.

She glanced up at him, and saw the weariness settling again on his waxy face, and the vast disillusion in his dark eyes, and the underlying indifference. He felt her glance, and said to himself:

"Now my own followers will want to do me to death again, for having risen up different from their expectation."

"But you will come to us, to see us, us who love you?" she said.

He laughed a little and said:

"Ah, yes." Then he added, "Have you a little money? Will you give me a little money? I owe it."

She had not much, but it pleased her to give it to him.

"Do you think," he said to her, "that I might come and live with you in your house?"

She looked up at him with large blue eyes, that gleamed strangely.

"Now?" she said, with peculiar triumph.

And he, who shrank now from triumph of any sort, his own or another's, said:

"Not now! Later, when I am healed, and . . . and I am in touch with the flesh."

The words faltered in him. And in his heart he knew he would never go to live in her house. For the flicker of triumph had gleamed in her eyes; the greed of giving. But she murmured in a humming rapture:

"Ah, you know I would give up everything to you."

"Nay!" he said. "I didn't ask that."

A revulsion from all the life he had known came over him again, the great nausea of disillusion, and the spear-thrust through his bowels. He crouched under the myrtle bushes, without strength. Yet his eyes were open. And she looked at him again, and she saw that it was not the Messiah. The Messiah had not risen. The enthusiasm and the burning purity were gone, and the rapt youth. His youth was dead. This man was middle-aged and disillusioned, with a certain terrible indifference, and a resoluteness which love would never conquer. This was not the Master she had so adored, the young, flamy, unphysical exalter of her soul. This was nearer to the lovers she had known of old, but with a greater indifference to the personal issue, and a lesser susceptibility.

She was thrown out of the balance of her rapturous, anguished adoration. This risen man was the death of her dream.

"You should go now," he said to her. "Do not touch me, I am in death. I shall come again here, on the third day. Come if you will, at dawn. And we will speak again."

She went away, perturbed and shattered. Yet as she went, her mind discarded the bitterness of the reality, and she conjured up rapture and wonder, that the Master was risen and was not dead. He was risen, the Saviour, the exalter, the wonder-worker! He was risen, but not as man; as pure God, who should not be touched by flesh, and who should be rapt away into Heaven. It was the most glorious and most ghostly of the miracles.

Meanwhile the man who had died gathered himself together at last, and slowly made his way to the peasant's house. He was glad to go back to them, and away from Madeleine and his own associates. For the peasants had the inertia of earth and would let him rest, and as yet, would put no compulsion on him.

The woman was on the roof, looking for him. She was afraid that he had gone away. His presence in the house had become like gentle wine to her. She hastened to the door, to him.

"Where have you been?" she said. "Why did you go away?"

"I have been to walk in a garden, and I have seen a friend, who gave me a little money. It is for you."

He held out his thin hand, with the small amount of money, all that Madeleine could give him. The peasant's wife's eyes glistened, for money was scarce, and she said:

"Oh, Master! And is it truly mine?"

"Take it!" he said. "It buys bread, and bread brings life."

So he lay down in the yard again, sick with relief at being alone again. For with the peasants he could be alone, but his own friends would never let him be alone. And in the safety of the yard, the young cock was dear to him, as it shouted in the helpless zest of life, and finished in helpless humiliation of being tied by the leg. This day the ass stood swishing her tail under the shed. The man who had died lay down and turned utterly away from life, in the sickness of death in life.

But the woman brought wine and water, and sweetened cakes, and roused him, so that he ate a little, to please her. The day was hot, and as she crouched to serve him, he saw her breasts sway from her humble body, under her smock. He knew she wished he would desire her, and she was youngish, and not unpleasant. And he, who had never known a woman, would have desired her if he could. But he could not want her, though he felt gently towards her soft, crouching, humble body. But it was her thoughts, her consciousness, he could not mingle with. She was pleased with the money, and now she wanted to take more from him. She wanted the embrace of his body. But her little soul was hard, and short-sighted, and grasping, her body had its little greed, and no gentle reverence of the return gift. So he spoke a quiet, pleasant word to her, and turned away. He could not touch the little, personal life of this woman, nor in any other. He turned away from it without hesitation.

Risen from the dead, he had realised at last that the body, too, has its little life, and beyond that, the greater life. He was virgin, in recoil from the little, greedy life of the body. But now he knew that virginity is a form of greed; and that the body rises again to give and to take, to take and to give, ungreedily. Now he knew that he had risen for the woman, or women, who knew the greater life of the body, not greedy to give, not greedy to take, and with whom he could mingle his body. But having died, he was patient, knowing there was time, an eternity of time. And he was driven by no greedy desire, either to give himself to others, or to grasp anything for himself. For he had died.

The peasant came home from work, and said:

"Master, I thank you for the money. But we did not want it. And all I have is yours."

But the man who had died was sad, because the peasant stood there in the little, personal body, and his eyes were cunning and sparkling with the hope of greater rewards in money, later on. True, the peasant had taken him in free, and had risked getting no reward. But the hope was cunning in him. Yet even this was as men are made. So when the peasant would have helped him to rise, for night had fallen, the man who had died said:

"Don't touch me, brother. I am not yet risen to the Father."

The sun burned with greater splendour, and burnished the young cock brighter. But the peasant kept the string renewed, and the bird was a prisoner. Yet the flame of life burned up to a sharp point in the cock, so that it eyed askance and haughtily the man who had died. And the man smiled and held the bird dear, and he said to it:

"Surely thou art risen to the Father, among birds." And the young cock, answering, crowed.

When at dawn on the third morning the man went to the garden, he was absorbed, thinking of the greater life of the body, beyond the little, narrow, personal life. So he came through the thick screen of laurel and myrtle bushes, near the rock, suddenly, and he saw three women near the tomb. One was Madeleine, and one was the woman who had been his mother, and third was a woman he knew, called Joan. He looked up, and saw them all, and they saw him, and they were all afraid.

He stood arrested in the distance, knowing they were there to claim him back, bodily. But he would in no wise return to them. Pallid, in the shadow of a grey morning that was blowing to rain, he saw them, and turned away. But Madeleine hastened towards him.

"I did not bring them," she said. "They have come of themselves. See, I have brought you money! . . . Will you not speak to them?"

She offered him some gold pieces and he took them, saying:

"May I have this money? I shall need it. I cannot speak to them, for I am not yet ascended to the Father. And I must leave you now."

"Ah! Where will you go?" she cried.

He looked at her, and saw she was clutching for the man in him who had died and was dead, the man of his youth and his mission, of his chastity and his fear, of his little life, his giving without taking.

"I must go to my Father!" he said.

"And you will leave us? There is your mother!" she cried, turning round with the old anguish, which yet was sweet to her.

"But now I must ascend to my Father," he said, and he drew back into the bushes, and so turned quickly, and went away, saying to himself:

"Now I belong to no one and have no connection, and mission or gospel is gone from me. Lo! I cannot make even my own life, and what have I to save? . . . I can learn to be alone."

So he went back to the peasant's house, to the yard where the young cock was tied by the leg, with a string. And he wanted no one, for it was best to be alone; for the presence of people made him lonely. The sun and the subtle salve of spring healed his wounds, even the gaping wound of disillusion through his bowels was closing up. And his need of men and women, his fever to have them and to be saved by them, this too was healing in him. Whatever came of touch between himself and the race of men, henceforth, should come without trespass or compulsion. For he said to himself:

"I tried to compel them to live, so they compelled me to die. It is always so, with compulsion. The recoil kills the advance. Now is my time to be alone."

Therefore he went no more to the garden, but lay still and saw the sun, or walked at dusk across the olive slopes, among the green wheat, that rose a palm-breadth higher every sunny day. And always he thought to himself:

"How good it is to have fulfilled my mission, and to be beyond it. Now I can be alone, and leave all things to themselves, and the fig-tree may be barren if it will, and the rich may be rich. My way is my own alone."

So the green jets of leaves unspread on the fig-tree, with the bright, translucent, green blood of the tree. And the young cock grew brighter, more lustrous with the sun's burnishing; yet always tied by the leg with a string. And the sun went down more and more in pomp, out of the gold and red-flushed air. The man who had died was aware of it all, and he thought:

"The Word is but the midge that bites at evening. Man is tormented with words like midges, and they follow him right into the tomb. But beyond the tomb they cannot go. Now I have passed the place where words can bite no more and the air is clear, and there is nothing to say, and I am alone within my own skin, which is the walls of all my domain."

So he healed of his wounds, and enjoyed his immortality of being alive without fret. For in the tomb he had slipped that noose which we call care. For in the tomb he had left his striving self, which cares and asserts itself. Now his uncaring self healed and became whole within his skin, and he smiled to himself with pure aloneness, which is one sort of immortality.

Then he said to himself: "I will wander the earth, and say nothing. For nothing is so marvellous as to be alone in the phenomenal world, which is raging, and yet apart. And I have not seen it, I was too much blinded by my confusion within it. Now I will wander among the stirring of the phenomenal world, for it is the stirring of all things among themselves which leaves me purely alone."

So he communed with himself, and decided to be a physician. Because the power was still in him to heal any man or child who touched his compassion. Therefore he cut his hair and his beard after the right fashion, and smiled to himself. And he bought himself shoes, and the right mantle, and put the right cloth over his head, hiding all the little scars. And the peasant said:

"Master, will you go forth from us?"

"Yes, for the time is come for me to return to men."

So he gave the peasant a piece of money, and said to him:

"Give me the cock that escaped and is now tied by the leg. For he shall go forth with me."

So for a piece of money the peasant gave the cock to the man who had died, and at dawn the man who had died set out into the phenomenal world, to be fulfilled in his own aloneness in the midst of it. For previously he had been too much mixed up in it. Then he had died. Now he must come back, to be alone in the midst. Yet even now he did not go quite alone, for under his arm, as he went, he carried the cock, whose tail fluttered gaily behind, and who craned his head excitedly, for he too was adventuring out for the first time into the wider phenomenal world, which is the stirring of the body of cocks also. And the peasant woman shed a few tears, but then went indoors, being a peasant, to look again at the pieces of money. And it seemed to her, a gleam came out of the pieces of money, wonderful.

The man who had had died wandered on, and it was a sunny day. He looked around as he went, and stood aside as the pack-train passed by, towards the city. And he said to himself:

"Strange is the phenomenal world, dirty and clean together! And I am the same. Yet I am apart! And life bubbles variously. Why should I have wanted it to bubble all alike? What a pity I preached to them! A sermon is so much more likely to cake into mud, and to close the fountains, than is a psalm or a song. I made a mistake. I understand that they executed me for preaching to them. Yet they could not finally execute me, for now I am risen in my own aloneness, and inherit the earth, since I lay no claim on it. And I will be alone in the seethe of all things; first and foremost, forever, I shall be alone. But I must toss this bird into the seethe of phenomena, for he must ride his wave. How hot he is with life! Soon, in some place, I shall leave him among the hens. And perhaps one evening, I shall meet a woman who can lure my risen body, yet leave me my aloneness. For the body of my desire has died, and I am not in touch anywhere. Yet how do I know! All at least is life. And this cock gleams with bright aloneness, though he answers the lure of hens. And I shall hasten on to that village on the hill ahead of me; already I am tired and weak, and want to close my eyes to everything."

Hastening a little with the desire to have finished going, he overtook two men going slowly, and talking. And being soft-footed, he heard they were speaking of himself. And he remembered them, for he had known them in his life, the life of his mission. So he greeted them, but did not disclose himself in the dusk, and they did not know him. He said to them:

"What then of him who would be king, and was put to death for it?"

They answered suspiciously: "Why ask you of him?"

"I have known him, and thought much about him," he said.

So they replied: "He has risen."

"Yea! And where is he, and how does he live?"

"We know not, for it is not revealed. Yet he is risen, and in a little while will ascend unto the Father."

"Yea! And where then is his Father?"

"Know ye not? You are then of the Gentiles! The Father is Heaven, above the cloud and the firmament."

"Truly? Then how will he ascend?"

"As Elijah the Prophet, he shall go up in a glory."

"Even into the sky?"

"Into the sky."

"Then is he not risen in the flesh?"

"He is risen in the flesh."

"And will he take flesh up into the sky?"

"The Father in Heaven will take him up."

The man who had died said no more, for his say was over, and words beget words, even as gnats. But the man asked him: "Why do you carry a cock?"

"I am a healer," he said, "and the bird hath virtue."

"You are not a believer?"

"Yea! I believe the bird is full of life and virtue."

They walked on in silence after this, and he felt they disliked his answer. So he smiled to himself, for a dangerous phenomenon in the world is a man of narrow belief, who denies the right of his neighbour to be alone. And as they came to the outskirts of the village, the man who had died stood still in the gloaming and said in his old voice:

"Know ye me not?"

And they cried in fear: "Master!"

"Yea!" he said, laughing softly. And he turned suddenly away, down a side lane, and was gone under the wall before they knew.

So he came to an inn where the asses stood in the yard. And he called for fritters, and they were made for him. So he slept under a shed. But in the morning he was wakened by a loud crowing, and his cock's voice ringing in his ears. So he saw the rooster of the inn walking forth to battle, with his hens, a goodly number, behind him. Then the cock of the man who had died sprang forth, and a battle began between the birds. The man of the inn ran to save his rooster, but the man who had died said:

"If my bird wins I will give him thee. And if he lose, thou shalt eat him."

So the birds fought savagely, and the cock of the man who had died killed the common cock of the yard. Then the man who had died said to his young cock:

"Thou at least hast found thy kingdom, and the females to thy body. Thy aloneness can take on splendour, polished by the lure of thy hens."

And he left his bird there, and went on deeper into the phenomenal world, which is a vast complexity of entanglements and allurements. And he asked himself a last question:

"From what, and to what, could this infinite whirl be saved?"

So he went his way, and was alone. But the way of the world was past

belief, as he saw the strange entanglement of passions and circumstance and compulsion everywhere, but always the dread insomnia of
compulsion. It was fear, the ultimate fear of death, that made men
mad. So always he must move on, for if he stayed, his neighbours
wound the strangling of their fear and bullying round him. There was
nothing he could touch, for all, in a mad assertion of the ego, wanted
to put a compulsion on him, and violate his intrinsic solitude. It was
the mania of cities and societies and hosts, to lay a compulsion upon
a man, upon all men. For men and women alike were mad with the
egoistic fear of their own nothingness. And he thought of his own mission, how he had tried to lay the compulsion of love on all men. And
the old nausea came back on him. For there was no contact without a
subtle attempt to inflict a compulsion. And already he had been compelled even into death. The nausea of the old wound broke out afresh,
and he looked again on the world with repulsion, dreading its mean
contacts.

The Gardener

by Rudyard Kipling

This Rudyard Kipling (1865–1936) story fea-

tures a character named Michael, whose fate

closely resembles that of Kipling's own son,

John. The title of the story refers to John 20:15.

One grave to me was given,
  One watch till Judgement Day;
And God looked down from Heaven
  And rolled the stone away.

One day in all the years,
  One hour in that one day,
His Angel saw my tears,
  And rolled the stone away!

Everyone in the village knew that Helen Turrel did her duty by all her world, and by none more honorably than by her only brother's unfortunate child. The village knew, too, that George Turrell had tried his family severely since early youth, and were not surprised to be told that, after many fresh starts given and thrown away, he, an Inspector of Indian Police, had entangled himself with the daughter of a retired non-commissioned officer, and had died of a fall from a horse a few weeks before his child was born. Mercifully, George's father and mother were both dead, and though Helen, thirty-five and independent, might well have washed her hands of the whole disgraceful affair, she most nobly took charge, though she was, at the time, under threat of lung trouble which had driven her to the South of France. She arranged for the passage of the child and a nurse from Bombay, met them at Marseilles, nursed the baby through an attack of infantile dysentery due to the carelessness of the nurse, whom she had had to dismiss, and at last, thin and worn but triumphant, brought the boy late in the autumn, wholly restored, to her Hampshire home.

All these details were public property, for Helen was as open as the day, and held that scandals are only increased by hushing them up. She admitted that George had always been rather a black sheep, but things might have been much worse if the mother had insisted on her right to keep the boy. Luckily, it seemed that people of that class would do almost anything for money, and, as George had always turned to her in his scrapes, she felt herself justified—her friends agreed with her—in cutting the whole non-commissioned officer connection, and giving the child every advantage. A christening, by the Rector, under the name of Michael, was the first step. So far as she knew herself, she was not, she said, a child-lover, but, for all his faults, she had been very fond of George, and she pointed out that little Michael had his father's mouth to a line; which made something to build upon.

As a matter of fact, it was the Turrell forehead, broad, low, and well-shaped, with the widely spaced eyes beneath it, that Michael had most faithfully reproduced. His mouth was somewhat better cut than the family type. But Helen, who would concede nothing good to his mother's side, vowed he was a Turrell all over, and, there being no one to contradict, the likeness was established.

In a few years Michael took his place, as accepted as Helen had always been—fearless, philosophical, and fairly good-looking. At six, he wished to know why he could not call her "Mummy," as other boys called their mothers. She explained that she was only his auntie, and that aunties were not quite the same as mummies, but, that if it gave him pleasure, he might call her "Mummy" at bedtime, for a pet-name between themselves.

Michael kept his secret most loyally, but Helen, as usual, explained the fact to her friends; which when Michael heard, he raged.

"Why did you tell? *Why* did you tell?" came at the end of the storm.

"Because it's always best to tell the truth," Helen answered, her arm round him as he shook in his cot.

"All right, but when the troof's ugly I don't think it's nice."

"Don't you, dear?"

"No, I don't, and"—she felt the small body stiffen—"now you've told, I won't call you 'Mummy' any more—not even at bedtimes."

"But isn't that rather unkind?" said Helen softly.

"I don't care! I don't care! You've hurted me in my insides and I'll hurt you back. I'll hurt you as long as I live."

"Don't, oh, don't talk like that, dear! You don't know what—"

"I will! And when I'm dead I'll hurt you worse!"

"Thank goodness, I shall be dead long before you, darling."

"Huh! Emma says, 'Never know your luck.'" (Michael had been talking to Helen's elderly, flat-faced maid.) "Lots of little boys die quite soon. So'll I. *Then* you'll see!"

Helen caught her breath and moved towards the door, but the wail of "Mummy! Mummy!" drew her back again, and the two wept together.

At ten years old, after two terms at a prep. school, something or some-body gave him the idea that his civil status was not quite regular. He attacked Helen on the subject, breaking down her stammered defences with the family directness.

"Don't believe a word of it," he said, cheerily, at the end. "People wouldn't have talked like they did if my people had been married. But don't you bother, Auntie. I've found out all about my sort in English Hist'ry and the Shakespeare bits. There was William the Conqueror to begin with, and—oh, heaps more, and they all got on first-rate. 'Twon't make any difference to you, my being *that*—will it?"

"As if anything could—" she began.

"All right. We won't talk about it any more if it makes you cry." He never mentioned the thing again of his own will; but when, two years later, he skillfully managed to have measles in the holidays, as his temperature went up to the appointed one hundred and four he muttered nothing else, till Helen's voice, piercing at last his delirium, reached him with assurance that nothing on earth or beyond could make any difference between them.

The terms at his public school and the wonderful Christmas, Easter, and Summer holidays followed each other, variegated and glorious as jewels on a string; and as jewels Helen treasured them. In due time Michael developed his own interests, which ran their courses and gave way to others; but his interest in Helen was constant and increasing throughout. She repaid it with all that she had of affection or could command of counsel and money; and since Michael was no fool, the War took him just before what was like to have been a most promising career.

He was to have gone up to Oxford, with a scholarship, in October. At the end of August he was on the edge of joining the first holocaust of public-school boys who threw themselves into the Line; but the captain of his O.T.C., where he had been sergeant for nearly a year, headed him off and steered him directly to a commission in a battalion so new that half of it still wore the old Army red, and the other half was breeding meningitis through living overcrowdedly in damp tents. Helen had been shocked at the idea of direct enlistment.

"But it's in the family," Michael laughed.

"You don't mean to tell me that you believed that old story all this time?" said Helen. (Emma, her maid, had been dead now several years.) "I gave you my word of honor—and I give it again—that—that it's all right. It is indeed."

"Oh, *that* doesn't worry me. It never did," he replied valiantly. "What I meant was, I should have got into the show earlier if I'd enlisted—like my grandfather."

"Don't talk like that! Are you afraid of its ending so soon, then?"

"No such luck. You know what K. says."

"Yes. But my banker told me last Monday it couldn't *possibly* last beyond Christmas—for financial reasons."

"Hope he's right, but our Colonel—and he's a Regular—says it's going to be a long job."

Michael's battalion was fortunate in that, by some chance which meant several "leaves," it was used for coast-defense among shallow trenches on the Norfolk coast; thence sent north to watch the mouth of a Scotch estuary, and, lastly, held for weeks on a baseless rumor of distant service. But, the very day that Michael was to have met Helen for four whole hours at a railway-junction up the line, it was hurled out, to help make good the wastage of Loos, and he had only just time to send her a wire of farewell.

In France luck again helped the battalion. It was put down near the Salient, where it led a meritorious and unexacting life, while the Somme was being manufactured; and enjoyed the peace of the Armentières and Laventie sectors when the battle began. Finding that it had sound views on protecting its own flanks and could dig, a prudent Commander stole it out of its own Division, under pretence of helping to lay telegraphs, and used it round Ypres at large.

A month later, and just after Michael had written Helen that there was nothing special doing and therefore no need to worry, a shell-splinter dropping out of a wet dawn killed him at once. The next shell uprooted and laid down over the body what had been the foundation of a barn wall, so neatly that none but an expert would have guessed that anything unpleasant had happened.

By this time the village was old in experience of war, and, English fashion, had evolved a ritual to meet it. When the postmistress handed her seven-year-old daughter the official telegram to take to Miss Turrell, she observed to the Rector's gardener: "It's Miss Helen's turn now." He replied, thinking of his own son: "Well, he's lasted longer than some." The child herself came to the front-door weeping aloud, because Master Michael had often given her sweets. Helen, presently, found herself pulling down the house-blinds one after one with great care, and saying earnestly to each: "Missing *always* means dead." Then she took her place in the dreary procession that was impelled to go through an inevitable series of unprofitable emotions. The Rector, of course, preached hope and prophesized word, very soon, from a prison camp. Several friends, too, told her perfectly truthful tales, but always about other women, to whom, after months and months of silence, their missing had been miraculously restored. Other people urged her to communicate with infallible Secretaries of organizations who could communicate with benevolent neutrals, who could extract accurate information from the most secretive of Hun prison commandants. Helen did and wrote and signed everything that was suggested or put before her.

Once, on one of Michael's leaves, he had taken her over a munition factory, where she saw the progress of a shell from a blank-iron to the all but finished article. It struck her at the time that the wretched thing was never left alone for a single second; and "I'm being manufactured into a bereaved next of kin," she told herself, as she prepared her documents.

In due course, when all the organizations had deeply or sincerely regretted their inability to trace, etc., something gave way within her and all sensation—save of thankfulness for the release—came to an end in blessed passivity. Michael had died and her world had stood still and she had been one with the full shock of that arrest. Now she was standing still and the world was going forward, but it did not concern her—in no way or relation did it touch her. She knew this by the ease with which she could slip Michael's name into talk and incline her head to the proper angle, at the proper murmur of sympathy.

In the blessed realization of that relief, the Armistice with all its bells broke over her and passed unheeded. At the end of another year she had overcome her physical loathing of the living and returned young, so that she could take them by the hand and almost sincerely wish them well. She had no interest in any aftermath, national or personal, of the war, but, moving at an immense distance, she sat on various relief committees and held strong views—she heard herself delivering them—about the site of the proposed village War Memorial.

Then there came to her, as next of kin, an official intimation, backed by a page of a letter to her in indelible pencil, a silver identity-disc, and a watch, to the effect that the body of Lieutenant Michael Turrell had been found, identified, and reinterred in Hagenzeele Third Military Cemetery—the letter of the row and the grave's number in that row duly given.

So Helen found herself moved on to another process of the manufacture—to a world full of exultant or broken relatives, now strong in the certainty that there was an altar upon earth where they might lay their love. These soon told her, and by means of time-tables made clear, how easy it was and how little it interfered with life's affairs to go and see one's grave.

"*So* different," as the Rector's wife said, "if he'd been killed in Mesopotamia, or even Gallipoli."

The agony of being waked up to some sort of second life drove Helen across the Channel, where, in a new world of abbreviated titles, she learnt that Hagenzeele Third could be comfortably reached by an afternoon train which fitted in with the morning boat, and that there was a comfortable little hotel not three kilometers from Hagenzeele itself, where one could spend quite a comfortable night and see one's grave next morning. All this she had from a Central Authority who lived in a board and tar-paper shed on the skirts of a razed city full of whirling lime-dust and blown papers.

"By the way," said he, "you know your grave, of course?"

"Yes, thank you," said Helen, and showed its row and number typed on Michael's own little typewriter. The officer would have checked it, out of one of his many books; but a large Lancashire woman thrust between them and bade him tell her where she might find her son, who had been corporal in the A.S.C. His proper name, she sobbed, was Anderson, but, coming of respectable folk, he had of course enlisted under the name of Smith; and had been killed at Dickiebush, in early 'Fifteen. She had not his number nor did she know which of his two

Christian names he might have used with his alias; but her Cook's tourist ticket expired at the end of Easter week, and if by then she could not find her child she should go mad. Whereupon she fell forward on Helen's breast; but the officer's wife came out quickly from a little bedroom behind the office, and the three of them lifted the woman on to the cot.

"They are often like this," said the officer's wife, loosening the tight bonnet-strings. "Yesterday she said he'd been killed at Hooge. Are you sure you know your grave? It makes such a difference."

"Yes, thank you," said Helen, and hurried out before the woman on the bed should begin to lament again.

Tea in a crowded mauve and blue striped wooden structure, with a false front, carried her still further into the nightmare. She paid her bill beside a stolid, plain-featured Englishwoman, who, hearing her inquire about the train to Hagenzeele, volunteered to come with her.

"I'm going to Hagenzeele myself," she explained. "Not to Hagenzeele Third; mine is Sugar Factory, but they call it La Rosière now. It's just south of Hagenzeele Three. Have you got your room at the hotel there?"

"Oh yes, thank you. I've wired."

"That's better. Sometimes the place is quite full, and at others there's hardly a soul. But they've put bathrooms into the old Lion d'Or—that's the hotel on the west side of Sugar Factory—and it draws off a lot of people, luckily."

"It's all new to me. This is the first time I've been over."

"Indeed! This is my ninth time since the Armistice. Not on my own account. I haven't lost anyone, thank God—but, like everyone else, I've a lot of friends at home who have. Coming over as often as I do, I find it helps them to have someone just look at the—the place and tell them about it afterwards. And one can take photos for them, too. I get quite a list of commissions to execute." She laughed nervously and tapped her slung Kodak. "There are two or three to see at Sugar Factory this time, and plenty of others in the cemeteries all about. My system is to save them up, and arrange them, you know. And when I've get enough commissions for one area to make it worth while, I pop over and execute them. It *does* comfort people."

"I suppose so," Helen answered, shivering as they entered the little train.

"Of course it does. (Isn't it lucky we've got window-seats?) It must do or they wouldn't ask one to do it, would they? I've a list of quite twelve or fifteen commissions here"—she rapped the Kodak again—"I must sort them out tonight. Oh, I forgot to ask you. What's yours?"

"My nephew," said Helen. "But I was very fond of him."

"Ah, yes! I sometimes wonder whether *they* know after death? What do you think?"

"Oh, I don't—I haven't dared to think much about that sort of thing," said Helen, almost lifting her hands to keep her off.

"Perhaps that's better," the woman answered. "The sense of loss must be enough, I expect. Well, I won't worry you anymore."

Helen was grateful, but when they reached the hotel Mrs. Scarsworth (they had exchanged names) insisted on dining at the same table with her, and after the meal, in the little, hideous salon full of low-voiced relatives, took Helen through her "commissions" with biographies of the dead, where she happened to know them, and sketches of their next of kin. Helen endured till nearly half-past nine, ere she fled to her room.

Almost at once there was a knock at her door and Mrs. Scarsworth entered; her hands, holding the dreadful list, clasped before her.

"Yes—yes—*I* know," she began. "You're sick of me, but I want to tell you something. You—you aren't married, are you? Then perhaps you won't . . . But it doesn't matter. I've *got* to tell someone. I can't go on any longer like this."

"But please—" Mrs. Scarsworth had backed against the shut door, and her mouth worked dryly.

"In a minute," she said. "You—you know about these graves of mine I was telling you about downstairs, just now? They really *are* commissions. At least several of them are." Her eye wandered round the room. "What extraordinary wall-papers they have in Belgium, don't you think? . . . Yes. I *swear* they are commissions. But there's *one*, d'you see, and—and he was more to me than anything else in the world. Do you understand?"

Helen nodded.

"More than anyone else. And, of course, he oughtn't to have been. He ought to have been nothing to me. But he *was*. He *is*. That's why I do the commissions, you see. That's all."

"But why do you tell me?" Helen asked desperately.

"Because I'm *so* tired of lying. Tired of lying—always lying—year in and year out. When I don't tell lies I've got to act 'em and I've got to think 'em, always. *You* don't know what that means. He was everything to me that he oughtn't to have been—the one real thing—the only thing that ever happened to me in all my life; and I've had to pretend he wasn't. I've had to watch every word I said, and think out what lie I'd tell next, for years and years!"

"How many years?" Helen asked.

"Six years and four months before, and two and three-quarters after. I've gone to him eight times, since. Tomorrow'll make the ninth, and—and I can't—I *can't* go to him again with nobody in the world knowing. I want to be honest with someone before I go. Do you understand? It doesn't matter about *me*. I was never truthful, even as a girl. But it isn't worthy of *him*. So—so I—I had to tell you. I can't keep it up any longer. Oh, I can't!"

She lifted her joined hands almost to the level of her mouth, and brought them down sharply, still joined, to full arms' length below her waist. Helen reached forward, caught them, bowed her head over them, and murmured: "Oh, my dear! My dear!" Mrs. Scarsworth stepped back, her face all mottled.

"My God!" said she. "Is *that* how you take it?"

Helen could not speak, and the woman went out; but it was a long while before Helen was able to sleep.

Next morning Mrs. Scarsworth left early on her round of commissions, and Helen walked alone to Hagenzeele Third. The place was still in the making, and stood some five or six feet above the metaled road, which it flanked for hundreds of yards. Culverts across a deep ditch served for entrances through the unfinished boundary wall. She climbed a few wooden-faced earthen steps and then met the entire crowded level of the thing in one held breath. She did not know that Hagenzeele Third counted twenty-one thousand dead already. All she saw was a merciless sea of black crosses, bearing little strips of stamped tin at all angles across their faces. She could distinguish no order or arrangement in their mass; nothing but a waist-high wilderness as of weeds stricken dead, rushing at her. She went forward, moved to the left and the right hopelessly, wondering by what guidance she should ever come to her own. A great distance away there was a line of whiteness. It proved to be a block of some two or three hundred graves whose headstones had already been set, whose flowers were planted out, and whose new-sown grass showed green. Here she could see clear-cut letters at the ends of the rows, and, referring to her slip, realized that it was not here she must look.

A man knelt behind a line of headstones—evidently a gardener, for he was firming a young plant in the soft earth. She went towards him, her paper in her hand. He rose at her approach and without prelude or salutation asked: "Who are you looking for?"

"Lieutenant Michael Turrell—my nephew," said Helen slowly and word for word, as she had many thousands of times in her life.

The man lifted his eyes and looked at her with infinite compassion before he turned from the fresh-sown grass toward the naked black crosses.

"Come with me," he said, "and I will show you where your son lies."

When Helen left the Cemetery she turned for a last look. In the distance she saw the man bending over his young plants; and she went away, supposing him to be the gardener.

acknowledgments

Many people made this anthology.

At Thunder's Mouth Press and Avalon Publishing Group:
Thanks to Will Balliett, Neil Ortenberg, Susan Reich, Dan O'Connor, Ghadah Alrawi, Maria Fernandez, Mike Walters, Paul Paddock, Simon Sullivan, Linda Kosarin and David Reidy for their support, dedication and hard work.

At Shawneric.com:
Thanks to Shawneric Hachey for his meticulous work on rights and photos.

At The Writing Company:
Thanks to Nat May, who did most of the research. Thanks to Nate Hardcastle, who ran the project. Thanks also to Taylor Smith, Mark Klimek and March Truedsson.

Among friends and family:
Thanks to Hampton Davis for his friendship and for his example. Thanks to Jennifer and Harper and Abner for their love and for their company.

Finally, I am grateful to the writers whose work appears in this book.

We gratefully acknowledge everyone who gave permission for written material to appear in this book. We have made every effort to trace and contact copyright holders. If an error or omission is brought to our notice we will be pleased to correct the situation in future editions of this book. For further information, please contact the publisher.

"The Conversion of the Jews" from *Goodbye, Columbus* by Philip Roth. Copyright © 1959, and renewed 1987 by Philip Roth. Reprinted by permission of Houghton Mifflin Company. All rights reserved. ❖ "The Annunciation" from *The Unknown Rilke: Expanded Edition. Selected Poems by Rainer Maria Rilke, translated with an Introduction by Franz Wright, FIELD Translation Series 17.* Copyright © 1990 by Oberlin College Press. Reprinted by permission of Oberlin College Press. ❖ "Notes from a Desert Sanctuary" by Heather King. Copyright © 2001 by Heather King. First appeared in *The Sun*, December 2001, issue 312. Reprinted by permission of the author. ❖ Excerpts from *The Seven Storey Mountain* by Thomas Merton. Copyright © 1948 by Harcourt, Inc. and renewed 1976 by the Trustees of The Merton Legacy Trust. Reprinted by permission of the publisher. ❖ "Old Man Joseph and His Family" from *Jesus Tales : A Novel* by Romulus Linney. Copyright © 1980 by Romulus Linney. Reprinted by permission of Farrar, Straus & Giroux, LLC. ❖ Excerpt from *The Last Temptation of Christ* by Nikos Kazantzakis. English translation by P.A. Bien. Translation Copyright © 1960 by Simon & Schuster, Inc. Copyright renewed © 1988 by Faber & Faber, Ltd. ❖ An Excerpt from "A Palpable God" from *Three Gospels* by Reynolds Price. Copyright © 1996 by Reynolds Price. Reprinted by permission of Scribner, a Division of Simon & Schuster, Inc. ❖ Excerpt from *The Lost Gospel: The Book of Q and Christian Origins* by Burton L. Mack. Copyright © 1993 by Burton L. Mack. Reprinted by permission of HarperCollins Publishers, Inc. ❖ Excerpts from *The Gospel According to Jesus Christ* by Stephen Mitchell. Copyright © 1991 by Stephen

Mitchell. Reprinted by permission of HarperCollins Publishers, Inc. ✤ Excerpt from *Jesus the Son of Man: His Words and His Deeds as Told by Those Who Knew Him* by Kahlil Gibran. Copyright © 1928 by Kahlil Gibran and renewed 1956 by Administrators C.T.A. of Kahlil Gibran Estate and Mary G. Gibran. Used by permission of Alfred A. Knopf, a division of Random House, Inc. ✤ Excerpt from *Jesus: A Revolutionary Biography* by John Dominic Crossan. Copyright © 1994 by John Dominic Crossan. Reprinted by permission of HarperCollins Publishers, Inc. ✤ Excerpt from *One Jesus, Many Christs* by Gregory J. Riley. Copyright © 1997 by Gregory J. Riley. Reprinted by permission of Harper Collins Publishers, Inc. ✤ Excerpt from *Christ: A Crisis in the Life of God* by Jack Miles. Copyright © 2001 by Jack Miles. Reprinted by permission of Alfred A. Knopf, a division of Random House, Inc. ✤ Excerpt from *Constantine's Sword* by James Carroll. Copyright © 2001 by James Carroll. Reprinted by permission of Houghton Mifflin Company. All rights reserved. ✤ Excerpt from *The Man Who Died* by D.H. Lawrence. Copyright © 1931, 1959 by Random House, Inc. Reprinted by permission of Alfred A. Knopf, a division of Random House, Inc.

b i b l i o g r a p h y

The selections used in this anthology were taken from the editions listed below. In some cases, other editions may be easier to find. Hard-to-find or out-of-print titles often are available through inter-library loan services or through Internet booksellers.

Carroll, James. *Constantine's Sword: The Church and the Jews: A History*. Boston: Houghton Mifflin, 2001.

Crossan, John Dominic. *Jesus: A Revolutionary Biography*. New York: HarperCollins, 1994.

Gibran, Kahlil. *Jesus the Son of Man: His Words and His Deeds as Told by Those Who Knew Him*. New York: Knopf, 1995.

Kazantzakis, Nikos. *The Last Temptation of Christ*. New York: Simon & Schuster, 1960.

King, Heather. "Notes from a Desert Sanctuary". First appeared in *The Sun*, December 2001, Issue 312.

Kipling, Rudyard. *Kipling's Fantasy Stories*. New York: Tom Doherty Associates, 1992.

Lawrence, D.H. *The Man Who Died*. Hopewell, New Jersey: Ecco Press, 1994.

Linney, Romulus. *Jesus Tales: A Novel*. San Francisco: North Point Press, 1980.

Mack, Burton L. *The Lost Gospel: The Book of Q and Christian Origins*. New York: HarperCollins, 1993.

Merton, Thomas. *The Seven Storey Mountain*. Orlando, FL: Harcourt, Brace, 1983.

Miles, Jack. *Christ: A Crisis in the Life of God*. New York: Alfred A.Knopf, 2001

Mitchell, Stephen. *The Gospel According to Jesus*. New York: HarperPerennial, 1993.

Nietzsche, Friedrich. *The Anti-Christ*. Tuscon, AZ: See Sharp Press, 1999.

Notovich, Nicolas. *The Unknown Life of Jesus Christ*. Santa Monica, CA: Tree of Life Publications, 1980.

Phillimore, Cecily Spencer-Smith. *By an Unknown Disciple*. New York: George H. Doran, 1919.

Price, Reynolds. *A Palpable God*. San Francisco: North Point Press, 1985.

Riley, Gregory J. *One Jesus, Many Christs*. San Francisco: Harper San Francisco, 1997.

Rilke, Rainer Maria, translated by Franz Wright. *The Unknown Rilke: The Expanded Edition*. Oberlin, Ohio: Oberlin College Press, 1990.

Roth, Philip. *Goodbye, Columbus*. Boston: Houghton Mifflin, 1959.

Thoreau, Henry David. *A Week on the Concord and Merrimack Rivers* and *Walden*. Cambridge, MA: The Riverside Press, 1929.

adrenaline lives

New from Adrenaline Lives Books

KENNEDYS

STORIES OF LIFE AND DEATH FROM AN AMERICAN FAMILY

EDITED BY CLINT WILLIS

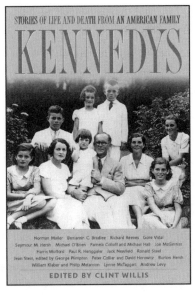

The Kennedy family for the past 50 years has lived at the intersection of politics, history, sex, fashion, gossip, war, murder, and Hollywood—all elements of a good and gripping story. *Kennedys* collects 21 of the best stories about the Kennedys, who during the century have shaped our public life while building private lives charged with purpose and passion—lives far more interesting and exciting than decades of gossip columns have managed to convey. First-rate writers from Norman Mailer to Gore Vidal capture the charm, intensity, and passion of the Kennedy family—brothers Jack, Bobby, and Ted and their parents, siblings, spouses, and children. Ultimately, they offer a surprisingly fresh vision of one of America's most compelling families. $17.95 ($28.95 Canada), 400 pages

"The writing here is suburb . . . gripping . . . unexpected. Into the Kennedy aura once more, but brightly."
—*Kirkus Reviews*